STEPPING Forward

Joshua Stepping Forward into the Jordan

Joshua leads priests into the Jordan River. He splits the waters.
Jericho is represented over his shoulder.

STEPPING Forward

Synagogue Visioning & Planning

ROBERT LEVENTHAL

THE
ALBAN INSTITUTE

Stepping Forward: Synagogue Visioning and Planning

The Alban Institute
2121 Cooperative Way, Suite 100
Herndon, VA 20171

Scripture quotations, unless otherwise noted, are reprinted from the Tanakh, copyright © 1999, The Jewish Publication Society, with the permission of the publisher, The Jewish Publication Society.

Other ancient sources are generally from Shlomo Toperoff, *Avot: A Comprehensive Commentary on the Ethics of Our Fathers* (Northvale, N.J.: Jason Aronson, 1997); *The Soncino Talmud* (Chicago: Judaica Press, 1995); Hayim Nahman Bialik and Yehoshua Hana Ravnitzky, eds., *The Book of Legends: Legends from the Talmud and Midrash*, translated by William G. Braude (New York: Schocken Books, 1992).

Transliterations are based on the romanization table of Yale University Press.

The Margulies map is reproduced by permission of Nancy Margulies of Mindscapes, Montana, California, nm@montana.com.

The frontispiece is reproduced with permission of the artist, Barbara Leventhal Stern, Palo Alto, California, artbabe51@aol.com.

Library of Congress Cataloging-in-Publication Data

Leventhal, Robert F.
   Stepping forward: synagogue visioning and planning / Robert Leventhal.
      p. cm.
   ISBN 978-1-56699-331-9
   1. Synagogues—Organization and administration.   2. Jewish leadership.
I. Title.

   BM653.L36 2007
   296.6'5—dc22

                                                          2007039645

12   11   10   09   08   1   2   3   4   5   6   7   8   9   10

This book is dedicated to those leaders
who have been willing to work through
the initial resistance and the short-term chaos of planning
to create something new, to step forward.

Contents

PART 1

Trumah: The Gifts of Synagogue Life

PART 2

Teshuvah: Getting on a New Path

PART 3

'Avodah: Putting Ideas of Planning into Action

PART 4

'Omets Lev: The Courage to Engage

PART 5

Hoḥma: Lessons Learned

Appendix

Background
and Acknowledgments

Stepping Forward is a book about hope. It gives leaders tools to gather a team and focus them on a hopeful future. When leaders step forward to address the important issues of the community, their questions and conversations change that community. New leadership should increase the *capacity* for ongoing conversations and community building. Just as Joshua demonstrated gifted leadership, so his leadership brought out the gifts in the people.

Starting new leadership practices is often a lonely task. The board has developed a way of doing things. Certain voices are louder than others. Some steps in the process are skipped when they are inconvenient. Management consultant Jim Collins, in *Good to Great*, calls for nonprofit leaders to practice disciplined planning, governance, and resource allocation. All too often these boards have neither the disciplined people nor the processes to manage the road ahead. The general board and other parts of the leadership community may have come to acquiesce in the status quo. They have reduced expectations. Breaking these patterns is lonely work.

As a consultant I have often experienced loneliness in my work. I am on the road eighty to ninety nights a year. At 7:00 p.m. I am full of hope and energy. Deep inside, as I make that long drive to the airport hotel at 10:30 p.m., I sometimes hear an anxious voice from the evening's leadership meeting: "How can we do this process? You are asking us to attend three workshops. You are asking us all to call ten people for parlor meetings. That is a lot to ask." It is like the grumblings of the ten spies who felt like grasshoppers when they were asked to scout out the challenges of entering the land of Canaan. Like consultants, synagogue presidents and rabbis know what it is like to be out on a limb. In the face of such complaining, you too can feel that your talents are too small and the task is too great. In those lonely minutes your practice hangs in the balance.

As the freeway signs come in and out of view, I wait for a sign, for some assurance from God. Sometimes deep down, a still small voice answers me as it answered the ancient psalmist, "The LORD is the stronghold of my life, whom should I dread? . . . still would I be confident" (Psalm 27:2, 3). Having faith and being confident are choices. Two spies, Joshua and Caleb, heard the voice of faith and voted to enter the land. Congregational leadership development and planning is a choice. Planners make the decision to embrace the rigors and disciplines of planning. They will also make the decision about what to do with what they learn. Dedicated leaders will have to commit to the process in order to maintain momentum and implement the plans.

My Alban colleagues are always asking, "What is God calling you to do in this place?" Joshua and Caleb could say that despite their fears they were still confident. There is much of which I am not certain. I am in agreement with Joshua and Caleb: our people's future cannot be played out in the wilderness of Paran. We are called to cross to the other side. One of the things that I believe God is calling many of our congregations to do is to take responsibility for their future. They are being called to plan.

In the mystical tradition angels on earth are here to encourage our goodness. Some believe that angel specialists encourage our faith, our study, and our service. As I stepped forward into uncertain waters, I needed a host of specialists. We are taught that when we see someone stranded on the roadside, we are to stop our journey and help them with theirs. These angels got off of their carts to help raise me up.

I started on the side of the road as a very peripheral Jew. In my thirties I became involved in my Jewish community center and in the Federation campaign. In my early forties I went on the national United Jewish Appeal (UJA) leadership cabinet and was involved in Israel advocacy. In my mid-forties I turned to the realm of Jewish education. I became the president of the board of my local day school. In my late forties I volunteered to be the seventh grade teacher in our supplementary two-day religious school. What makes someone move from the periphery of Jewish practice and community to the center? I will return to this question throughout the book. My interest is more than academic. I am trying to look at my own road map and understand how a Jewish businessman from Dayton, Ohio, journeyed to the nation's largest Protestant consulting firm and created a practice of synagogue consulting. I am convinced that my journey was shaped by various angels.

I was first encouraged in Jewish communal life by our Federation's executive director, Peter Wells. I was recruited to develop a temple leadership program by my rabbi, Irving Bloom. I was supported in my Judaic training by my Hebrew tutor, Ilana Wolpert; my teacher at Ulpan Akiva, Mora Shoshi; and my advisor at Spertus Institute, Dr. Elliot Lefkovitz. As a seventh grade teacher, I was mentored by Temple Israel's educator, Rabbi Jennifer Marx Asch. I also want to thank the entire faculty of the Union for Reform Judaism's Sh'liach Kehillah program for two extraordinary summer workshops.

My synagogue consulting practice could not have developed without the generous support of STAR (Synagogue Transformation and Renewal). I would like to thank the Charles H. Schusterman Foundation, the Bronfman Foundation, and the Jewish Life Network (Michael Steinhardt) for their early support of the Alban consulting project.

As I developed my consulting, I was supported by the Rev. John Janka and Dr. Gil Rendle of the Alban Institute. My guide to the world of synagogue conflict was the Rev. Speed Leas. I was inspired by the workshop I took on Future Search with Marvin Weisbord and Sandra Janoff. This gave me a vision of the energy of large-group stakeholder workshops. I have adapted their tools and blended them with others. I would never claim that I am doing a Future Search, but I am indebted to their writings and work. I received input from such thoughtful readers as Jerry Garfield, Alice Mann, Susan Beaumont, Kathryn Palen, and Larry Peers. Rabbi Tsvi Blanchard and Rabbi Alfredo Borodowski read key Judaic segments. Early denominational collaborations were extremely important. I would like to particularly thank Rabbi Jerome Epstein, Dr. Moshe Edelman, Dr. Stephen Huberman, Dr. Richard Lederman, and Rabbi Paul Drazen of United Synagogues of Conservative Judaism (USCJ). I would also like to thank Rabbi Sean Zevit of the Jewish Reconstructionist Federation (JRF). My Midwest regional director, Rabbi Elliot Kleinman, his successor, Rabbi Steven Mills, and past regional president Dr. David Davidson were helpful in my initial workshops. In July 2003 I began an important grant with the UJA Federation of New York. They have supported the development of my work and encouraged me to offer my leadership workshops to the Long Island community. I would like to

קדימה I am in agreement with Joshua and Caleb: our people's future cannot be played out in the wilderness of Paran.

thank Rabbi Deborah Josleow, Elliot Forchheimer, Dru Greenwood, Janet Bienenfeld, Donna Divon, Ilana Slawitsky, and Erika Witover for their support of the program.

I would like to mention the Alban editorial team of Richard Bass, Kristy Pullen, and Ann Delgehausen of Trio Bookworks.

Finally, I would like to thank my wife, Sarah, and my three boys, Daniel, Micah, and Eli, for their support, and my mother, Shirley Leventhal, and father, Harry Leventhal, of blessed memory, for my love of Judaism.

Introduction:
The Leadership Seder

And it shall be, when he sits on the throne of kingship, that he shall write for himself a copy of the teachings in a book before the levitical priests. And it shall be with him and he shall read in it all the days of his life, so that he may learn to fear the LORD his God, to keep all of the words of his teaching and these statutes.

—Deuteronomy 17:18-19

Stepping Forward is a call for more intentional synagogue leadership. It argues that like the biblical kings, leaders must regularly revisit their mission, values, and purpose. They must "step forward" and write their own scroll. Leaders continuously strive to connect God's will, their will, and the people's will within the context of their times, so that the Torah wisdom will guide their path "all of the days" of their life.

I know some of you have been frustrated as you try to develop leaders. While it may be difficult to teach leadership, people can step forward and learn it together. Some scholars argue that the king was actually supposed to create two scrolls. The first was for his personal spiritual practice. The second was for the public, that is, to be placed "before the levitical priests." From this we learn that Jewish leadership is a journey of both personal and communal growth.

> קדימה **Leaders must regularly revisit their mission, values, and purpose. They must "step forward" and write their own scroll.**

Leaders Are Challenged to "Turn It"

Like the king, today's leaders need to revisit ancient truths and share their learning with the public. The tradition says we are to take the Torah and "turn it": to look at it from different angles and with the perspective of our times. When I speak of the Torah, I am referring to the ḥumash (five books) or Jewish Bible, the oral tradition (Mishnah, the Talmud), the Bible commentaries, and the midrash (interpretations). I believe the Torah is living literature. The Torah tradition evolves in seminaries and universities, in the presence of contemporary rabbis who wrestle with its ancient truths and their current realties. It is enriched by serious Jews who seek to step forward like the king and turn it and the stories they weave together about their journey.

Stepping Forward explains the stepping stones of synagogue planning. Leaders are tasked to plan the agenda of the board. They need a plan to develop leaders. They need to create long-term plans. Whatever the scope of your planning, you will need to learn to look at issues from multiple angles and consider multiple paths. You will have to turn it!

Some leaders will respond, "We all know what we do here. We have services, we do life cycle events, we celebrate the holidays, we have a school. . . ." What more needs to be said? Some congregational leaders have a very strong sense of their culture, their context, and their purpose. Most will find it helpful to reflect on how the congregation makes the connection between ancient truths and current realties. This effort to make the connection is the writing of a new congregational scroll.

Jim Collins argues in *Good to Great* (2005) that organizations need to connect what they are passionate about, the communities they can best serve, and the things they do best. Each leadership team must look at their situation from every angle so that they can honestly address these leadership questions. When leaders step forward with answers to these questions, they can help congregations develop a compelling language for current members, prospects, and staff.

קדימה I will not describe an ideal rabbi or a model congregation, but I offer stories about synagogue leadership that will help you step forward.

In order to promote their mission with passion, leaders need to have the hands-on experience of "writing their scroll." *Stepping Forward* takes its title from the moment when Joshua and the priests step into the waters of the Jordan. Like the king they have the Torah at their side. They carry the Ark of the Covenant, which will guide them on the road ahead. When Joshua enters the land, like the king he will write his own scroll. He ritualizes their covenanting process by circumcising the males, having the Torah read, and writing the law on giant pillars. This book provides tools for leadership development and for a more in-depth planning process that I call Synagogue Visioning and Planning (SVP). Using this book, you will write down some of your covenants and engage your people with the challenge of building a covenantal community. You will learn new rituals that will guide you on the stepping stones to accomplish your synagogue's plan.

New Rituals: The Leadership Seder

How can leaders ritualize their leadership journey? The text above argues that these Torah principles require constant reflection. We don't tell the story of the Exodus at Passover every five years. Even though many know it well, we revisit it every year. We are challenged to remember and experience what it would have been like to be a slave. The Passover seder seeks to help us feel as if we actually had been slaves, to experience that bondage.

Leadership development programs can learn a great deal from the Passover seder. It is a showcase of experiential learning. There is something for everyone. There are very concrete things we can do. We have prayers to read, texts to hear, objects to touch, things to smell and taste, songs to hear. We are challenged to engage all of our senses and all types of learners.

Hagadot are books that guide us through the Passover seder, like workbooks to help us understand the holiday. (Hagadah means "to tell.") I enjoy using several hagadot to guide our Passover table. I hope this workbook will make a contribution to your leadership seder. In this book I will not describe an ideal rabbi or a model congregation, but I offer stories about synagogue leadership that will help you step forward.

Studies show that 80 percent of American Jews find their way to a Passover seder. The leadership seder is not such a well-developed ritual. Like any new ritual it will take extra energy to bring people to the table. Just as the seder has its narrative (magid) and its cast of characters, so we revisit several well-known biblical narratives to tell our leadership story.

Reluctant and Courageous Leaders

Consider the biblical story of the twelve spies whom Moses asked to scout out the land. All but two (Joshua and Caleb) came back with a depressing story that in the so-called land of milk and honey "the people who inhabit the country are powerful, and the cities are fortified and very large" (Numbers 13:28). They report that the country that they "traversed and scouted is one that devours its settlers" (Numbers 13:32). They were reluctant leaders. They reported that they felt like grasshoppers as they looked at their adversaries and contemplated the future. When the people received this report, they were frightened. They saw the land as full of forces of resistance and were reluctant to step forward. To proceed into the land without adequate information would be reckless. Moses had asked the spies to be sure to bring back a taste of the possibilities of the new land. They were to share their experience of joy in the land.

קדימה Throughout the tradition we find those who were reluctant and those who were willing to step forward.

Contrast the spies with Joshua's leadership as he led the people to step forward into the Jordan and enter Canaan, the land of promise. Think of the courageous leadership of Abraham. Throughout the tradition we find those who were reluctant and those who were willing to step forward. This book is dedicated to leadership champions who call out, "All of you who are hungry for leadership, come and join us at this table. Let the seder begin!"

Our Hero: Joshua

One of the key narratives in our magid is the story of Joshua's leadership. The Israelites wandered for forty years in the desert. God had punished them with a forty-year exile because their leaders (the spies) gave a report that showed a lack of hope and heart in God's land of milk and honey. As you see in the frontispiece illustration, Joshua's procession is blessed because the priests carry the Ark of the Covenant. Joshua is able to part the waters of resistance because his mission is for the sake of heaven, not for his self-interest. Joshua has many tasks to do when he crosses into the new land, but all of the tasks are connected to a central document of values and goals: the Torah.

The first half of *Stepping Forward* will help leaders write down some leadership lessons for the journey. Most synagogue leaders are caught up in the day-to-day managerial details of sustaining the congregation. This book challenges you to be more like Abraham and take some risks to find out what's next. The second half of the book will provide you with several different exercises you can try out on your congregational practice field.

Engaging in a structured process of conversations is neither easy nor without the possibility of conflict. It takes strength. Joshua was well suited for the challenge he faced. Today's leaders will need to marshal deep reservoirs of patience and strength to help their congregations step forward into the future. While this book offers a vision of stepping forward, its chapters provide an honest accounting of some of the very concrete challenges and opportunities you will encounter.

From Strength to Strength—
One Chapter at a Time

Each congregation is different, so these leadership development campaigns all have their own character. Each congregation will move through the seder at their own speed. Some will skip around, and others will savor each page and welcome every commentary. My hope is that they all find tools to build capacity. I am not a scholar of synagogue history, but I have walked side by side with many rabbis and leaders. I believe that if you turn to this book enough, you will find in these pages some tools and perspectives to build your capacity—to go from strength to strength.

- Some will use this book just to help them review how they gather data (chapter 5).
- Some will use this book to plan a one-day retreat on values or goals (chapters 13 and 14).
- Some will use the steering committee development chapter to support a new long-range planning team (chapter 9).
- Some will identify recommended reading for membership committees and volunteer development teams (chapter 1).
- Some will use a variety of chapters to support a three- to four-session leadership development plan.

- Some may have the readiness do a complete project. They
  may be attracted to an organized "step-by-step" approach to
  help sustain them for a more in-depth twelve- to fifteen-month
  process.

This book summarizes a variety of approaches that have been tried in the last three years. No congregation has used all of these tools.

In my experience most congregations have done little if any planning in the last five years. Few have conducted an organized leadership development program of more than one session. They have been reluctant to set the leadership seder table. I encourage you to set the table and welcome your guests. The leadership seder offers synagogue members a chance to make the connections between their personal stories, the congregation's story, and the story of the Jewish people.

Just One Hagadah among Many

As I said, at my Passover table, I like to multitask with several hagadot. I am not trying to have everyone follow me page by page. I seldom go in a straight line. I often fumble between my various hagadot and may have to be reminded that I left something out. Similarly, in this workbook, I do not hold up one rabbi or one congregation as a model. I am not picking winners. I am not qualified or comfortable trying to discuss the many theological questions that rabbis, denominational officials, and Jewish studies professors might debate in relation to a congregation's purpose. While I have held many positions in the Jewish community and have been a congregational consultant for six years, I am still learning. I really only got serious about Jewish learning at age thirty-seven (eighteen years ago), when I went on a young leadership mission to Israel.

קדימה **All of the tasks are connected to a central document of values and goals: the Torah.**

There is much I don't know. I do know something about the journey of an emerging leader. I know something about the joys and oys of stepping forward.

I have had some experience helping leaders have meaningful conversations about what their strengths are, what they are passionate about, what drives their organization, and who their community is. My background makes me comfortable in all of those conversations. I am prepared to step forward with my observations and experiences as a businessman, educator, consultant, fundraiser, and lay leader. I try to show the connection between my experiences and the challenges of synagogue leadership. As I go though the leadership seder, I hope that others at the table are encouraged to make their connections. I am prepared to share my observations about volunteerism, commitment, leadership, vision, and courage. Those who are hungry for leadership, come and connect!

Some of you who are chairing your board meetings may be a little anxious about creating new leadership rituals. I believe if you are transparent, your team will learn from your own efforts to develop a leadership agenda. In 1999–2000 I stepped forward to volunteer as our congregation's seventh grade religious school teacher. As a new teacher, I was inspired to become a more transparent leader by the words of educator Parker J. Palmer in his book *The Courage to Teach* (1998, 11):

> Good teachers possess the capacity for connectedness. They are able to weave a complex web of connections among themselves, their subjects, and their students so that students can learn to weave a world for themselves.
>
> The methods used by weavers vary widely: lectures, Socratic dialogue, laboratory experiments, collaborative problem solving, creative chaos. The connection made by good teachers are held not in their methods but in their hearts—meaning heart in its ancient sense, the place where intellect and emotion and spirit and will converge in the human self.

This book is for planning committees, leadership development teams, and boards. Like the gifted teacher, they have been challenged to work to make the connections. As they make these connections, they will help others learn how to make the connections between their will, the congregation's will, and God's will.

Who Leads the Synagogue Visioning and Planning Journey?

The SVP process is led by a group of about twelve members of the SVP steering committee, which includes the rabbi and the executive director. It meets at least monthly for about twelve months to gather data, recruit participants, conduct workshops, and debrief their experiences. The steering committee is composed of proven leaders of the board, such as the past president and committee chairs. It is seasoned with prospective leaders who have demonstrated spiritual maturity, have helpful planning skills, and have shown a commitment to Jewish communal life. Steering committee members recruit various segments (such as new members, long-standing members, worship-focused members, empty nesters) of the congregation to participate in parlor meetings. They go on to recruit members to become co-planners, who are called stakeholders. The steering committee, the professional staff, and some fifty stakeholders representing different groups, go though various planning exercises.

Rabbis

This book is for rabbis who want to encourage leaders to jump into the water of new learning. They want to help design a forum to talk about what matters and to be accessible to talk about what the experience was like. SVP rabbis believe that, in order to part the sea of resistance and inertia, they need to allow the free flow of feedback from parlor meetings and planning workshops. They strive to be open to hearing reflections and suggestions, even if these do not exactly fit their vision. We all bring our assumptions to our work. SVP was influenced by my experience as a liberal Jew. Many of the workshops and tools have been helpful to more traditional communities.

SVP rabbis learn to be less reactive. Just because members provide input about what they would like the congregation to do, the rabbi is not bound to respond to every suggestion. SVP rabbis are optimistic that, as a key member of the SVP steering committee, they can help shape the leadership conversation. They can listen with empathy and develop a plan that connects the will of members to God's will. Even if they are not always in authority in the process, they feel comfortable that they can be appreciated as an authority. Like Bezalel, the master craftsman of the tabernacle, they welcome the unique contributions and gifts of each member. They understand that they have a unique responsibility to step forward and organize these gifts for the creation of a sacred and dedicated community.

Lay Leaders

SVP is for lay leaders who want to expand the size of their core leadership. They feel it is important to invest in developing new leaders. They want to find a way to integrate new and seasoned leaders by helping them work together on an engaging and important project. They believe that by developing shared facts, shared values, shared goals, and shared accountability, they will build the kind of team that breaks through the force of resistance and helps the congregation step forward. They know that the rabbi is particularly well positioned to help them understand how the tradition informs this journey. They are open to sharing their thoughts and reflections with the rabbi and other staff. They understand that the process of dialogue can be as important as the end products (the plans).

Executive Directors and Administrators

SVP calls on the leadership expertise of executive directors, who will help with recruitment and logistics. They will anticipate administrative barriers to success. They will build volunteer relationships. They will look for opportunities to put some of the creative ideas on a fast track. They will ensure that important documents are treated with respect, filed, and distributed. They help drive SVP.

Who Goes on the Journey?

SVP will require that the steering committee attempt to recruit approximately nine stakeholder groups. These might include new members, long-standing members, families with young children, empty nesters, etc. SVP workshops thus take courage to recruit for and to conduct. Synagogue leaders are often shocked by the level of commitment I ask for. "You want our steering committee of twelve to recruit forty to sixty planners? How can we do that?" Leaders know that if they aim too high, the goal will seem unattainable. If they aim too low, there will be no urgency to step forward. I don't expect leaders to leap tall buildings, but I do ask them to stretch—to take some bigger steps.

The biggest complaint I heard in my early work with synagogues was that the mission and vision statements developed by long-range planning committees were not implemented or anchored in the culture. Too often the documents were left in a three-ring binder in the synagogue office. Small planning groups did not have the critical mass to change the leadership or congregational culture. Research has shown that "the fate of the congregation is intertwined with the percentage of its members who choose to be actively involved. The high correlation suggests that a change in the size of the active core *ipso facto* changes the nature of the congregation" (Sales 2006, 3). By including a high participation requirement in the SVP design, I am encouraging congregations to increase their overall capacity for leadership, which will produce longer lasting benefits. The involvement of a large group (up to seventy) will help the congregation take some bigger steps. That is the ideal.

The number seventy often stands for a holistic community. Jacob moved his family of seventy to Egypt; this group would lay the foundation for the Israelite nation. When Moses traveled up the mountain to accept the Torah, he brought seventy leaders with him to the foot of the mountain; the number seventy stands for the nation receiving the law. The highest assembly of rabbis is the Sanhedrin, which has seventy members, plus one to break the tie. Seventy is the result of multiplying seven times ten: Seven is associated with the seven days of the week—a complete week. Ten is associated with a complete congregation (i.e., minyan). Of course, in smaller congregations or ones with less history of leadership development, I have sometimes worked with groups of forty to fifty. The large leadership group idea is inspired by the idea of wholeness.

קדימה SVP is about people, not just paper! It doesn't just create documents; it calls forward the gifts of the membership.

Some congregations do not have a strong history of volunteerism and engagement, and they are fearful that they cannot recruit a large planning group. Others are at a stage of development when planning is not a critical issue. Some congregations feel their first priority is training their current boards. These groups are often looking for smaller steps. The tools in this book can be applied to the issue of leadership and board development. I have also developed one-day retreats that incorporate some of the exercises from the values and goals workshop.

Setting the Table:
Synagogue Visioning and Planning Process

Synagogue Visioning and Planning is about hope and heart. It is a collaborative process that uses a steering committee and three large stakeholder group workshops to create a *values statement*; a set of *strategic goals*; and a series of *vision statements and action plans* to implement the goals. SVP is about people, not just paper! It doesn't just create documents; it calls forward the gifts of the membership.

What Does the Journey Look Like?

Joshua knew that the steps on a journey need to be commemorated. That is why he took the stones from the river Jordan and made a monument on the other side of the river. The following is a quick look at some of the key stepping stones for SVP:

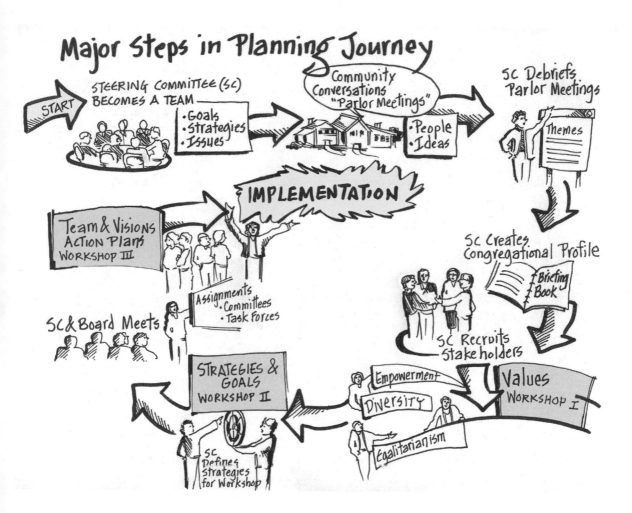

Major Steps in Planning the Journey

SVP Cases

As you follow the stepping stones through this book, you will hear leadership stories from the journey—stories of learning and insight, stories of heroes who stepped forward.

Planning Turns Up Hidden Talents

One congregation was convinced that they would never be able to recruit a steering committee to do this work for the next year. They found, however, that they had many talented members who were energized by the prospect of bringing their talents to the service of the congregation they loved. Many were not active at the time. Many of them had significant experience in strategy and planning. They were so proactive that they took ownership of the project and reshaped the process to meet their unique congregational context.

Imagining the Future Helps Healing in the Present

One congregation had some long-standing divisions. They had generational issues and ideological difference. These issues had never been resolved with the rabbi. The SVP provided a container to hold these complex issues. Out of this process the rabbi was better able to understand the members' concerns, and they were able to be more hopeful that they could mediate their differences. A prominent leader was motivated to become president, and key organizational issues, long unresolved, began to be addressed.

Bringing Diverse Members Together Keeps Their Needs in View

One congregation in the Southwest had a core group of long-standing members who lived near the synagogue. Over the years most new members were coming from new exurbs that were some distance away. There was an ongoing discussion about the needs of new members but no focused campaign. As the members from these areas continued to share their feelings throughout SVP, the issues became clearer. Addressing the needs of all of the synagogues' members, they began to explore satellite services and programs. They looked into transportation for seniors.

SVP CASE

The Basics of SVP

Major Workshops

You can be sure that when leaders sign up for a year-long process, they want to see some results, or what some business leaders call "deliverables" (goals, actions, working groups, etc.). Below I outline the workshops and some of their goals and offer case studies that show how the goals are achieved.

Workshop 1: Values

The workshop reviews the existing culture. Participants are assigned to stakeholder *segment* groups (e.g., new members, long-standing members) to explore the values they feel should guide the community. The groups produce a "values statement in process."

Workshop 2: Strategic Goals

This workshop looks at the past and the present. It explores congregational history. It uses an SVP briefing book to review important internal data about revenue and expenses, enrollment, membership, and demographics. It captures learning from the parlor meetings. It provides important data about the external environment. The stakeholders share their observations about the data. In the first workshop, they participated simply as stakeholder segments. In this workshop, they are empowered to work on the goal topics that most interest them. These goal discussion groups create "goals statements in process."

SVP CASE

The Rabbi's Voice

The rabbi of one congregation had exceptional teaching skills, but he was a little introverted. He was reluctant to bring his teaching skills to the areas of leadership and board development. In the parlor meetings it was clear that members saw him as the congregation's number one asset, but on key issues his voice was not fully heard. When it came time to write the values statement, he became the senior partner. He worked with the workshop notes and captured the aspirations of the planners. He infused these ideas with great Jewish learning and wove key elements of the transition into the plan. The planners felt that the rabbi's contribution to the values statement in process reflected where they were but more importantly captured the rabbi's voice about where they might want to be. The SVP values workshop provided a vehicle to strengthen that voice.

Workshop 3: Vision and Action Planning

In this workshop stakeholders are assigned to specific committees and task forces to address the emerging ("in process") values and goals. They form their groups and create a vision for their task force or committee. They look for short-term initiatives that can be fast-tracked. They lay the foundation for longer term goals and objectives.

Leadership Rituals

In order for the leadership seder to work, it needs its rituals just like the worship service. Steering committee members fill out their membership profiles so that they are ready to ask a member to fill out theirs. This ritualizes the feedback process. Members commit to disclose something of themselves, and leaders commit to listen. When the whole community brainstorms descriptions of the congregations' culture, they are stimulated and connected by the thoughts of others. When the stakeholders post their observations about the briefing book on the thirty-foot wall of butcher paper, some may sense that they are like supplicants sticking notes into the bricks of the kotel—a place for every idea and prayer. The ritual of the profile, the values brainstorming session, or the posting of thoughts will have different meanings for different people, but experience has shown that the rituals and symbols of the workshops evoke powerful feelings.

Keeping a Conversation Going

One congregation struggled with governance issues. After SVP, the governance task force continued to meet. At first there was little progress, but over time new approaches to board planning and executive committee–board relationships began to evolve. SVP brought the issue to the surface (posted it on the wall), and the task force worked on the issue long enough to see change slowly take root.

SVP CASE

Duration and Schedule

It usually takes two months to get approval for the process from the board. The steering committee will meet for three months to help plan the process and conduct parlor meetings. The rest of the stakeholders will participate for about four to five months. Thus, the initial process normally runs from nine to twelve months. Task forces and committees then will work for another three to twelve months.

Final Products

All plans have a congregational profile briefing book, a values statement, a set of strategic goals, a set of assignments to committees and task forces, and at least some of the early task force work.

The briefing book (see chapter 5) contains information on the community context (economics, Jewish population trends, schools, housing issues, etc.). It also contains internal information about the congregation's membership history, ages of members, types of membership units,

enrollment in the school, etc. Some create profiles of their most important types of prospective members. They may even try to articulate the
compelling benefits that would appeal to them. The briefing book also
provides financial information, including the sources and uses of the congregation's funds and the key drivers of its business model. It describes
key programs (worship, adult education, social actions, etc.) and signa-
ture events. It outlines the synagogue organization, governance, and
committees.

SVP is designed to develop new leadership disciplines. Each congregation is different, and there is wide variation in the detail and sophisti-
cation of the plans that result from SVP. I encourage congregations to see
this as more than a twelve- to eighteen-month planning process and to
build stronger planning disciplines. One of these disciplines is to put the
assumptions and the priorities of the plans into a future budget (ideally
a five-year budget forecast). As new insights come from committees and
task forces, the plan may need to be updated, but the planners will have
built a planning mentality and a framework to hold their learning. These
will serve the leadership well.

Outcomes

SVP has been tried in its current form with seven congregations. The
individual workshops on values and goals have been used for leadership
development, conflict resolution, and team building with another ten
congregations. The model in this book was formalized in 2003; thus SVP
is still very much an experiment in process. Based on this admittedly
limited experience, I do believe that the following kinds of outcomes
are realistic for congregations with enough readiness to be candidates
for SVP.

1. The process should identify and engage new leaders. Their
   talents will be immediately leveraged through new task forces
   and current committees.
2. It should help provide leadership skills for the steering
   committee (gathering data, debriefing congregational
   meetings, active listening, managing conflict, communication
   skills, decision making).
3. It should provide shared facts (i.e., briefing book, group
   learning) about the current situation. This should help build
   greater consensus for action.

4. It should provide leaders with insight into their culture (dominant themes document). This should provide a better sense of strategic challenges and directions.

5. It should yield some specific community agreements: values statement, goals statement, and a detailed plan for several task forces and committees.

6. It should develop disciplines for planning, decision making, and resource allocation. It should provide the finance committee with critical assumptions and priority goals to build a five-year financial business plan.

7. It should stimulate both leadership and financial gifts.

8. It should provide motivation to develop an ongoing leadership development program.

9. The whole SVP process should help leaders reflect on their accountability to God, fellow leaders, and the congregation.

10. It should provide some new practices to encourage accountability (committee charters, committee plans, key initiative tracking).

11. It should provide a framework for a communications plan to the membership, prospective members, and the community.

Is SVP for Everyone?

The SVP model is deeply rooted in the values of empowerment, account-ability, collaboration, creativity, and innovation. SVP seeks to listen to a wide array of congregational voices so that it can honor what members value. It seeks to encourage new leaders while respecting long-standing leaders. It works hard to ensure that existing leaders do not inadvertently block the path of new leaders and ideas. In chapter 7 I discuss some of the factors that determine the readiness of a congregation to do visioning and planning. Leaders should read chapter 7 to make an honest assessment of their readiness.

I come from an entrepreneurial family. My grandfather was entrepreneurial enough to get on a boat and come to America. My father started a cleaning products business with one employee and saw it grow into a major business. I had a chance to reflect on this entrepreneurial family history when I taught entrepreneurial marketing at the University of Dayton. One of the definitions of an entrepreneur was "one who steps forward." Developing experiments to encourage leaders to step forward was the passion that motivated me to write this book.

Is SVP Only for Synagogues?

The SVP model was designed for synagogues, and the case studies and examples are drawn from that environment. I believe these tools can be effective in developing leadership for Hillel chapters, Jewish community enters, Federation teams, camp boards, other Jewish agencies, and nonprofits.

Do You Have to Be Jewish to Use SVP?

As the first Jewish consultant at Alban, I had to jump into unknown waters. I often had to translate Alban theories and learning to the specific environment of synagogues. Most of it was very applicable, but there were some major differences that had to be understood and honored. Can this book be helpful to churches? I believe there are some insights and tools here that could be adapted for churches. You just have to be willing to make some translations and build some bridges from our context to yours. I hope that you will then find joy in learning how one faith tradition can raise helpful questions for another.

How Is This Book Organized?

Part 1 of the book is dedicated to the building blocks of congregational leadership. In chapter 1 I discuss the leadership challenge of bringing the community's gifts to the service of the tabernacle. In chapter 2 I discuss the kinds of things that leaders do.

Part 2 looks at elements of planning and techniques to manage change. In chapter 3 I present several different approaches to planning. In chapter 4 I review the critical need to understand the synagogue environment. Chapter 5 looks at ways to gather data. Chapter 6 discusses authority and decision making in times of change. In chapter 7 I then look at the congregation's overall readiness for change. Chapter 8 describes planning as a campaign to manage change.

Part 3 deals with the process of getting the planning process started. In chapter 9 I review the composition and characteristics of the steering committee, including members' roles and responsibilities. I then go into detail on recruitment for parlor meetings (chapter 10) and strategies for training members of the steering committee and the stakeholders, and interpreting the parlor meetings they hold (chapter 11).

Part 4 details the planning workshops and other meetings necessary to gain consensus on the plan to implement it. These include, after the overview (chapter 12), the workshop on values (chapter 13), the workshop on strategies and goals (chapter 14), the delegation of responsibilities related to the plan (chapter 15), and accountability and feedback (chapter 16).

Part 5, chapter 17, addresses what I have learned from planning and leadership development projects, presented as eighteen lessons.

Welcome to Stepping Forward!
I hope that whatever part of this journey you embrace,
it will be encouraging and productive—a journey of hope and heart.

Traveler's Prayer (Tefilat HaDerekh)

May it be Your will, Lord my God, to lead me on the way of peace and guide and direct my steps in peace, so that You will bring me happily to my destination, safe and sound. Save me from danger on the way. Give me good grace, kindness and favor in both Your eyes and in the eyes of all whom I may meet. Hear this my prayer, for You are a God who hears the heart's supplication and communion. Blessed are You, Lord our God, who hears prayer.

PART 1

Trumah: The Gifts of Synagogue Life

R Judah said in the name of Rav,
Bezalel knew how to combine the letters
by which heaven and earth were created.

—*b. Berakhot 55a*

The SVP process is dedicated to exploring creative ways to engage synagogue members, to draw out their gifts and talents. *Stepping Forward* brings some of the practical leadership, management, and communications skills of the business world to the service of the sacred. We challenge steering committees to combine their gifts for theory and practical knowledge—to combine heaven and earth. As leaders better understand the gifts of synagogue membership, they can bring their special gifts to the congregation and welcome the gifts of others.

1.

The Gifts of
Synagogue Membership

*The L*ord *spoke to Moses, saying: Tell the Israelite people to bring Me gifts; you shall accept gifts for Me from every person whose heart so moves him. . . . And let them make Me a sanctuary that I may dwell among them.*

— Exodus 25:1-8

"Stepping forward" means bringing one's gift to the service of the community. I will discuss various types of leadership in this book, but most leaders are challenged to create a compelling and inspirational vision that will attract followers. Our biblical texts tell of such a vision: God asked the Israelites to step forward to build a spiritual home. The building of the tabernacle is a beautiful and comforting part of the Exodus narrative. It comes right after the incident of the golden calf. In the story of the golden calf, the people did not have the courage to wait for Moses to return. They were frightened and felt they needed to make an image of God to comfort them. Moses, as we know, broke the first tablets when he saw this idolatry. Then he calmed down and convinced God to create a second set of tablets. After he returned, the people affirmed their commitment to God by following God's instructions for the building of the mishkan, the desert tabernacle.

In the story of the golden calf the people panicked because they couldn't feel God's presence. The story of the spies (Numbers 13) repeats this theme: they felt unsupported. In contrast, the story of the mishkan tells how God promised that if they built a sanctuary, God would abide with them.

In the Bible God facilitated this process by inspiring a master crafts-man to coordinate the building of the tabernacle. God provided a gifted leader, Bezalel.

> And Moses said to the Israelites: See, the Lord has singled out by name Bezalel, son of Uri, son of Hur, of the tribe of Judah. He has endowed him with a divine spirit of *skill, ability, and knowledge* in every kind of craft . . . to make designs for work in gold, silver, and copper, to cut stones for setting . . . to work in every kind of designer's craft. (Exodus 35:30-33, italics added)

Bezalel knows how to motivate the people and mold their talent into great art—the tabernacle. The text tells that he has three kinds of knowl-edge. He is endowed with the knowledge to learn from others (ḥokhma), to apply that knowledge (tevunah), and to inspire others (Da'at) to step forward. The Sages said of Bezalel's gift that he could bring heaven (shamayim) and earth ('erets) together. He could take God's inspiration and help the people put the worldly task into action.

Contrast the leadership of Bezalel with that of the twelve spies who are sent to scout out the land. They have a similar opportunity to Bezalel's. They have to do a worldly task—scout out the land, identify the oppor-tunities and challenges, make a fair report. They also have a spiritual challenge. They are to bear witness to the land that God has promised the people. They are to look at it with awe. They are to feel blessed and protected. They are to bring a hopeful report that comes from the mouth of those who have born witness and who believe. They are to inspire the people.

Bezalel accepts the gifts of the mixed multitudes of Egypt. He sees their heart, not their shabby garments. He sees their strengths, not just their weaknesses. In our parlor meetings, we will ask members to describe the congregation's strengths and weaknesses. As we discuss these, we invite participants, like Bezalel, to connect our gifts to the opportunities for mission.

Bezalel maintains a hopeful vision of how all of these small offerings can come together. The spies see the challenges (enemies, fortresses, etc.) of the land but cannot see how the mission can come to fruition. They have no faithful vision.

In the end, the spies are punished because they have no faith in God's mission or God's gifts. In the mishkan story we see how people can be encouraged and empowered to give. We see how two different leaderships handle their God-appointed missions. Even in the earliest part of the biblical narrative people have choices about the gifts they bring. They can be reluctant, or they can step forward.

In the building of the tabernacle every gift was welcome (Exodus 25), but God had a master craftsman, Bezalel (see Exodus 35:30-34), to ensure that all of the individual talent and gifts contributed to something beautiful—something that honored God's design. In the building of the tabernacle we have the model for how the individual and the community can come together. An individual's gifts are honored when they are offered for the sake of heaven.

What does it mean to be called to bring your personal gifts to the service of God and community? Synagogue leaders need to understand the gifts they bring. I believe that if they can learn how to bring their own personal gifts to the service of the community, they will be better able to see how others' gifts could be woven into the overall plan. If they know their own story, they will be better at reading the hearts of others.

Leaders need to understand why members join and why they leave. They need to know what gives meaning to synagogue membership. Rabbi Eric Yoffie raised these issues in his biennial address to the Union of Reform Congregations' convention. He noted that 50 percent of new members leave five years after they join (Yoffie 2004). He pointed out that there are key decision points when members question the value of their membership: when their children leave religious school, when their children go off to college, after they are no longer active in leadership positions, etc.

The Gifts of Synagogue Membership

Leaders need to fully reflect on the gifts of synagogue community. What gives meaning to members? How can we build on this? Before you launch a campaign for leadership and change, you as a leader need to know what you are promoting. What is your synagogue's compelling proposition? The chart below (Fig. 2) comes from a study of sixteen congregations. About 1,300 members of these congregations completed a survey about their relationship to Judaism, to the congregation, and to the community. What's important methodologically is that the survey was distributed to a random sample drawn from the membership lists of each of the congregations, thereby increasing our confidence that results can be generalized to the full membership.

Each number below indicates the percentage of the 1,300 respondents who said that an element of synagogue membership was not at all, somewhat, or extremely important to them.

Elements That Give Meaning to Synagogue Membership

Adapted from Sales 2004, 21–22

Element	Not at all important	Somewhat important	Extremely important
1. High Holiday Services	3	19	78
2. Life Cycle Events (baby naming, yartseit, bar/bat mitsvah)	6	26	68
3. Other Holiday Celebrations (Sukkot, Purim, Passover)	11	51	37
4. Children's Education (preschool, nursery, or religious school)	33	15	52
5. Family Activities at the Synagogue	28	45	28
6. Social and Cultural Activities at the Synagogue	22	57	21
7. Adult Education or Torah Study	32	46	22
8. Volunteer or Social Action Projects	28	56	17
9. Youth Group/Youth Activities	40	31	30
10. Caring for or Receiving Care	36	45	19
11. Daily minyan or Weekly Shabbat service	42	34	24

Element	Not at all important	Somewhat important	Extremely important
12. Board and Committee Work	56	30	13
13. Sisterhood or Brotherhood	57	35	9
14. Volunteer Work (library, gift shop, school)	58	33	9

"So often," writes Luther Snow (2004, 5), "we make lists of the things we have done and problems we haven't fixed. We get so accustomed to dealing with the negatives that we forget what it feels like to focus on the positives." Planners must balance a focus on what needs to be improved with an appreciation of what is *working well*. Leaders need to be able to talk about what is bringing meaning to their own membership. They should look at different segments of the congregation and inquire about what is bringing meaning for them.

Rabbi Harold Kushner argues that we must remember we were a people before we were a formal religion. Our ancestors were a family with a relationship with God. We had this relationship long before the Torah was revealed at Sinai. Congregational leaders may debate issues about ideology, but when a member resigns (for a reason other than moving away), we will often find that a failure to build relationships with staff and/or community was a critical factor. Look at the exit interviews. They left because the community was not compelling, not because of theological differences.

I would like to offer a personal reflection on the survey's findings. I will work to articulate how these elements bring meaning to me and invite you to do the same.

The Gifts and Possibilities of Membership

1. The Gift of Keruv at High Holidays:
Our Relationship with God

Members may have a tough time describing their theology, but most believe in God. Many members have little interest, skill, or energy when it comes to debating theological ideas, but they have a fundamental need to be touched by the divine. Awe of God (yir'at Hashem) is a core value of prayer, or tefilah. Members may struggle most of the year to feel the presence of God. Rabbi Alan Lew's book on the high holidays is titled *This Is Real and You Are Completely Unprepared: The Days of Awe as a Journey of Transformation* (2003). I can certainly relate to this. Most leaders I meet are not comfortable talking about what God is challenging them to do—they are not prepared.

At times of crisis they turn to God. During the high holidays they become more aware of their limitations; they come to grips with fear, loss, and failure. One of the great things about synagogue life is to see how such moments such as the high holidays memorial service, yiskor, offer transcendence to members. Members rank high holidays as the number one thing that gives meaning to membership. The high holidays make a difference. Only about 40 percent of American Jews belong to a congregation, but 67 percent fast on Yom Kippur. They know there is something special about that day.

In the study, respondents said they value regular worship much further down the list (eleventh). One of the challenges for leadership is to find a way to capture the power and transcendence of the high holidays at other times. In a recent workshop with Protestant pastors of large congregations I asked them about worship. They reported that about 50 percent of their members regularly attend one of their Sunday worship services. Several described how these spiritual practices changed how leaders work. Many Jewish members are seeking, but they have not found how weekly prayer can make a difference in their lives. Many leaders are serving congregations but have not found how Jewish values and practices might change the shape of their boardroom.

2. The Gift of Community:
Celebrating Key Life Cycle Events

The synagogue is a place for members to celebrate beney mitsvah, weddings, and funerals. Members value the chance to mark their important life cycle events and those of friends. The synagogue helps bring meaning to these events. Members see the synagogue as the place where you can celebrate your joys and get support to bear your grief. Leaders who value the gift of community, or kehilah, will want to ensure that this gift is available for future generations. Whether members are active or not, most have a sense that the Jewish people need to continue to be there for each other.

3. The Gift of Holiday Celebrations:
Living with a Jewish Calendar

Members find that the holidays provide an opportunity to come together to celebrate ancient rituals and practices. In our busy world, time is scarce. Anyone who has tried to get people to agree on meeting dates will attest to the challenge of aligning all of those Palm Pilots and Blackberries. The Jewish calendar creates holy days for us to share parts of our Jewish history together. Tradition helps us make space on our calendars for these special days. Even those who don't belong to a synagogue feel called to light Hanukah candles or find themselves looking for a Passover seder to hear the story of the Exodus with friends and co-religionists.

If Judaism is a family, then part of what gives meaning to a membership is the deep trust that as members we will have a place at the holiday table. We may be joined at Pesach by a cantankerous uncle or a cousin who has done little to keep up. We may have a nephew who has become quite observant and a wayward sister who comes to the table with a cynical attitude. We even have the country cousins who come from the unfashionable part of town.

Many congregations lament the lack of attendance at daily minyan. The minyan regulars may complain about nonattendees, but when they are asked about when they started to attend, they may share that it was after a parent's passing. Some criticize those who don't come to adult education, but when asked, they may say that they started to attend class when they became involved in their child's bar mitsvah. SVP appreciates that members are moved at different times in their lives. Some come early, and some come late, but when synagogues value inclusion, the table is still set for them. Dedicated minyanaires ensure others have the opportunity to give minyan a try throughout the year.

4. The Gift to Children: Helping Them
Understand Their Relationship to Judaism

In order for children to develop a relationship with God and Jewish practice, it takes both Jewish literacy and a positive exposure to Jewish living. Many members make the decision to join a synagogue to ensure these gifts "for the kids." Many congregations are providing excellent bar mitsvah preparation and religious school education. The conventional wisdom has been to focus on competing for young families and their school-age children. The Jewish world has changed in recent decades, however, and many women are not having their first child until age thirty-five. This has delayed the membership engagement process. A minority of Jewish families have children under seventeen at home (only 24 percent, according to a recent National Jewish Population Survey).

Leaders can explore ways to enrich membership for adults and children. The value of synagogue education for children will be enhanced if adult members are finding meaning for themselves. Adults must demonstrate that they value the study of Torah, or Limud Torah. One congregation role-modeled this by having their parents participate in bar mitsvah family education, which led to their providing the dvar torah as their child's service. I experienced the joys of adult study in my forties, and it made a difference in how I looked at my synagogue membership. A community solely focused on what some call "pediatric Judaism" fails to come to grips with the changing demographics and the need to encourage adults to step forward.

5. The Gift of Family Activities:
Shalom Bayit, Joy at Home

Judaism is very family oriented. In many families husbands and wives work long hours. Children are under great pressure to succeed academically and socially and are often involved in multiple activities. It is easy for family members to pass like ships in the night. Synagogue activities that bring multiple families together deeply enrich the lives of members. Members can develop the skills and understanding to perform these rituals in their home. When they encounter other families at their best, they can bring some of this shalom bayit to their homes.

6. The Gifts of Social and Cultural Activities: Simḥah

Members are looking for relationships. The synagogue creates events that bring people together around common interests. Friends, family, and food and drink help enrich life. The tradition says that one of the questions we will be asked in heaven is whether we enjoyed life's permissible pleasure. We are to serve God in joy (Psalm 100:2).

7. The Gift of Adult Education and Torah Study

Members enjoy learning. Jewish learning combines American Jews' love of learning with ancient rituals of Jewish study and dialogue. We see this passion in formal education at Torah study, lectures, and small discussion groups. We also see it in informal dialogue in the board-room or the parking lot. Jews like to learn. By convening conversations around Torah values, the synagogue allows members to take their cur-rent interests and connect them with a two-thousand-year history of rabbinic learning.

8. The Gift of Volunteer or Social Action Projects

Our Torah portions, our liturgy, and our holidays remind us that we were slaves in the land of Egypt, or 'avadim hayinu bemitzrayim (Deuteronomy 6:21). Our liturgy and rituals build empathy for other oppressed peoples and drive synagogue social action. Tsedakah, or justice, is the value that calls us all to do our part in setting things right. Many members have the need to "make a difference." They want to make their contribution to the synagogue. They are looking for opportunities. Some want to work "hands-on," as they honor the value of repairing the world, or tikun olam. The act of making a commitment to give to those in need is a great syna-gogue obligation. The synagogue can help members share their feelings about service with other committed members and find ways to put these aspirations into action.

9. The Gift of Youth Activities

Parents want their children to continue to connect with other Jewish chil-dren and with Jewish learning. Synagogues have the capacity to nurture these youth communities and keep them growing. Many of these youth will attend college. How prepared are they to deal with anti-Semitism on campus, secularism, and intermarriage. Do they know why it is impor-tant to be Jewish? Parents have every reason to be concerned about Jew-ish continuity. Synagogue youth programs that engage children until they leave for college help young people develop pride in their Jewish identity and an ability to handle challenges to that identity. Synagogue leaders can channel parents' anxiety into constructive efforts to build a vibrant youth community. There are wonderful resources to help prepare our children for college. They need to be able to answer the question, Why be Jewish? They need to be able to speak in support of Judaism. I recom-mend *A Letter in the Scroll* by Jonathan Sacks. Synagogues can be a place to hold these conversations before kids leave their congregations.

10. The Gift of Participating in a Caring Community

Members want to feel they are cared for. They take joy in being connected to others. When I have observed leadership groups, I have seen people who are clearly very connected to some fellow members. They look forward to working together; they walk out to the parking lot together. They take joy in these relationships. These family bonds are a pillar of effective Jewish community. Synagogue affiliation processes that do not allow these friendships to blossom are missing a huge opportunity. Alban scholars have found that the major reason people leave churches is that after a year they have failed to make friends. There is the old story about the man who regularly attended Shabbat worship. When he was asked if he enjoyed the services, he replied, "Not really." Why did he come every Shabbat? Because he comes to sit with Saul, and Saul loves services. Most people are reluctant to leave congregations when they have good friends like Saul.

When you help members bring their gifts, you also help them find each other. In an affluent consumer society we can purchase most of the things we want. Synagogue friendships are valued because members derive special meaning in the great moments of life.

Synagogue caring is more than just feeling. It is based on the value of covenantal caring. We care for others as God cares for us. We are part of a chain of caring that goes back to our parents, our grandparents, and the patriarchs and matriarchs. The synagogue calls for caring even when we aren't in the mood. This tradition is a gift.

11. The Gift of Inspiring Worship

More than 90 percent of synagogue members believe in God. They may have trouble finding the words or the way to connect, but there is a fundamental need to do something with this belief. Only about 40 percent of Jews affiliate with a congregation at any time. Even those who don't belong to synagogues find themselves drawn to high holiday services and rituals. According to a recent National Jewish Population Survey, 67 percent fast on Yom Kippur, 77 percent light Hanukah candles, and 67 percent attend a seder. Rabbi Eric Yoffie talks about the failure of the synagogue to engage more members.

> Nearly 80 percent of North American Jews will join a synagogue at some point in their lives. But here is the problem: About half

of them will leave, usually in three to five years, often right after celebrating a child's bar or bat mitsvah. Approximately one million North American Jews once belonged to a synagogue but no longer do. If we could put an end to this exodus, Jewish life would be immeasurably strengthened.

Our challenge, then, is to create a synagogue whose message of Torah is so inspiring, whose spiritual energy is so transforming, and whose web of kinship and caring is so embracing that no one who enters its gates will ever consider forsaking the holy community that it provides. (Yoffie 2005)

Many members and nonmembers have clearly not embraced the disciplines of regular worship; they have not experienced its joys. The tradition values spiritual intention (kavanah). It values gratitude (hodaya). We learn in the service that God has given us the Torah and the liturgy out of love ('ahavah). It is hard to experience these values if members don't slow down enough to enter worship. Most synagogues have an undeveloped group of core worshippers. Synagogue leaders have the potential to build on the spiritual commitment the members exhibit at high holidays and other events.

Conclusion

Leaders try to capture these gifts in a brochure. They try to remind people of these gifts in their high holiday speeches. But most adults learn about these gifts from their own experience. SVP is designed to help the planning group see the gifts from a new perspective. If SVP is successful, leaders will be able to communicate their story more effectively. Recall that Joshua re-educated the people about the covenant. He had them build a memorial from the stones of the river Jordan to commemorate God's parting of the waters. The men were circumcised. He retold God's covenant from Mount Ebal and Gerizim. Joshua reflected the value of preserving the tradition, or shalshelet ha-kabalah.

קֵדִּימָה Leaders should explain how the synagogue maintains the chain of tradition and brings the gifts of its past to the service of its future.

Leaders should explain how the synagogue maintains the chain of tradition and brings the gifts of its past to the service of its future. Leaders need to reflect on what gives meaning to their membership so that they are better able to articulate what might be compelling to their prospective members. Ultimately the leadership, the membership, and marketing and communications committees need to agree on a communications platform that describes some of the most important gifts and of belonging to their synagogue community. Communications need to be creative and compelling, not a string of tired clichés. Where do these committees find inspiration for creating compelling messages? They need to look inward, to their own experiences—what gives meaning to their membership. They also need to look outward, to the needs of prospective members and to the various programs and organizations that are trying to compete for the hearts and minds of their families.

Questions for Reflection

1. What gives meaning to your synagogue membership?
2. How would members of your congregation answer this?
3. If you were writing a brochure for your congregation, what would be the three most compelling gifts you would mention?

2.
Developing Leadership Gifts

It is a tree of life to them that hold fast to it.

—Proverbs 3:18

Most of my clients have some advanced notice of my strange vocation. They know I was a business executive before I was a congregational consultant, so when I arrive at a synagogue to teach a workshop, it is not uncommon for the treasurer to corner me in the hall and say, "Thank God you're here. I've been trying to convince this group that the synagogue needs to be run like a business, and I know you understand how important business is." Later on, in the workshop, this same treasurer often appears crestfallen when I announce that the synagogue is not, in fact, something that can be run solely as a business.

Leadership Can't Be Business as Usual

I believe that if members try to bring their briefcase straight from the office, they will not create a plan that will bring the congregation together. The gifts of the synagogue cannot be fully understood through the lens of business. Jim Collins writes, "We need to reject the naïve imposition of the language of business on the social sectors and instead jointly embrace the language of greatness" (2005, 2). The Torah provides a language of greatness for those who "hold fast to it."

Charles Olsen, in writing about church boards, cites Robert Kreider, who challenges congregation leaders "to resist the seductive drag of modernity—individualism, competition, compartmentalization, special-ization, secularization and professionalism—to create community" (cited in Olsen 1995, vi). When leaders become a nucleus of renewal (an inspired core), according to Kreider, congregation building becomes serious busi-ness—not just a hobby. One church I visited had a giant pegboard with photos and profiles of volunteers. One profile read: "I'm Bob. My day job is being an electrician—my real job is our congregation's youth minister." That is not business as usual.

Leaders need to find ways to bridge ancient values and contemporary leadership principles—to create a language of shared values and vision. They are a tree of life. The synagogue is not simply a business, but it is in great need of the disciplines, skills, and tools that many business lead-ers have. The congregation's leaders need a strategic map, but it doesn't come from just one of the professional disciplines around the table. If leaders try to bring their maps directly from their business to the syna-gogue boardroom, their work will be frustrating.

Unfortunately, there are nights where everyone on the board has brought their own personal maps for the 7:00 p.m. meeting. As it gets close to Jewish starting time (7:14), leaders may find they are at cross pur-poses. Some are looking at their watches and asking, "With a little work why couldn't we make this a one-hour meeting?" Others are happy to socialize. I have been overwhelmed by the pressure to reduce the amount of time for SVP workshops. While I have made many adjustments for the sake of practicality, I have held my position that it takes time to gain con-sensus, to learn the culture, and to understand the different perspectives of members. If the calendar for leaders involved in planning mirrors the rhythms of the Jewish calendar, planners will be more aligned with Jew-ish time.

Some individual leaders can be overconfident. They feel called to change the historic norms for how the rabbi and/or executive director will do their work. They may arrive in June and begin to suddenly reshape the expectations and practices that have been established through four presidencies over eight years, ignoring the collective wisdom of previous leadership teams. Can you imagine a work environment in which you had a new boss every two years? The tradition says that God weeps when a communal leader "lords it over the community" (*b. Hagigah 5b*). Lead-ers need to move carefully, collaboratively, and respectfully. Even those with smaller, more humble synagogue roles on the staff or board are to be respected for their service (*b. Bava Batra 71*). Leaders should avoid creating unnecessary resistance by their careless comments because all change efforts are going to meet natural congregational resistance. Why make the situation worse?

Twelve Leadership Principles

When leaders challenge others to raise their commitment to worship, study, leadership, and community, they will meet resistance. These insights led me to develop twelve leadership principles you can put to work. They provide some key coordinates on my map for leaders. The synagogue organization has been described as voluntary. You cannot compel leaders to develop self-awareness and self-management skills. You cannot compel them to stay involved with the organization long enough to practice new skills. Most congregations don't have resources to send their individual members to executive development programs. For all of these reasons I have chosen to focus on encouraging synagogue teams to develop better leadership practices rather than focusing on the individual journeys of leaders.

1. Leaders Step Forward
to Help the Congregations Be Less Reluctant

Dr. Gil Rendle encourages leaders to make a careful assessment of their environment when they embark on change (Rendle 1998). He tries to help them understand how congregations naturally resist change and how to help people be less reluctant about change.

Vibrant systems need to be steady in purpose and flexible in strategy. That is why you spend so much time trying to define purpose through the values and goals workshops. A shared purpose will help leaders focus as they look at a wide range of strategic action plans.

When a system doesn't know what went wrong, it wants to know who went wrong. Under pressure some leaders will look for someone to blame. The membership blames the leadership for declining membership or higher dues. The leadership may blame the membership for their apathy. Both may turn on the professional staff. One of the benefits of planning is to reverse this blaming pattern by developing a better collective sense from the leadership about appropriate roles and responsibilities.

Congregations collude with themselves to change in ways that do not change them. Congregations may feel they are under more pressure to welcome new members. They create a welcoming committee and give them all the responsibility for this cultural change while the rest of the leaders sit back. They may ask the school to engage post–bar mitsvah students, but they don't create the resources for the new programs (staff, money, etc.). They may hire a consultant but put the wrong people on the steering committee. They may allow the steering committee to do the workshops, but the board continues to review issues and make important decisions outside of the planning process, thus undermining the process. When they are fearful, congregations set up a stumbling block before planning leaders.

Congregational learning requires flexibility and experimentation. When leaders get anxious, they become rigid and slow down. I recommend that the board get a consensus from a large leadership group so that any pressure from the congregation does not focus on a few people. These moments of resistance are extraordinary learning opportunities for the leadership. They must treat the resistance as an opportunity to learn about the congregation (they should not take it personally), and they must protect important experiments from those opposing change.

Congregations expect the leaders to maintain the status quo. If the leaders do not do this, they may be attacked or replaced. The normal congregational system is in some kind of equilibrium. Some issues can force the leadership out of their comfort zone. As a consultant I am often called in, for example, to help rabbis who try to do too much in their first six months on the job. They often come face to face with all of these natural forms of resistance. The congregations are not yet ready to accept their leadership. Leaders can certainly make managers nervous but openness, humility, and a careful plan make the relationships more manageable.

Jim Collins talks about extraordinary leaders who combine "personal humility and professional will" (2005, 12). It is difficult to honor previous leadership teams if you are ready to make major changes in the lay-staff relationship in the first month in your presidency. Our rituals encourage people to slow down and to be open to the holy—to God and to our fellow members, made in God's image. The steps of the south entrance to the old Temple were made uneven so that the people would not rush up the steps. We are to come to synagogue work with reverence and patience.

If you look around the typical board table, you see many different individual gifts. They have all come with their personal maps under their arms, but they have not agreed how they will mount the Temple steps together. What they lack is the master craftsman, like Bezalel, who can work with their practical skills ('erets) and their spiritual gifts (shamayim). As you develop stronger leadership, you will need to give them the time it takes to develop new approaches.

2. Leaders Are Strategic

Although strategic skills are not common, they are critical in times of change, according to leadership expert and Harvard professor John Kotter (1999). Strategic planning skills help leaders overcome their internal focus, learn from the changing environment, and manage the inefficiencies of the synagogue organization. A successful planning model must simplify the process enough to ensure that the volunteer organization can be successful with strategic work. Remember, volunteers want to know that their projects will succeed.

While it is clear that strategic thinking is important today, the history of strategic and long-range planning in congregations is mixed. It is not uncommon for congregations to do facility planning with a fundraising consultant in preparation for a capital campaign. In this case, planning is tied to a very concrete goal. But when congregations face size transitions, changes in demographics, cultural changes, increased diversity, or generational changes, they are less likely to see these as planning opportunities. Elite and relatively small leadership groups have sometimes gone through reflection and written plans only to find that their plans are never implemented. One major obstacle to new planning efforts is the disturbing narrative of past attempts that failed. The visioning and planning process must be able to translate abstract ideas about values and strategic goals into specific actions that can be tracked and implemented.

Judaism argues that we gain major insights about God, holiness, and righteousness by "doing" things. At Mount Sinai, the Jewish people answered God's challenge by saying, "All that the LORD has spoken we will faithfully do" (Exodus 24:7). We comprehend the abstract by doing the concrete—observing mitsvot (commandments). One of the ways leaders can attain such qualities as credibility, integrity, authenticity, and foresight is by doing leadership tasks.

3. Leaders Use Different Frameworks

One important leadership task is the ability to reframe our leadership work. According to Lee Bolman and Terrence Deal, in their book *Reframing Organizations* (2003, 15), organizations provide several frameworks for leaders: the structural, the human, the political, and the symbolic. In this book I will discuss situations that call on all of these frameworks.

When you design the steering committee and clarify its relationship with the board, you are using the structural frame. When you look for the right mix of people and try to build them into the planning process, you are using the human frame. When you recruit the diverse stakeholders and help find some common ground, you are working in the political frame. When you let members tell their stories in parlor meetings and in the workshop on historical reflection, you are emphasizing the symbolic frame. Not everyone was born a natural leader, but many volunteers can gain a leadership perspective by learning to use different frameworks.

Leaders focus on the human relationships among people and not just on the goals. God breathes life into Adam, not into his work plan. As Peter Drucker explains in *Managing the Nonprofit Organization* (1990), the process is also the organization's product. Judaism believes that each person is made in the image of God (betselem elohim). Judaism believes that leaders strive to understand that everyone comes to the table with different levels of experience, understanding, and motivation.

At the Passover seder the leader models these Jewish educational values. Everyone is encouraged to participate. Everyone is encouraged to share the same story. In the Jewish community there are individuals who can work with the larger community. They are open, curious, and engaged: these are the wise ones. There are those who are willing but less knowledgeable: these are the simple ones. There are those who have little motivation: these are the apathetic ones. Still others have turned their backs on the community; they do not feel that the community conversation (or seder) matters: these are the evil ones. Synagogue leaders must manage all four types of people.

The Passover provides a symbolic framework to help leaders understand our communal story and to go beyond what is happening at our table. We are reminded that we are a part of a people and share the experience of having been in slavery. We open our door to Elijah because we all want to be part of the communal vision of redemption. We honor the gifts of individuals, but our unique calling is to be a nation. The wicked son in the hagadah scoffs at this communal focus when he says, "What is this to you?" When leaders fail to use the full range of frames, they may focus too much on the political frame—advocacy, winning and losing.

When boards are too tactical, they often fail to define and communicate the board's essential mission, values, and strategies. They may fail to get the clergy and other staff involved in designing a synagogue leadership agenda. It is popular today to remind board members that their tactical managerial efforts are sacred work because they serve a sacred purpose. Unfortunately, if the board's culture, processes, and rituals look like any other secular task, the idea of the management of the sacred can look in fact quite secular. A five-minute text commentary (dvar Torah), however well-intended, does not symbolically transform board workers into a dynamic leadership community. The whole design of the board's work needs to be reviewed if it is going to work effectively on the synagogue agenda.

4. Leaders Seek Out the Sacred

In order to inspire others to make the journey from consumer to member to disciple, synagogue leaders need to become more familiar with the whole range of synagogue gifts (chapter 1). Many churches see their leaders as disciples. These are people with both extraordinary commitment and passion. Disciples are more than their secular portfolios. Synagogue leaders need to strive to be more than the lawyers, accountants, or social workers on the board. They need to be able to find sacred places within the leadership by connecting texts to real-life situations, inviting spiritual reflections, taking a Minḥah moment in an afternoon workshop, or connecting their work with an upcoming holiday. How do you attract new members? You introduce them to leaders who love Jewish living.

According to Irwin Kula, rabbi and president of CLAL (the National Jewish Center for Learning and Leadership), leaders need to be able to see the sacred in new places. You can see the sacred in how leaders support the staff or give each other loving feedback for the sake of the community. You can see the sacred when people give financial gifts that are beyond what is expected. You can see the sacred when people struggle to learn new things—even when it's a little embarrassing. The sacred is not just in the siddur; it is on the walls of the workshop sessions and in the homes of parlor meetings. It is in the notes that debrief the steering committees. Leaders have the capacity to find the meaning in old and new places.

5. Leaders Are Aware of Trends in Jewish Community Life

A number of trends, factors, and forces are affecting Jewish life in general and synagogue life in particular, so an awareness of these trends—as well as the challenges and opportunities they represent—is essential for effective synagogue leadership.

In the preface I discussed the challenges of mobility, assimilation, the cost of Jewish living, the stresses of two-income households, intermarriage, and a general reluctance to commit to traditional organizations. These are the well-known forces that synagogue leaders discuss in my workshops. What is mentioned less often, however, is that the Jewish community has been extraordinarily successful. Jewish immigrants came to America for economic opportunity and political freedom. They have achieved both. Jews have prospered and gained respected positions in government, the professions, and business, and anti-Semitism has substantially declined in the sixty years since World War II.

While Jewish leaders are concerned about intermarriage, one of the reasons it is so prevalent is that non-Jews are far more accepting of Jews than they once were. Some Jews may look with nostalgia at the old pre-emancipation Jewish world of the eighteenth century. That was a time when Jews were more frequently on the same page, but, on the other hand, they had never been allowed to freely choose what page they wanted to be on. Today Jews have greater access to resources of Western knowledge and commerce than they ever have before but must relearn the skills of Jewish community building.

In recent years, Jewish knowledge has expanded exponentially. Few cities are without significant adult study opportunities, and anyone with an Internet connection can quickly access a host of Jewish Web sites offering everything from commentaries on the week's Torah portion to essays on Jewish communal issues. This has given the people ways to enrich their membership. It has also empowered them to review religious practices, synagogue authority, leadership priorities, and denominational relationships.

Regardless of whether a trend is positive or negative, it needs to be understood and managed. Jonah studied the trends at Nineveh and concluded they were negative. How do we look at tough challenges without panic, without jumping on the first boat out of town? Even strengths like the Internet create challenges: How do we use this tool? How do we leverage it? How do we avoid some of the negative side effects associated with it—its impersonality and intemperate e-mail, for instance? In times of change, managing the environment takes work.

6. Leaders Learn By Doing

There is much about the sacred that leaders may not know. According to Malcolm S. Knowles (1973), adults need to apply their life experiences and professional expertise to their new congregational work. Leaders need to assure adult learners they will have a "practice field" where they can bring their life experiences and talents to the work of building sacred community.

Most volunteers step forward because they have experienced the leadership of another person. They did not respond to an ad; they responded out of admiration. The right person asked them.

Successful leadership development processes involve the creation of small groups in which individuals can get "hands-on" with synagogue learning and deeds. In these communities they can bounce ideas off each other and gain an appreciation for each other's contributions. The Passover seder offers a model for experiential learning: we hear stories; we smell the food; we taste the bitter herbs; we see the seder plate; we feel the matsah. We learn by doing.

7. Leaders Are Reflective

Synagogue leaders consistently tell me that they do not have a method for identifying the skills, talents, and interests of their members or a way to make appropriate leadership opportunities available to them. In order to be a more effective leader you need to understand yourself. What are your needs and how do you express them? What makes you step forward? What makes you reluctant?

As they share their Jewish journeys and leadership development experiences, they will be more able to hear what other people are saying about their next steps.

A 2003 Urban Institute survey of volunteer management capacity among charities and congregations found that more than 40 percent of those who were no longer volunteering had withdrawn their efforts because of poor experiences they had had as volunteers (Urban Institute 2004). Not only has there been a decline in association, but those who have tried to "step forward" have often been disappointed. In the Urban Institute study, volunteers reported that their volunteer tasks were often poorly designed and were inadequately supervised or supported. Volunteers with little discretionary time often found the work did not meet their expectations.

There are clearly barriers to volunteerism. What helps? One Jewish Federation did extensive interviews with prospective leaders between the ages of twenty-five and thirty-five. The following is a composite portrait of the members' discussions:

Interviewer: Would you consider volunteering with the federation?

Prospect: I don't really have the time.

Interviewer: Would you consider making time for this?

Prospect: I might if the work was really important.

Interviewer: What would it mean for the work to be important?

Prospect: I would want to know that this work will make a difference. I would also want to know that the work would be a good match for my talents.

Interviewer: What else would make you consider volunteering?

Prospect: I want to have staff support so that I can be confident that the project will be a success. On the other hand, I don't want the staff person to try to control everything. I'd want to have some autonomy.

As a former leader, my first instinct upon hearing this demanding agenda was to mutter (rather grumpily), "Is that *all* they want?" But if you use your active listening skills—and a little patience—you can gain some insights about these potential volunteers. And by listening to their thoughts you can better manage their conflicting desires, such as the need for both support and autonomy, or the desire to do important work while not spending a great deal of time on it. Recruitment efforts face challenges today, and the next generation of potential volunteers (in their twenties and thirties) are even more independent.

As they look for committed volunteers, Jewish organizations are always appealing for more financial support. What helps inspire philanthropy today? Dr. Steven Windmueller (2006) has found that contemporary funders are inspired by local causes to create new initiatives or to reinvent traditional funding methods to make them relevant to today's communities.

According to Windmueller leaders who are willing to step forward and take risks are less focused on denominations and institutions and more on learning firsthand about their causes. They don't just want to join an organization; they want to move in and out of organizations and groups that meet their needs. They look for projects they feel passionate about, with partners they want to work with. They judge by their own experience rather than by the norms of the past or the organization.

Leaders want to use their talents; they want to be heard as individuals; they want to make a difference; they want to personally connect with the programs they develop. They value innovation, and they are less patient with bureaucratic responses. If this portrait is true of many of today's emerging leaders, and I think it is accurate, then tomorrow's leadership development will need to look different.

8. Leaders Have Hope for the Future

Most planning processes identify strengths and weaknesses. They look at the gap between the leader's expectations and congregational performance. Most congregations that agree to embark on planning feel some pressing need to invest the time and money to do so. Rob Weinberg, director of the Experiment in Congregational Education, one of several pioneering synagogue transformation projects, has discovered that the elements that create a "readiness for change" are dissatisfaction with the present, a vision of the future, a belief that change is possible, and practical first steps (personal communication).

I believe a hopeful, positive vision of the future is instrumental in increasing the belief that change is possible. The belief that change is possible reinforces and energizes the ability to create a vision. For this reason, when leaders are overly focused on gaps and deficits, congregational planning will be weakened. Most congregational leaderships excel in certain areas (sermons, social action, facility, board, etc.) or segments (young families, older families, etc.). Part of the art of planning is to review the congregational landscape and to bring these various strengths into focus and inspire hope. Leaders should be able to tell prospects what is great about worship, religious school, leadership, and social action (the gifts of membership). They need to create scripts they can communicate with authenticity and integrity. They need to learn to communicate their passions and strengths to new prospects and current members. The biblical spies who were sent to do reconnaissance of the promised land of Canaan were encouraged to "take pains to bring back some of the fruit of the land" (Numbers 13:20). God knew that leaders needed to promise a sweet future to help sustain the people's hopes.

9. Leaders Seek Assistance from Professionals

Consultants and facilitators can be helpful (okay, I'm a little biased) in creating a sense of urgency by identifying areas of concern and opportunity. They can help maintain momentum and energy by helping planning leaders imagine a promising future. Management tends to have an equilibrium. Leadership often requires that the status quo be challenged. Leaders need to get help to overcome the disruption in the process when unanticipated events take center stage, or when leadership changes leave the board with a short-term deficit of energy. While the economics of synagogues do not ensure much steady work, it is my hope that this book encourages an array of people to take on roles as coaches, mentors, and consultants in their areas.

When synagogues use facilitators to help institute effective volunteer processes, they can increase volunteer satisfaction in leadership work and increase expectations for volunteer effectiveness. SVP participants are ensured that their efforts will be supported by a facilitator and a practical, well-tested model. Their valuable time will be honored.

I do not specialize in coaching, but the same economics are at work. When you think of the total costs of a rabbi's salary and benefits, it is a small cost to set up a monthly coaching call. Coaches can help rabbis reflect on situations. They can help rabbis communicate their goals and action plans. Coaches can help rabbis be less reactive to the different personalities and situations they encounter. As the rabbis become less anxious, they help make the whole system less anxious and reactive.

Consultants can also help set up resources that build long-term capacity. Leaders can be connected to peer leaders from other congregations. Past presidents and other experienced leaders can be groomed to be mentors to members in their own congregation.

10. Leaders Build Effective Collaborative Teams

Contemporary organizational experts emphasize the importance of building more effective teams. The Center for Creative Leadership calls teamwork "the most frequently valued managerial competence," and, according to John Seely Brown, head of Xerox's Research Park, "If you ask successful people, they will tell you that they learned the most from and with each other" (Goleman 1995, 202).

Synagogues have diverse members, so their leadership needs to reflect this diversity. Members can learn from each other if their talents are meshed with a worthwhile mission and team-building processes. Planning can address key elements of the team-building process.

In SVP you hold parlor meetings to hear about members' concerns and needs. You gather congregational data. You interview the staff to understand their perspectives. The steering committee is encouraged to read books that help make them more sensitive to the needs of team members. I particularly recommend *Practicing Right Relationship* (Sellon and Smith 2005), which helps leaders understand the building blocks of building interpersonal relationships. I also like *Please Understand Me II: Temperament, Character, Intelligence* by David Kiersey (1998). This book is based on the author's development of the Myers Briggs Type Inventory assessment. He provides an assessment of certain temperament preferences that can be helpful in developing an understanding of team members' ways of gathering information, learning, and making decisions. His book will give you insight about how boards communicate, make decisions, and manage conflicts.

Members have heard religious leaders challenge them to embrace core Jewish values of loving kindness (ḥesed) and mutual respect (betselem elohim). They may know the "should do" but don't understand the "how to do." SVP seeks to honor the value of making peace (rodef shalom). We do this by trying to see the best in others.

When people quiet their judgmental selves, they are more able to hear diverse voices. They are more able to see the good in everyone. Aaron was a role model of this style of collaborative leadership.

> When two men quarreled, Aaron would go and sit with one of them, and say, "My son, look how your friend beats his breast and tears his hair out as he says, Woe is me, how can I raise my eyes and face my friend? I would be too embarrassed, for it is I who acted offensively toward him." Aaron would sit with him until he had removed all rancor from his heart. Then, Aaron would go and say the same thing to the other man. (*Hukat 764*)

The Sages so admired Aaron's character that it was said the people mourned for him longer than Moses. Thus it was said that Aaron "loved peace and pursued peace and made peace between man and man" (*Sanhedrin 6b*). Each steering committee is different, but each one is encouraged to focus on developing as a team as they go about doing the SVP planning tasks.

11. Leaders Recruit a Critical Mass of Participants in the Planning Process

One of the problems with strategic planning efforts by long-range planning groups is that they may create a document that has little buy-in. In an era of declining volunteerism, planning efforts need to create new energy and momentum. If only eight people go into the boardroom and "knock the plan out," who will implement it? How will this work engage new leadership prospects? The top complaints of core leaders are "we cannot engage new leaders" and "we feel burned out."

How does the work of a small elite planning group change that dynamic? Effective leadership development and change management will involve a wide array of current and potential leadership to build a critical mass for change. SVP differs from much traditional planning approaches because it is front loaded. If the group is successful in recruiting the Steering Committee and the stakes, the planning process will be halfway home. These groups represent a substantial increase in the total amount of energy that is available for planning.

12. Leaders Are Matchmakers, Connecting the Right Volunteers to the Right Jobs

Some observers emphasize the importance of recruiting people with natural leadership qualities. I agree that talent matters, but the synagogue is not like corporate America. You will not always be able to ensure the most talented are, in Jim Collins's words, "driving the bus" (2005). Some leadership positions will be occupied by major givers, long-standing past leaders, and loyal workers of modest ability, many of whom may lack a capacity for change.

Leaders sometimes survey their memberships to "find out what programs they want," then initiate the most commonly mentioned ideas. To their surprise, few members respond. How can this be? What makes a program compelling? Yes, content matters, but people matter also. Collins contends that if one has the right people on the bus "it matters less if the bus has to change directions" (2005).

I start leadership development groups by asking participants why they have agreed to participate. They seldom cite philosophical or intellectual (content) reasons. They come because someone they respect has volunteered in the past or asked them to help now. The right people asked.

The synagogue will often need to work with people who are not natural leaders. Ronald Heifetz, cofounder and director of the Center for Public Leadership at Harvard University, has argued that leaders can be developed by doing leadership tasks (1999). The most important of these tasks are recruiting talented people and finding the right work for them. The Gallup Organization directed an extensive twenty-five-year research project involving more than eighty thousand managers; Marcus Buckingham and Curt Coffman report on the results in their book *First, Break All the*

Rules (1999). They argue that leaders must stop trying to put a square block into a round hole. Part of creating a great team is working to make sure people have the right assignments, ones that utilize their gifts.

Finding the right assignment for volunteers is a core Jewish value. In his "Eight-Step Ladder" of tsedakah (righteous deeds), twelfth-century Jewish philosopher, scholar, and leader Maimonides offers a spiritual hierarchy of acts that move up a ladder (sulam) to the most selfless of deeds. One of the highest forms is to empower others to find a vocation. Gallup's research indicated that one of the qualities of great supervisors was a focus on supporting and developing their employees' strengths. They made this a priority rather than always trying to "fix" employees' weaknesses. Most adults have limited potential to change their weaknesses. Leaders can strive to make a "good shittac" (match) between a prospect's strengths and the volunteer work available.

SVP is clearly in the business of recruiting talent. It has a broad vision of what constitutes talent. SVP looks to identify people's passions and then connect them to the planning process and ultimately to committees and tasks forces (and even projects) where their strengths can be applied. Leaders need to look at a broad array of individual or short-term projects. Many prospects are willing to step forward, but they don't want to make a long-term commitment. Effective leaders find a way to meet them where they are!

Conclusion: Synagogue Leadership Development Is Ongoing

Synagogue leadership is an ongoing challenge. New leaders must be oriented every year. You may not be able to have an impact on every individual, but you hope to create a commitment to develop the team. Boards need to do major team building every two to three years. Even if they have an exciting vision or a charismatic period of leadership, they must keep reviewing and integrating that vision. In our tradition, Isaac follows his charismatic father Abraham (Genesis 26) and finds that he has to re-dig the wells his father dug before. In order to unleash the life-giving energy from the wells, they must be reworked.

I began my exploration of synagogue leadership by asking, "Can leadership make a difference? Can it help synagogues be more effective and efficient? Can synagogue leaders learn from business and non-profit organization?" Susan Shevitz, associate professor and director of

Brandeis University's Hornstein Program in Jewish Communal Service, has described synagogues as pluralistic, diverse, voluntary, and loosely coupled. All of these qualities make it harder to be "on the same page" (1995). Shevitz also noted that synagogues keep poor records and have few written agreements. Even when they try to get people on the same page, they often fail to record the agreements, communicate them to others, or ensure a transition of their agreements from one president to another, let alone from generation to generation.

Boards often allocate training to a half-day workshop every two or three years. In these settings they learn a few new ideas and do a little planning, and there are usually some exhortations to take a fresh look at the "sacred work" of congregational governance. Though well-intended, these workshops are usually too limited to make much of an impact on the synagogue culture. Church consultant Thomas Holland argues that exhortations to improve board attitudes and performance are largely unsuccessful. What he believes works is changing what board members do (Holland 2000). I agree! Boards need to shift away from the managerial pole and migrate to the leadership pole. They can do this by putting more leadership work on the synagogue board agenda. The SVP agenda helps recruit, motivate, and train members to do the foundational work that ensures ongoing leadership development. In order to begin this work, some leaders need to step forward and be prepared, like Isaac, to re-dig those wells.

Questions for Reflection

1. When did you feel like a leader?
2. What skills were you using?
3. Who has helped you learn to lead others?
4. How did they help you grow as a leader?

PART 2

Teshuvah: Getting on a New Path

The repentant sinner should strive to do good
with the same faculties with which he sinned.
With whatever part of the body he sinned, he should
now engage in good deeds. If his feet had run to sin,
let them now run to the performance of the good.

—*Joseph Gerondi*, The Gates of Repentance

I use the term "teshuvah" to capture the spirit of these chapters about change. I see teshuvah as a turning process in which one seeks to get back on the right path. There is a fundamental optimism in the teshuvah literature. It assumes that there is a good path and that we can return to it. It also assumes that we have the capacity to change. Here I will focus on the ways in which leaders may have gotten off the path. They may have failed to properly assess their environment and to communicate their vision. They may have been unable to bring out the special gifts of others. These chapters do not focus on the traditional practice of repentance, but they very much challenge leaders to work harder to do the things they have avoided. If they have avoided taking time to reflect on their synagogue values, I encourage them to throw themselves into such a process. If they have avoided going out to meet their fellow members face to face, I ask them to run to the phones and set up those meetings. The tradition suggests that as we step forward, these efforts will be blessed. If they are continued, they will become habits.

3.

Planning:
Using Different Approaches

Go out and see which is the good way to which [one] should cleave.

—Avot 2:13

There are significant consequences for a lack of foresight. The spies condemned their generation to wander in the wilderness. The sages realized that adults needed to learn how to make decisions. The fear of the unknown had to be balanced by faith in the possibility of the Jewish mission. There are critical forks in the road where leaders must make choices. People will look where their leaders are looking. At such moments it matters a lot where the leaders are looking.

Joshua is charged with putting the people on the right path. He shows them where to cross the river. He commemorates their path by making a memorial of the stones they crossed on. Before they get too far on their journey, he reminds them of the covenant—the good path. Where can you find the good path for your congregation? I believe that path can be defined by three plans: a Leadership Plan, a Delegation/Management Plan, and an Accountability Plan.

The Leadership Plan

It is helpful to consider the relationship between management and leadership. Management refers to how things are to be done (effective, efficient, timely). Good management means doing things right. Leadership focuses on what is to be done (direction, mission). Good leadership means doing

53

the right thing. While leaders define goals and policies, managers implement plans. Both leadership and management are important in synagogues, but during times of change leadership skills need to be better developed.

Given the challenges of the synagogue environment and the complexity of synagogue organizational culture (chapter 4), it makes sense to invest in some planning. Ronald Heifetz (1999) describes one of the benefits of planning as achieving the vantage point of "balcony space." High above the organizational stage a group of people can get out of "reactive space" and move on to the balcony to get the big picture and see how they fit into a much larger pattern. On the balcony they become empowered to look at things in a new way.

In SVP they are joined by others who are looking and learning. In visioning work this shared vantage point builds teamwork among planners. They work hard to motivate a large cross section of stakeholders to take the time to come out on the balcony. Chapter 4 discusses some of the data they might review from that vantage point.

You need to motivate a group of planners in a reflective process to assess and explore the implications of this data. Dr. Steven Covey tells the story of a woodsman who was trying to cut a tree with an old rusty saw. The woodsman was exhausted and frustrated. The day was almost gone, and he had made little progress. A stranger walked by and observed the intense work effort of the woodsman. From his vantage point he suggested the woodsman walk over and use the sharpening stone. In anger the woodsman replied, "I don't have time to sharpen the saw" (1999, 287). Jewish texts often reflect the wisdom of our people's agricultural past. One states: "If one does not plow in the summer, what will one eat in the winter?" (Midrash Misle 6). Effective leaders take time to ensure they have the right tools and the right habits.

Leaders climb up the tallest palm tree in the jungle to get their bearings. Managers are often busy cutting a path through the jungle. The leader's role is to let the managers know if they are going in the right direction. The leader must know where the goal is. In today's complex world, it is easy to take the wrong trail. Too often the managers reply, "Yes, we may be lost, but we are making good time."

The Leadership Pole

Alban has an instrument that evaluates congregations using systems theory, the Congregational Systems Inventory (CSI), developed by George

Parsons and Speed Leas (1993). One of the seven dimensions that is analyzed is leadership. On one end of the continuum is the managerial pole, which is practical and tactical. On the other end is the leadership or transformational pole, which is visionary and strategic. Most congregational leadership groups are managerial and tactical. On a scale of one to ten, where one is managerial and ten is transformational, they will be about a two.

The Leadership Continuum

Managerial									Transformational
1	2	3	4	5	6	7	8	9	10

According to Parsons and Leas, both styles of leadership are important. If you only think about mission and purposes, you might fail to balance the budget or pay the utility bill. If you are only focused on the utility bills you may not pay enough attention to why you are maintaining the building. In Jewish terms, you need to balance the tension between 'erets (practical, earthly) and shamayim (spiritual, visionary). Without a vision the people perish. You will need to ask, What are we trying to achieve? Who are we trying to invite?

Management and leadership are polarities: they are not problems to be solved but tensions to be managed. If leadership goes too far to one side of the pole, it is harder to stay in touch with the imperatives of the other pole. When you get too far on the managerial pole, you simply forget what it's like to dream. When someone comes with an idea from the visionary realm, you may not recognize the gift they bring. Leaders are not consciously trying to be reluctant; they simply can't hear the message from the other pole.

Managers will not move to the leadership pole without an argument. I hear synagogue leaders say, "We have important financial issues to review. Our meetings are too long already. We don't have time for this planning stuff," etc. Like the woodsman they feel they don't have time to plan. They don't feel they have time to invest in preparing for the future.

What happens when there is no one at the top of the tree? Perhaps you don't have anyone who likes to climb. Perhaps no one thinks there is a view up there. Most groups are a 2 on the scale, but what happens if they don't have some who like to visit the 6 or 7 positions? Groups will look where the leader looks. One leader noted that board meetings always turned negative after the treasurer's report. Everyone focused on what couldn't be done. I suggested they move the report later on the agenda.

If the leader is down at the jungle floor hacking away, that is where the organization will be. When congregations are stuck or in decline, they tend to avoid looking from the tops of trees. They are afraid to.

SVP CASE

We Built It and They Came

One congregation had gone through rapid growth from a small ḥavurah of fifty to a congregation of five hundred. The congregation was full of young families. There were more than ninety beney mitsvahs. Underneath this dynamic growth there were developing tensions. Leaders had many unanswered questions.

- Should we have become so staff driven?
- Should we have become so child focused?
- Should we have taken on so much debt?

Through visioning exercises they developed new ways to leverage their staff better. They began to reallocate some of their energy from the bar mitsvah business and to develop their adult members more. This laid a better foundation for financial support from the adult members.

Delegation/Management Plan

Any kind of strategic or visioning work needs to take the planner from the Leadership Plan with its question, "Where are we going?" to the Delegation Plan with its question, "Who will do what?" In chapter 15 we will explore how SVP deals with issues of delegation in making assignments to committees and task forces and defining the scope of these assignments.

Accountability Plan

If your planning group is committed to the same values and strategic goals, you will have sufficient energy to make the assignments in the delegation and management plan. Delegation is the first step. It defines the task and empowers the team to work on the issue for a defined time frame. It encourages them to address certain issues and make recommendations. The planning process will only be really effective if there is a process of accountability. The planners need to develop strategies, goals, and actions for all of their recommendations and to communicate them to the board and planning leaders. In this way they develop accountability to themselves, their teams, to the congregation, and ultimately to God.

Three Approaches to Planning

Alban consultants Gil Rendle and Alice Mann have described three kinds of planning in their book *Holy Conversations* (2003, 2).

1. Problem-Solving Planning

Problem-solving planning is for very specific concrete problems that can be solved in a short period of time. Examples: "Which bid on the paving should we take?" "Should we shorten the length of the congregational bulletin?" "What night should we have the book club?" These should be relatively short-term processes.

2. Developmental Planning

Many challenging congregational issues require developmental planning. The leadership needs to determine what the next stage is. There are now new congregational questions: "We have a new building. We have grown. What's next? How do we integrate the new members? Now that our larger membership units provide us with more money, where should we allocate it?"

3. Frame-Bending Planning

Other congregations require "frame-bending planning," which involves looking at the congregation's culture, its mission, its facility, and its neighborhood. There are often complex positions: those who want a one-day Hebrew School and those who want to keep raising the bar of what can be taught; those who want more spirituality and innovation and those who want the services to be exactly as they remembered them growing up. Long-standing members talk about how things have "always been," and newer members seem to show little reverence for the past.

In some cases I am dealing with a congregation in decline. It cannot come out of decline by working on a list of tactical issues, like reorganizing the office or changing the newsletter. The planning group must revisit the synagogue's original mission and see if it still makes sense with this community in this place. This is a frame-bending planning review.

These are not "problems to be solved." These are issues that require new learning and understanding. Leaders need to reflect on these diverse views before they can plan how these members can live more successfully and "Jewishly" together. Most congregations require some measure of all three types of planning. There are some who always want to go directly to problem solving. When it comes to developmental and frame-bending issues, it doesn't pay to rush.

Technical Change versus Adaptive Change

Ronald Heifetz (1999) encourages planners to look at the roles of participants in the change process. He draws a distinction between technical change and adaptive change. Some changes can be done by experts. Some changes require that the people actively participate in the process of change. He calls these "adaptive changes." While problem-solving planning tends to be more technical, developmental and frame-bending planning is more adaptive.

Technical Change

Should we replace the air conditioning? Who should cut the grass? Should we increase the hours of the janitorial staff? These issues are common committee tasks with technical solutions. The executive director, the house chair, or the service provider can usually describe the problem, look at alternative solutions, and make a decision without much input from the system.

In a technical change, a few people can be responsible for all of the knowledge and skills. Consider the work of a surgeon. In terms of the operating procedure, the level of participation by the patient is usually relatively low, and the concentration of power in the expert specialist is relatively high.

Adaptive Change

Adaptive change is more like a therapeutic relationship. The patient must make an effort to share important information and insights with the therapist. The work cannot be done to them. In a congregational setting, this means that a wide array of congregational stakeholders must agree to learn from the process and to practice the new skills they have acquired.

How Many Classrooms Will We Need?

Let's imagine a congregational debate about the best way to manage significant growth in enrollment in the religious school. Leaders using a technical approach might move immediately to get the class sizes for every grade. They would then recommend how many classrooms should be built. This could lead the team to move quickly to request bids for construction. Now, let's look at how this task might be managed in a developmental or frame-bending process. The broader issues of the school would be explored.

- If we expand the school, what will be the implications for overall membership size? How big does the congregation want to be? What kinds of feelings are associated with growth? What kinds of staff will be required to manage this growth?
- What will be the impact on the role of the rabbi? How many more beney mitsvahs will we have? How will they be scheduled and managed?
- What is our vision for Jewish education? What will happen to the child post–beney mitsvah? The parents? Do we have a well-defined vision for teens, or is most of our energy directed at children in kindergarten through seventh grade?
- How will the school staff be affected? Will changes in size affect how teachers relate to each other? Will changes affect how teachers relate to parents?
- Is the cost of the building a religious school parents' problem? Should the cost be reflected in higher fees?

SVP CASE

- Can we use this issue as a way to educate our board and stakeholders about our mission in Jewish education?

The list of questions, which could be even longer, gives a sense of how the conversation might expand beyond technical questions relative to school rooms. The more questions raised, the more planners become aware of different constituencies that need to be involved. In order to get the input from different groups you need to broaden the process. In order to get the commitments of different groups you have to do a more intentional effort to educate them. This requires that the staff, leaders, and members go through a process of adaptive change. The leadership and the community are slowly changed by this process. It is very different from having a top-down process in which a few committee members "solve the problem" of building rooms.

The SVP process does not develop the specs for building the rooms. That is a technical task that can be managed by the building committee, the architect, and the contractor. If the SVP process has done its job, the leaders should fully understand the issues. SVP should help leaders devise alternative scenarios for the community to consider. The task force can then move on to problem solving. How many rooms?

Conclusion

In order to plan, you need to know if you are trying to problem solve, do developmental planning, or do frame-bending planning. Frame-bending planning requires adaptive change. These adaptive processes take longer and require that more people be engaged in the learning.

Questions for Reflection

1. What type of planning do you need?
2. Where do you need to see adaptive change?
3. What have you tried that helps address this?

4.

Foresight: Anticipating the Challenge of the Synagogue Organization's Future

If people do not plow in the summer, what will they eat in the winter?

—Midrash Misle 6

Synagogue leaders are responsible for looking to the future. As planners you have been blessed with the opportunity to look at your data and make some assumptions about the future. The most admired leadership quality, according to management scholars James Kouzes and Barry Posner (2002), is to provide an honest assessment of the environment. Our biblical ancestors had an agricultural tradition. They had to understand the changes in the seasons; they had to have a sense of planning to survive. Synagogue leaders need to take time to understand their environment, to reflect on the seasons, and to invest in their communities. They need to explore guiding principles and find ways to adapt them to their congregations' needs. God willing, they will be able to celebrate the harvest of new leaders, new projects, and new spirit (ruaḥ).

Why Plan? To Encourage Alignment

When leaders have shared data, shared values, and shared goals, they can guide the volunteer and paid staff to work in the same direction. This is called alignment. We all know the term from car care. When our tires are unaligned, they create a bumpier ride. The characteristic of an unaligned organization is waste. When organizational work is unaligned, it creates additional wear and tear.

In our biblical tradition we are taught not to put an ox and an ass in the same yoke to pull a wagon. We are to think ahead. The stronger ox might exhaust and overwhelm the smaller ass. When congregations have no plan to address the challenges of the twenty-first century, they are often putting their communities at risk. They may have different parts of the leadership pulling in different directions. When that happens, the organization may be hindered.

Why Plan? To Help Leaders Tell a Forward-Looking Story

Opponents of planning often focus on the negative. They become experts at listing why people won't come. A forward-looking and self-confident style has a powerful impact on followers. Kouzas and Posner note that the characteristic of being forward looking is the second most admired leadership trait after honesty (2002, 44). Leaders must overcome the negativity and fear that haunts so many communities. Like Joshua they need to be able to help the people tell a new story.

Leaders tell me about their current synagogue story. They tell of a litany of excuses they receive from fellow members. They often hear

- "People won't come out on a weeknight."
- "They are too tired after a long day at work."
- "They don't want to commit."
- "They just want to drop their kids off"

I do a variety of brainstorming exercises with boards. I asked one group to tell me about the synagogue community. Almost all of the comments were about weaknesses and problems. The rabbi observed this and asked, "Why do any of you belong here?" In focusing on only the negatives this group had lost focus of the "sweet fruits" of congregational life: high holidays, life cycle events, relationships, dedicated teachers, etc. It is essential that leaders balance an appreciation for what is working with that which needs to be improved (see chapter 2). Too much negativity makes leaders reluctant to try new things. It hinders their ability to think about the future.

To have a plan makes sense, but planning is difficult. Plans often break down because the hard work of the present overwhelms the hopes of the future. Perhaps this is why God asked the spies not just to report on the "cities, soil and forests" but also to "bring back some of the fruit of the land" of Canaan. According to the tradition, the spies did not want to move forward into the land. They could not see how this work would lead to fruition. They thus resisted bringing the fruit back (*b. Sotah 34b*).

God wanted to motivate the people by giving them a taste (the "fruit") of a positive future life on the land. SVP creates future scenarios, in Workshop 3, that give the planners a "taste of the fruit" of the land—the congregation to come. SVP also works to create a taste of success by achieving short-term victories. Management experts agree that celebrating success helps maintain morale. SVP leaders tell a forward-looking story: they create communications (newsletters, letters, sermons, briefings) that focus the community on future opportunities and become advocates and "cheerleaders" for different approaches to planning. This campaign is necessary because many congregational members fear change.

It is helpful to consider contextual issues such as the congregational size, culture, and life cycle stage. These are important factors affecting the nature of synagogue leadership. To increase their effectiveness synagogue leaders must learn to manage the synagogue environment, the synagogue organization, and the synagogue context.

1. Understanding the Synagogue Environment: Situation Analysis

Synagogue leaders often say to me, "It's just a shul. How complex can it be?" From a business perspective even small businesses can be complex to manage. In business you try to look at some of the forces that are creating threats or opportunities for your organization. You try to develop a situation analysis. Most congregations avoid the in-depth analysis of business planning, but it can be helpful to fill in some of the blanks.

Trends and Forces

Business leaders try to get a good list of the forces that they can agree on. They can then productively debate the implications of these forces. If you can't even convene a conversation on the forces, how can you get to the more nuanced debate of implications? As you consider these trends and forces in your community, do you see them as having a high, medium, or low impact?

Trends and Forces Worksheet

Trends and Forces	Impact		
	High	**Medium**	**Low**
Mobility			
High cost of Jewish living (home, schools, camps, congregations)			
Husband and wife working			
Less ethnic identity			
Less trust in Jewish organizations			
Intermarriage			
More day school students			
Members seeking spirituality			

These are a few of the well-known forces that synagogue leaders discuss in my workshops. Today's Jews have greater access to resources of Western knowledge and commerce than they ever had before, but we must relearn the skills of Jewish community building.

Today's members are more mobile and have more competing interests. Today's seekers may be challenging to please, but the good news for synagogues is that they are seeking. They are in motion. They may be seeking friendship or spiritual connection. They may be trying to use their talents in a new way. They hunger for relationships.

Many trends cut both ways. There has been a dramatic increase in the number of Jewish family foundations (opportunity), but the majority of Jewish giving is going to non-Jewish causes (threat). In times of change, managing the environment takes work. SVP is about identifying these trends and forces and learning how to manage them as a team.

In Sales's study of Westchester's congregations (2004) not one congregation had a majority of respondents who agreed that their congregation was good at taking advantage of the talents and interests of members. Few agreed that the right leadership opportunities were being made available. Leaders need to better understand the needs of prospective leaders.

2. Understanding Prospects

Later on in the process I will discuss the development of strategies that usually involve targeting some prospects or addressing the needs of some segment of the congregation that is not adequately served. Developing targets is a key strategic approach. Targeting raises several questions:

- Who are our target prospects?
- How will this target prospect look at our programs and benefits?
- How big is the target segment? We may want to attract young families, but there may not be many in our area.
- Do we have the programs to meet this segment's needs?
- Who else is competing for this group (or might choose to)?
- If we choose a target, where will this population be in five or ten years? Is it growing or declining? What is the trend?

קדימה Developing targets is a key strategic approach.

3. Understanding the Synagogue Organization

Synagogue organizations present challenges to leaders trying to create cohesive communities in a world of change. According to Susan Shevitz (1995), synagogues are distinguished by five characteristics: they are voluntary, pluralistic, loosely coupled, nonrational, and technologically weak. The following are my reflections on these characteristics.

Voluntary

Volunteers go into and out of the organization. They are interested in some issues and not others. They may have a period of high energy and then fade when other competing interests capture their attention. Their motivations and energies are often inconsistent. Authority in a voluntary environment is diffuse, writes Jim Collins (2005). There is not enough concentrated authority to ensure executive leadership. Leaders cannot coerce action or pay incentives for performance.

Pluralistic

Congregations have diverse members, and the members have diverse needs. Unlike some businesses that can specialize, most congregations have to serve a broad constituency. They are not able to fully segment their programs and focus on a just few profitable niches. They have a blueprint for community that comes from Torah, not from a business plan. Congregational leaders must find a way to hear the voice of families with preschool children and empty nesters. They need to anticipate the needs of singles and seniors.

SVP CASE

Honoring Our Traditions

I was conducting a visioning workshop with a large historic multigenerational congregation. The older, more long-standing members were frustrated. They felt there had been too many changes in the congregation. At first they complained that new members were trying to "water down" Conservative Judaism. This charge tended to create conflict because it devalued the ideas of some newer members. As the process developed the older members became more explicit about their concerns.

They were upset that their tunes had been changed by the cantor. Others were concerned that their high holiday seats had been changed. Others were uncomfortable with some of the new approaches of the board. When they were asked to express all of these feelings as values, they argued that the congregation should "honor the synagogue's traditions." This was no longer a debate about who was a Conservative Jew. It was now developing into the issue of how to manage the rate of change.

I then asked them about the notes from the first workshop, when the planning group had decided that the synagogue needed to attract new members. The older members had all agreed this was a top priority. I asked if new members would want to come into a culture and agree not to change anything. The older members all laughed. They saw the absurdity of trying to hold on so tight. In fact, all the stakeholders saw the irony of this. They realized that they would have to find ways to honor long-standing members while respecting the perspectives of new members if they were to achieve their goals.

Loosely Affiliated Congregation

Congregants may connect to some individuals and not to others. They may identify with some elements of the congregation's mission and not others. Synagogue observers have noted that many members have a "consumer orientation" rather than a membership orientation. The consumer is "loosely coupled." They focus on the service they are trying to procure. They may like a certain program or may enjoy some social events. They may be focused on getting their child a bar mitsvah. They do not see the holistic mission of the congregation and all of the diverse voices that make up the community.

Dedicated Core of Leaders

In reviewing Shevitz's organizational characteristics I have decided to add one feature I see often: the dedicated core leadership. While 81 percent of the congregation may not be consistently engaged with the congregation, there is a core group of members who are described by themselves and others as dedicated. Sales's study of Westchester congregations (2004) found that 5 percent were greatly active and another 14 percent were very active. This study thus found a core group of 19 percent. When I am speaking with groups, I often give a slightly lower estimate for the active core, 10 to 15 percent. Most groups concur with this assessment. These are the people you can count on to see at services at least twice a month. They come to major events. They are working with some committee or group each year.

One of the challenges of synagogue life is to help the inner circle find ways for the less engaged to connect and be more active. It is not uncommon for the very active to spend years overfunctioning to keep the synagogue running. As they do this, they often become set in their ways. They develop a style of doing business. When new ideas are presented, they may say, "That won't work. We've tried that before." Some dominant leaders may interrupt a conversation and redirect the discussion to their approach. Intentionally or unconsciously, core leaders can resist innovation. In contrast, congregational creativity occurs when core leaders interact with motivated, gifted leaders who come from the periphery.

Developing leaders entails not only the challenge of recruiting and orienting new leaders but also ensuring that there are real leadership opportunities available for them. This means term limits for current members and structuring board meetings so that they elicit new ideas. It means that good manners (derekh 'erets) be maintained to protect new ideas and new leaders.

Nonrational

Scholars note that in business organizations there is a great deal of irrationality. Managers bring complex emotions to their work. Today, business leaders speak of organizations as "swamps," where the footing is unstable and the visibility blocked, metaphorically speaking, by "heavy foliage and mist." If businesses are sometimes swamps, what are congregational environments like?

In business organizations, at least people share professional training as engineers, accountants, marketers, and lawyers. In contrast, synagogue leaders have a wide array of talents, experiences, and beliefs. Volunteers come with strong attachments, memories, beliefs, and positions. Many of these feelings lie below the surface and are not known

SVP CASE

The Unexpected Agenda Item

Synagogue leaders have talked about the dread they have about certain issues. They recall how at their dinner table at home they shared their anxiety with their spouse. "Issue three is on the agenda tonight. It is going to be hot. We have heard the buzz about this for months, and now it's coming to the board. I will be late tonight, dear." When they get to the meeting, issue three sails through with only modest discussion. It turns out that issue four, the religious school field trip, is the hot one. How can this be? Why are experienced board members often so wrong about which issues will be controversial? It is the irrational character of so much synagogue work.

Unbeknownst to the board members, issue four is an important personal issue to a few congregational members. They remember the poorly planned school field trip from three years ago. Their children were on the bus that came late and did not have enough box lunches. It is an emotional issue for them. They forget about lay-staff boundaries. They do not give the rabbi time to consult with the educator, even though she has the logistical details that might put their concerns to rest. They want to hash these out in the middle of the meeting of the entire board. They forget the board's agenda and its priorities, even though other issues clearly are of greater weight to the vast majority of the room. Issue four "turns out to be hot." Who would have guessed?

to their congregational teammates. These emotions can come forward unexpectedly and without warning.

Weak Information Technology

In order to lead, modern organizational leaders must learn from their mistakes. They must be more reflective about their work. In order for leaders to grow from their leadership experiences, they must document their leadership lessons. Unfortunately most congregations keep very poor records of committees and task forces. They invest little in orienting new team members so that prior learning can be transmitted.

File on a Holiday

When I do SVP, I have several pre-contracting discussions about the process. One task is to identify the kind of data the planners need and determine what is available. As I begin to go down my checklist, the other party often goes silent. I have to check to see if the person is still on the line. I sense some anxiety about the depth and accessibility of the congregation's data.

In one instance I tried to offer a simple confidence-building request. I asked, "Can I get a copy of the minutes of the education committee?" My planning partner answered, "I will check, but I think she went to Boca." Went to Boca? I wonder. How can the education committee's records have gone to Boca?

The answer is that, like in so many congregations, there are few central files for the committees. They are the special preserve of individuals. The process is highly informal. Some take good minutes. Some hold on to them. Few ensure they are maintained or transferred to new leadership groups.

Historically Jewish learning was extremely serious about preserving the legal debates between scholars. We read about this rabbi and that rabbi's views. Even the minority views that did not prevail were maintained ('eduyot). Despite this deep historic concern for honoring the past work of others, most synagogue leaders have very inconsistent and sketchy records. What few are available may have headed south to Boca.

SVP CASE

3. The Synagogue Context

All synagogue leadership approaches are affected by the synagogue's context. In SVP context is the congregation's history and culture. It is the stories that members tell. Context is the memories that members have and the meaning they make from memorial plaques and other artifacts that they encounter. Context is the size of the congregation and its history of size changes. Context is the way the governance functions and the table where decisions are processes. Context is the way that the rabbi has chosen or not chosen to lead. It is the authority the congregation gives to the rabbi, to Torah, and to halakhah. Context is the informal set of customs and practices that members observe when they do their synagogue work. Leaders must be aware of the congregation's size, culture, and life cycle stage.

Congregational Size

Arlin Rothauge has described four congregational size types (Gaede 2001, 15). They are family (up to 50), pastoral (50 to 150), program (150 to 350), and corporate (larger than 350). These are just general estimates. Many congregations operate with "one foot in several size cultures." As congregations change in size, they will make transitions into larger congregational structures or decline back to a previous size structure. While I am not going to try to explore all of these issues, you need to be aware that size affects the relationship of lay leaders to the professional staff, lay leaders to the clergy, and the clergy to each other. For example, pastoral congregations require a great deal more hands-on managerial work by the lay leaders than a program congregation because there is inadequate staff to manage the work. Rabbis often describe themselves as jacks of all trades in such congregations.

Congregational Life Cycle Stages

Congregations have various stages in their lives. Alice Mann (1999, 2) describes congregational birth, formation, growth, stability, decline, and death. Different strategies and leadership styles are "appropriate" at each stage. Congregations "like biological organisms manifest a pattern of emergence and decline," which can be described with the following developmental arch. I have combined the stages that Mann discusses (in bold) with some of the language that Gil Rendle (1998) uses for these stages (in bold italics).

1. Birth/*The Dream:* This stage reflects the earliest moments of a congregation's story. It may be the first meeting at someone's home or in a meeting room at the JCC. It may include the first Friday night Shabbat dinner when a service was put together.

2. Formation/*Beliefs and Goals:* During this phase the basic identity of the congregation takes form. For many congregations this starts with the family-size congregation, which is often lay led. At this stage the leaders are asking the following questions: Who are we? What are we here for? Who is our community?

3. Stability/*Structure:* The formative period paves the way for a period of sustainable congregational life. If the congregation has come through the formative stage and made the transition from family to pastoral, then years of stability may be supported on a firm foundation. This period includes the development of professional staff, operating procedures, facilities, financial resources, and governance processes. As time goes on, even stable congregations may come to a point of stagnation. At this point they need to develop self-renewing processes, or they may slip into decline. When congregations are at the height of stability, it is hard to motivate them to plan. These congregations are often quite satisfied with their situation. They lack the sense of urgency to work on long-term planning. They may prefer "problem solving planning."

When congregations begin to stagnate, they are ready for developmental planning that asks them, "What is the next step for you?" When congregations are in significant decline, they may need frame-bending planning, which puts all of the issues on the table and is open to taking a fresh look at their missions.

4. Decline/*Nostalgia, Questioning, and Polarization:* At some point stagnation can turn into decline. As decline begins, writes Mann, "the congregation finds that it can no longer dismiss as temporary or random the noticeable falloff" (1999, 6). This falloff may be in members, worship attendance, life cycle events, religious school enrollment, or high holiday appeals.

Many of the consulting interventions that I am called in for have to do with congregations moving from stagnation to periods of decline. As Mann notes, the most common response is to blame someone. The rabbi may be blamed for a lack of vision; the lay leadership may be blamed for a lack of fundraising; the congregation may be blamed for its apathy. As Mann observes, "the cycle of blaming tends to accelerate decline." One of the first things I try to do in such congregations is to shift the focus from blaming to looking at the entire congregational system to see how all of the elements contribute to the situation.

I try to shift the focus of leaders from fighting over tactical issues to exploring strategic ones. This is not easy because, as Mann writes, "these congregations feel helpless about the changes in the external context so they are more likely to focus their attention on matters they feel they can control" (1999, 6).

In Rendle's model, during the decline stage leaders have the option of restructuring their congregations or revisioning them. The restructuring approach is tactical. Leaders can roll up their sleeves and recommit to the hard work of the congregation with the hope that what they did in the past will be able to repeat that ministry. The alternative approach, revisioning, calls for leaders to interrupt nostalgia in order to find new energy. There may be some chaos and transition, but eventually a new dream will emerge and members can respond to that challenge.

Congregational Culture

Rabbi Sam Joseph of Hebrew Union College once told me that every congregation has a DNA, an underlying character and culture. Congregations may change, but there are usually limits to their flexibility. There will be strong internal pressure to pull them back to where they were. Leadership should use the process of reflection to become more aware of their underlying culture. They will find it helpful to reflect on how they "do synagogue." We have a major exercise on this in Workshop 1.

Communal scholars talk about congregations that are "all encompassing." When you join, you enter a community. You embrace its vision and goals. You become a "Member by Choice." Many congregations have very diverse members. Some join for convenience. Some join because their friends or family are there. Some join for a program, such as a good religious school. Given the nature of synagogue organizations most congregations, according to Isa Aron, are not likely to be all encompassing communities with "Members by Choice": "All encompassing congregations tend to be very traditional, very new or very small. It is nearly impossible to rewind the clock and turn large and/or heterogeneous synagogue back into communities of choice" (2002, 135).

SVP was specifically designed to provide these heterogeneous communities with tools to gain more common ground.

The Individual

I strongly believe in the systems approach to congregational analysis and leadership. While I have noted the importance of congregational development stages, size, and context, I want to note here the important role played by key leaders of the congregation. Key leaders can create bold new directions, and they can plunge the congregation into conflict. Leadership is a function of the gifts of leaders (intelligence, awareness, self management, etc.) and the challenges of their context (environment, leadership culture). The Jewish tradition appreciates the interplay of these factors. "According to one opinion, the character of a generation is determined by the leader. According to the other opinion the character of the leader is defined by the generation" (*b. Arakhin 17a*).

Look below the surface of a congregational conflict, and you will see some powerful personal style issues that dominate certain chapters of the story. Individual behaviors matter. Leaders are driven by a range of motivations. Some seek control. Some are trying to work though another issue with a member or staff person. Some need status. Some will stir things up to be in the limelight. Others are lonely and afraid to lose their place in the community. The factors are many. Some are aware of their motivations. For most they remain unconscious. Anyone who has worked with congregations in depth will attest to the impact that a few people can have on the direction of a congregational conversation.

Conclusion

Many of the factors affecting synagogues are outside of the leadership's control. In a world of changes there are weaknesses to address and strengths to leverage. The synagogue organization is not a large business, but because of diverse membership and special mission it is complex. Leaders must learn to understand the synagogue context so that they can choose the right path (planning steps) to manage their congregation.

Questions for Reflection

1. If a reporter were doing a story on your congregation, how would he describe the environment or context around the congregation?
2. How would he describe the organization or culture inside the synagogue?
3. How do the environment and culture affect your leadership?
4. What could you do to better manage your congregational culture?

5.

Gathering Data: Understanding the Land

See what the land is . . . and whether the land is rich or poor.

—Numbers 13:18–20

The lack of consensus among leaders is a serious hindrance to effective planning. Shared facts help create alignment. You may debate the implications of the facts, but what happens if you don't even agree on the facts? Shared facts allow us, as one friend of mine said, "to stand shoulder to shoulder even if we don't see eye to eye." Without shared facts planners can wander aimlessly without a map. Each SVP planning group is challenged to create a congregational profile briefing book that includes internal and external data about the congregation and its context. This provides leaders with a portrait of the current situation, that is, a situation analysis.

Why the Lack of Data?

Leaders Often Don't Know What Questions to Ask

Many of the factors facing the congregation are outside the control of leaders. What is happening in your environment? What are the key demographic questions you should be asking? (e.g., Is the population growing? Are young families moving in? Is the population aging?) What psychographic questions should you be asking about the lifestyles of people in your area? (e.g., Do you have young families with children? Do you have single urban professionals? Do you have working class ethnic groups?) What are the trends?

Leaders Don't Know Where to Get External Data

Planners are not used to gathering data. They often don't know where to start. There are various ways to capture data.

Percept. One helpful resource that churches use is Percept (www.perceptgroup.com). They work with census data to provide an area ministry profile based on the zip codes you request to be sampled. You may find the profile provides a helpful portrait of your surrounding area.

Jewish Mailing Lists. There are a variety of organizations that gather data from census information, credit cards, warranties, etc. Some claim that they have up to 60 percent of the Jewish names in an area. Working with these lists provides several opportunities. You get an immediate sense of how many Jews might be in your surrounding zip code area. This can be invaluable in areas with low affiliation (20 to 30 percent) where the population lacks visibility.

Federations. Federations often have community studies. When Federation studies are properly done and current they can be particularly helpful because they can provide specific data on denominational segments and Jewish practices.

National Jewish Population Study. The most recent version of the National Jewish Population Study (NJPS) was published in 2002. (It was previously published in 1990.) In seeks to estimate the Jewish population and to provide insights into such areas as the family structure of Jewish households, affiliation, attitudes toward giving, and beliefs and practices (www.ujc.org/njps). The national data may not exactly apply to your specific congregation, but the categories that are featured raise great questions. How does the congregation compare to the national data? Why is the congregation different from the average? Some federations, like UJA Federation of New York, have taken this data and made it available for specific geographic areas such as Northern Westchester or Southern Westchester County.

Other Studies. There are a host of books and articles that talk about Jewish identity and the needs and wants of prospective members. I find the data from the book *The Jew Within* (Eisen and Cohen 2000) very helpful. The insights from such books as Dr. Bethamie Horowitz's study "Connections and Journeys" (2000) or Dr. Jack Wertheimer's book on Conservative Jews, *Jews in the Center* (2000) shed light on different types of Jewish attitudes and practices. Leaders are always asking me about the 70 percent of their members who are only minimally engaged. What's on their minds? You can do surveys, polls, and parlor meetings, but one good place to start are sociological studies of typical congregational members. Synagogue 3000 has a site with many helpful studies and stories (s3k.org). These portraits are, in my experience, very descriptive of many of the attitudes and beliefs I encounter. Start from these overviews, and then drill down to the unique issues of your congregation. By analyzing a book or study's portrait of attitudes toward worship or ritual practice, you can ask how your congregational attitudes compare.

USA Congregational Life Study. There are also a wide variety of studies of Christian churches that provide insights into religion in America. One excellent resource for this is the USA Congregational Life Survey, conducted by U.S. Congregations, a research group staffed by religious researchers and sociologists. It is housed in the offices of the Presbyterian Church (USA) in Louisville, Kentucky. It studies 300,000 worshippers in 2,000 churches. One of the things I most enjoy about being at Alban is the ability to look at data from churches and ask about the lessons they hold for synagogues. Like so much of the data I have discussed, these studies may not exactly apply to Jewish congregations, but they pose fascinating questions.

Leaders Get the Wrong Data

Lawrence Butler identifies challenges of data management for nonprofit boards: being overloaded with data; having inappropriate data, having anecdotal data, and lacking the relevant context for the data (Butler 2000, 170).

Overload

Some synagogue software programs gather data about members' interests. They claim that if you push a button, you can find all the information you need about the membership.

The Misguided Mailing

One executive director was proud that he had gathered data and created a list of over 100 members whom he thought would be interested in a social action program. He then sent out a mailer to them about the program. I asked him what the response was. He said "zero." The data was not current; it had come from the membership applications they filled out when they joined. This data had not been filtered; it was too raw. He needed to know who was very interested in social action and had expressed some interest in a specific program, but what he had gotten from the software program was data overload.

Inappropriate Data

We have all watched the scene when the treasurer brings in detailed budget reports and presents them to the whole congregation. He dumps the spreadsheets with their ten-point font on the table, and people's eyes roll. This is often inappropriate data. It is too dense. It is in a format that is alien to many. It is in a font that is hard to read. I recommend, instead, creating one-page executive summaries that highlight some of the key variances and encourage the finance team to offer an explanation. Leaders are challenged to speak clearly and effectively. If the budget is working, the board probably doesn't need to see all of the background. If there is an emerging issue with great importance, I want to see the issue highlighted (for example, in a large font) in a helpful manner so that I can give it the respect it deserves. I call this "managing by exception."

Anecdotal Data

In the absence of a data gathering plan you often get anecdotes from various leaders. I once worked with a day school that was concerned about losses in enrollment. One leader insisted that people were leaving because the school was too religious. After I reviewed her exit interviews, I found that 60 percent of the members left because they moved out of the area. Another 20 percent left because of financial considerations. The remainder left because the school was too religious or not religious enough.

So are you committed to getting those exit interviews before you make the wrong assumptions?

Why Do They Leave?

One group was complaining about how difficult getting exit interviews was. "We can't get it." "We don't have time." "Why bother? Will they ever really tell us?" "They are leaving—they won't take the time." I knew there was some truth in this. Some members had a bad experience with exit interviews. In my experience as a marketer however, I found that if I was persistent and resourceful, I could get invaluable information. What were the barriers to getting good data? The group eventually conceded that the data was important. They then realized that they had assigned this task to a member who had very limited interpersonal skills—he intimidated people. The board realized that they had assigned important work to the wrong person.

Data without Context

Leaders are quick to talk about membership trends. If they are declining, they will express anxiety about the future and look to me for some inspiring strategies. It is thus very important for me to understand the "real numbers." After review, it is not uncommon to find a recent year with a significant (10 percent or more) decline in members. I ask, what happened here? Did they have really bad food at the "break the fast"? Did the president offend the faithful in the high holiday appeal? Often what has happened is that a new membership chair or executive director has reviewed the membership rolls and found a whole group that had not paid in two years and who are showing little interest in paying this year. He does what most good businesspeople do. He takes the "write down" and thus provides a more accurate picture of the true membership. There is usually a great deal of emotion surrounding this adjustment.

One leader described the prior executive director as simply not having a grip on the numbers. Another past president confided that he knew the numbers were not accurate but he was trying to be sensitive to the rabbi (the rabbi got upset when a member left). This is what Susan Shevitz means when she calls synagogue organizations "nonrational" (1999). Many essential management facts are covered over to avoid the emotional pain of managing.

In other cases I will see a blip in growth only to find there was a "special discount offer" for young families for two years. If you look at data without reference to the congregational culture and context, you might think you are doing better or worse than you really are. Remember, the most admired leadership trait is *honesty*. Leaders need to help the team make an honest assessment of the situation.

Leaders Get Survey Data They Can't Manage

Surveys can tell us something about members' past behavior. Have they volunteered in the past? Have they attended the family seder? Surveys, in my experience, are weaker in predicting whether people will attend next year or whether they will support a new program. Will they come to a book club on Tuesday? Would they go on a holiday retreat? Marketers are often tricked by focus groups who suggest that they like a product. When it gets to the shelf, people walk by.

Raised Expectations

In the twenty-first century members have little discretionary time and many competing interests. The things that they identify as of moderate ("some") interest may actually translate into a "no show." Surveys also create great concerns for leaders. They produce anxiety for staff. Once the "great survey" is in, there is pressure to respond to the data. "Rabbi, we spent all of this money on research, and now we must show that we can respond." The rabbi looks at the programming ideas that are listed in a great "data dump" and asks, "What should I do with this data?"

Findings That Are Not Actionable

Many times the data cannot be acted upon. Some members may want a very short service that the congregation's minhag cannot accept. The rabbi is not going to be willing or able to cut major sections of the traditional liturgy. Others may want multiple services, but the congregation is not staffed to manage these. Some may want improvement in the facility, but when the leadership comes back with higher dues, a building fund, or other sacrifices, that desire may become less urgent for many.

Giving Planning a Bad Name

When the planning team is not able to explain how they are using the survey data, the congregation may be confused. Lay leaders are now concerned that they may have not responded to the "wants and needs of the community," however confusing and impractical the data.

Leaders Don't Share Data

The budget may be circulated, but key facts are withheld. Much of the data is not in a user-friendly form, so that is difficult for the average member to read and almost impossible for them to retain. Data is presented without a historical trend so it is hard to see patterns.

Leaders Fail to Make the Connection

Leaders often fail to connect data and develop possible implications. When we discuss the forces affecting congregations, I ask leaders to define if these were having a low, medium, or high impact on the congregation. This question should be asked about the most important data that the steering committee identifies. What is the forecast for household income—is it growing? What will these trends mean for local school systems or housing prices? Time and again I find that the most basic facts are not known or shared.

Clarifying Critical Data

I was called to work with a long-term planning group considering various building options. One idea was to expand the preschool. There was some debate about the viability of this. I asked the group what percent of the revenue came from the preschool. The guesses ran from 20 to 30 percent. The actual number was 39 percent. Expanding the preschool was an obvious opportunity. It warranted significant staff and lay leadership time.

SVP CASE

Gathering Useful Data

Learning about Competitors and Customers

I suggest some exercises to sharpen your strategic lens. Review your steering committee responses to the satisfaction survey (pages 143–44), and come up with an average score. You can later compare the steering committee's assessment with the results from the parlor meetings. Identify up to three congregations that you feel you have to compete with. Have the steering committee provide their assumptions about how these congregations would score using your survey. Obviously your congregational assessments are subjective. It is not easy to assess your performance or others, but you must. Jim Collins writes, "What matters is that you rigorously assemble evidence—quantitative or qualitative—to track your progress" (2005, 7). Michael Hammer implores leaders to "measure like you really mean it" (2001, 100). He argues that we show what we value by what we track.

Your knowledge of other congregations may be sketchy, but you are not without sources of information. You and your planners have friends at these congregations. Many have visited there for holidays and life cycle events. This is a healthy exercise and always provides some insights.

Learning about Prospects: The Affiliation Process

Leaders need to gather data on how members experience the congregation at the various stages of affiliation. This data contributes to developing a membership strategy.

Affiliation Stage: Prospects' Needs	Welcoming: What Leaders Should Do	What Data Should We Gather?
Seek: Prospects are looking to meet basic needs.	**Build Awareness:** Make prospects aware of values, identity, programs (by advertising, special events, open houses, etc.)	What is our image in the community? Community interviews. Parlor meetings of prospects, recent members.
Test: Prospects visit the congregation, talk to members, observe and interact with clergy.	**Welcome:** Every member should be an ambassador. Demonstrate that we welcome new members and care about them. Committee members develop intentional methods to facilitate this.	What are members' first impressions? What do they say to office staff, educators, clergy, or welcoming committee members?

Affiliation Stage: Prospects' Needs	Welcoming: What Leaders Should Do	What Data Should We Gather?
Return: They come back; they follow up with questions.	**Follow Up:** We need to assign someone to build on their interest and educate them about the congregation.	What are the key decision-making criteria of our prospects? Why do they join? What makes them reluctant?
Join: They sign up.	**Engage:** Help connect them to other groups and individuals. Mentors welcome baskets/ dinners.	What data do we gather when they join? Who uses it? What is done with it?
Deepen: They hope to become included. They reflect on whether the congregational experience was what they hoped it would be.	**Monitor and Maintain:** Create a welcoming committee charter. Recruit a diverse team. Define data to gather. Define programs.	What data do we monitor? What percent get a follow-up letter or a call? What percent go to new member Shabbat? What percent connect with a mentor? What percent join a group? What percent of new members get involved in committees or projects in the first two years? Why do people leave (use exit interviews)?

Targeting Prospects

Targeting usually involves identifying some prospects you hope to attract or addressing the needs of some segment of the congregation that is not adequately served. Targeting raises several questions. Let's see how one congregation's planners might answer these questions for one segment: young families with school-age children.

Group 1: Young Families with School-Age Children

What are the target's attributes? Parents are ages thirty to forty; their children are in religious school and/or preschool. Many have husband and wife working. Busy schedules. Building careers.

What is our unique appeal to them (positioning)? We are a large congregation, and we are known for our resources (clergy, facility, etc.). We have a top-rated school. Our grade sizes are sixty to eighty children, so students will have the opportunity to make friends. We are close to where most of these families are buying homes. The public schools are excellent. We have beautiful and secure grounds. Some of the children in this segment have already participated in our summer camp program. We have an image of excellence with children.

What do we need to do to make them aware? Encourage more of them to come to our open house. Consider offering a second date. Run articles in Jewish media about the great programs we run. Have current members bring friends. Do more to increase socialization of young families. Create small family groups. Have them bring nonmembers to family Shabbats.

What do we need to do to meet their expectations? We need to continue to offer the same outstanding programs we have in the past. We need to increase the social networks in the congregations so families don't get lost.

Learning about the Congregation and Staff

SVP Interviews with Staff

The staff will play a central role in the SVP process. They will be one of the stakeholder groups. They will also be asked to support task forces and committees in the implementation phase. It is very helpful to get staff input early in the process. The staff will be integral in helping planners understand how our programs provide the benefits that members want; they can also help define who the best prospects are. By meeting with the staff I get background information about staff concerns that contributes to the design of the workshops and other planning processes.

Parlor Meetings with Members

In the parlor meetings you will ask current members to rate their satisfaction with current programs. In the values and goals workshops I will challenge the planners to define the goals they want to work on. What segments are underserved? What programs need to be strengthened? You will also want to look at who your most promising perspective members are. You might identify several groups, such as young couples with children in religious school or empty nesters. Once you identify these groups you will need to ask some basic questions about how to target them.

Leaders may find it intellectually interesting to look at the difference between how connected new members feel and how more long-standing members feel, but those who fund, create, and implement the survey are usually looking for insights that will produce some bottom-line results:

- More volunteers
- More attendance at programs
- More engagement
- New members

The Targeted Congregational Survey

You will not want to invest a great deal of energy into gathering survey data until the steering committee has developed some idea about the critical or driving issues. Data gathering is a very exhausting process, and if you go right to this, you may miss the opportunity to frame the proper conversations. I recommend parlor meetings to identify key themes (see chapter 8).

If you plan to do a survey, focus it on some *specific areas* where you have refined the questions and have a team prepared to focus in on the data and act on them. I prefer to do this at the task force action planning stage (see Workshop 3 in chapter 15). Some typical surveys would focus on worship or religious school. Some congregations want to learn about attitudes about the facility for capital budget planning. This sometimes follows an SVP plan as leaders begin to test the readiness of stakeholders to fund changes in support of values, strategies, and goals.

Intuitive or Empathetic Marketing

Some marketers conduct what they call "empathetic marketing." This process assumes that people often struggle to articulate how they are feeling about programs. They may say they are uncomfortable in services but not describe what would be more comfortable. They may want better services but they don't know what better means.

Empathetic marketers might observe members in worship. When do they arrive, and when do they leave? When do they read or sing? When are they silent? When are they disengaged, and when do they seem most alive? From these observations planners might develop some working ideas about increasing members' engagement in the congregation. They could test these in small groups or use their insights in designing a future worship survey. Many SVP workshop exercises are designed to help leaders capture these insights.

Synagogue Engagement Group

The Synagogue Engagement Group is a model I first observed at Temple Emunah in Lexington, Massachusetts. I see this as a truly values-driven approach. It uses the intuitive learning of congregational leaders, internal data, community surveys, leadership experience, and rabbinic vision to imagine a range of possible programs that might address members' wants and needs. These program ideas can be posted on the Internet, included in congregational bulletins, or displayed in the congregation's foyer on easels or bulletin boards. The engagement group process seeks members who are interested in designing, leading, or participating in one of the activities. Members who respond are given resources and support by paid and volunteer staff. The process connects intuitive ideas about members' needs and wants, leadership support for new programs, and the willing members who step forward. By connecting the creative ideas of leaders to the passions of members, the Synagogue Engagement Group collects people, not just paper.

The Volunteer Profile System

The Volunteer Profile System identifies what volunteers might want to do. The system is set up to solicit these individuals and put them to work, rather than just reflect on their data. It also helps group them based on their interests so that they can be a part of creating the new program. Instead of dreaming about new programmatic ideas, the staff can dream about new volunteer partners to help them plan and recruit for these programs. The programs should be conceptually viable. What makes them actionable is that you will have leaders who want to drive them.

Making a Start:
Working with Available Data

The president and the planning chairs are asked to review the Data Availability Worksheet (see page 247, part of Resource 1 in the Appendix). Your goal is to identify the data you have and put it into user-friendly form. You also want to decide what other data might be useful. If there was a worship survey, can you find it? If you had some focus groups, can you obtain the results? Some data may take more effort to generate. The administrator can help planners understand how much effort is involved in getting each item on the list. Synagogues do not have an abundance of staff. They need to prioritize their efforts. If there is something that you feel is essential, you can explore whether you want to invest the time and energy to gather and organize the data.

Data may not always be available or well organized, but the problem is exacerbated because the data is not consistently shared or discussed. If twelve steering committee members have a discussion about why people join, in my experience, a good deal of insight will emerge. A structured dialogue process will tap the intuitive knowledge of the participants. SVP believes that the combination of basic facts, committed and experienced leaders, and representative stakeholders accelerates learning.

Conclusion

I have argued that leaders can be developed by doing more leadership-oriented tasks. One of the most important is determining the kinds of data needed. As Hammer noted, we value what we measure. Data gathering encourages leaders to ask the tough questions about what matters. With shared facts they can begin to deal with the implications. These debates lay the foundation for future strategies.

Questions

1. What is the most important data that you need?
2. What would it help you do?
3. Choose one area. How might you go about gathering this data?

6.
Authority:
Learning to Lead

If a person picks up a bundle of reeds, do you think he can break them all at once? But if he takes them one at a time, even a small child could break them.

—Tanhuma Nitzabim 1:23

If all the leaders are going in different directions, they will be less effective. Planning seeks to create alignment so that the collective efforts of leaders are strengthened. In order to build trust and consensus, leaders must be able to understand each other's assumptions about authority, leadership, and decision making.

Leaders Must Learn to Use Authority and Power

Edgar Schein argues that there are several sources of authority (1988, 88). It's important to understand the sources of authority that leaders can draw on and how to use authority effectively with followers and peers.

Coercive Authority

B has no choice but to obey A. There are few examples of coercive authority in synagogues. The rabbi can compel a bar mitsvah student to attend a certain number of services during the year. The board can compel a member to pay his back dues or deny him his high holiday seats. Some synagogue employees can be directed to fulfill their obligations. Rabbis are usually empowered to ensure dietary policies are observed in the facility.

Traditional Authority

B goes along with A because A has traditional authority. Rabbis are historically empowered with this type of authority. Jill Hudson (2004) has noted that "congregations are born from a spark of intention between a faith tradition and a particular context." Rabbis understand the power of this spark, and they are trained in the tradition's intentions. Their challenge is to rekindle the flame and re-present the tradition in the context of the synagogue. SVP is designed to create a forum in which rabbis can use their traditional authority to influence leadership recruitment, training, decision making, and action. Some lay leaders, past presidents, and long-standing members may also be able to exert traditional authority. They are able to persuade others to follow them on behalf of Jewish or congregational traditions.

Rabbis need processes that enable them to reframe the congregational conversation in ways that allow traditional values to shape the community's practices and provide direction for important communal decisions.

Legitimate Authority

B accepts A as legitimate authority (employer, expert consultant, etc.). In a voluntary organization leaders must strive to gain legitimate authority by clarifying their roles and responsibilities and demonstrating that they have the personal characteristics to create results for the organization. Legitimate authority is fragile. It depends on continuous performance of the leadership to maintain credibility. When membership declines, when the financial commitment of members ebb, when the leadership cannot recruit and develop new leaders, the leadership will lose some of their legitimate authority. This creates a downward cycle in which leaders have less capacity to turn things around. When SVP leaders help define key governance issues, values, and goals, they can enhance the leadership's legitimate authority.

Derivative Authority

B accepts A because A is a friend or ally of someone who B respects. This is a very common characteristic in synagogues. The synagogue will have

various groups organized around certain leaders. These leaders can influence their allies and friends. Groups can be moved to positive action by
appealing to their leaders. The same phenomenon can be seen in resistance to change. B resists change because B's friend A is against it. SVP
creates a large planning group so that the planning process will gain
derivative authority. The stakeholders influence their friends.

Expert Authority

B goes along with A because B respects A's knowledge or skills. Synagogue
leaders depend on the legitimacy that starts at the top. The rabbi, president, and officers must be perceived as having the proper knowledge,
skills, and religious practices to lead the congregation.

Personality and Charisma

*B goes along with A because A has a powerful and attractive personal-
ity.* Charisma certainly helps, but few volunteer boards can assume that
they will have a continuous stream of charismatic leaders. In fact, strong
charisma is somewhat rare in lay leaders or clergy. When a rabbi has
strong charisma, followers talk about how inspired they are to work with
the rabbi on a project. It's exciting and meaningful. In the absence of a
charismatic rabbi, the rabbi–lay leadership team must work together to
increase their collective expertise and legitimate authority.

Concentrated and Dispersed Authority

In business school I was taught rules about delegation. When I got into
management, I learned that there was a great deal of art in real management. Sometimes it made sense to empower people to work indepen-
dently. Other times I needed to give much more specific instruction and
monitor performance more closely. The tradition understood that leaders had to know when to delegate and empower and when to hold fast to
their authority.

Delegate

When Moses is trying to manage the people in the desert, his father-in-
law tells him that he must delegate some of this responsibility. "'The
thing you are doing is not right; you will surely wear yourself out'" (Exodus 18:17-18). He then challenges Moses to create a chain of command.

Empower

In another section Joshua challenged two men, Medad and Eldad, who were feeling very empowered and spiritual. They felt called and began to prophesy in the camp: "And Joshua, son of Nun, Moses' attendant from his youth, spoke up and said, 'My lord Moses, restrain them'" (Numbers 11:28). Joshua had been working in the hierarchical system with Moses. Now he saw new people who felt they could be trusted to hear God's voice and describe God's plan. He didn't like it. There is in Jewish history a grave concern about false prophets. We can understand Joshua wanting to maintain "concentrated authority." You will see long-standing leaders in SVP who become concerned as relatively new arrivals begin to brainstorm and vision (prophesy in the camp). "But Moses said to him, 'Are you wrought up on my account? Would that all the Lord's people were prophets'" (Numbers 11:29). Like a good workshop leader, Moses understood that there are times when you need more energized participation.

Hold Fast and Maintain Boundaries

While the tradition established the importance of delegation and empowerment, it also established the importance of concentrated authority. Leaders must maintain boundaries. In SVP the rabbi establishes one boundary, and the board establishes the other. SVP is not a pure democracy, but it is collaborative, inclusive, and democratic.

The narrative of the desert wandering is full of chapters where the people are complaining about the mission and the leadership. There are several people running on the "Let's go back to Egypt" platform! Korah made a direct challenge to Moses. He asked who had appointed Moses to be over everyone. "They combined against Moses and Aaron and said to them, 'You have gone too far! For all the community are holy, all of them, and the Lord is in their midst. Why then do you raise yourself above the Lord's congregation?'" (Numbers 16:3).

While the tradition warns leaders not to lord it over the community, it also understands that some leaders understand God's mission better. Korah and his followers are punished and laid low. In this case Moses's credentials (legitimate authority) are well established. He was chosen by God. He has a relationship with God. He has provided extraordinary leadership. He has been selfless and sacrificing. In this story, Moses's leadership is concentrated, but it is for a noble purpose—for the sake of heaven. The survival of the Jewish people is on the line. Let's look at the tension between concentrated and dispersed authority.

Concentrated versus Dispersed Authority

Adapted from Parsons and Leas 1993, 24

Concentrated	**Dispersed**
Decisive leadership	Consult larger congregation
Continuity of leadership	Bring new people into leadership
Expertise, experience	Grassroots decision making, experiments
Tradition-established stakeholders	New stakeholders
Official leadership	Gifted leadership
Maturity	Spontaneity, Energy

Excesses at the Concentrated End of the Scale

- Small groups have the power to derail initiatives.
- Leadership is recycled.
- Leadership becomes burned out.
- Power groups become entrenched.
- Existence of in group/out group feelings.
- Those in authority become insensitive to diverse groups, new members, and changing environment.

Excess at the Dispersed End of the Scale

- People are confused about proper role of rabbi, staff, executive director, board, and congregation.
- Leaders turn over.
- Strong leadership distrusted.
- Decision-making process is slow.
- People pursue own agenda.
- They pick and choose, watering down the plan.

Choose Your Battles

Leaders must decide the key issues they need to focus on. There is only so much authority in the system, and leaders must marshal their efforts for the things that matter most. I often talk to boards about developing an A-B-C decision-making framework. A decisions need the most consensus. They may require congregational approval. B decisions may require that recommendations are sent back for further review. Extensive board debate is appropriate. C decisions should be delegated to committees and staff. They should be able to make these decisions within acceptable budget and policy frameworks.

Synagogue boards have been criticized for their structure. In his book *Boards That Make a Difference* (1997), John Carver tells boards to focus on ends and not become so involved in implementation (means). Charles Olson, discussing church boards (1995), challenges boards that are too bureaucratic, parliamentary, and business-like ("stone-like"). He wants leaders to make room to hear people's stories, to pray and reflect, to create sacred spaces, to be more nurturing. Whether one is inclined to choose Carver's model or explore more spiritual practices, one thing is clear. You have to stop doing some old things if you are going to start doing some new things. One thing to stop doing now is micromanaging C issues. Let's define what you will delegate and what the board should have on its agenda.

קדימה You have to stop doing some old things if you are going to start doing some new things.

Changing Board Practices: Reports

Board Practice	Stop Doing	Start Doing
Reviewing committee reports	Review all at meeting. Invite comments on each.	Only review ones with pressing issues to decide. Use time for looking into other issues in more depth.
Debating C issues	Debate "C" issues. If they are within the committee budget and have no major policy issues, they should not be considered by the board—period!	If over the budget but under a certain dollar level (say, $500), allow committee and executive director to decide. Create a small contingency fund in budget.

Board Practice	Stop Doing	Start Doing
Agenda	Have untimed, informal agenda. Where some items get too much time. Other items are cut short.	Use timed agenda that clearly reflects the amount of time the executive committee thinks is appropriate for the item.

Decision-Making Roles

One of the things that helps improve decision making is understanding the different roles people may play. Paul Rogers and Marcia Blenko (2006, 55) list five roles. In the following section I will show how SVP communicates these roles in planning.

1. Resources

These people give input. In SVP this is the steering committee, the parlor meeting participants, the stakeholders, and the community. They publish the values and goals in process and may offer town meetings to get more input. They may present updates at annual meetings.

2. Recommenders

Some have responsibility to gather data and make recommendations. The steering committee and the executive director are the leaders in data gathering. The SVP stakeholders make some general recommendations, and the steering committee refines these for approval.

3. Approvers

These are the people who can send a recommendation back for revision. In SVP the steering committee has this role in relation to the stakeholders' recommendations. The rabbi and to some degree the other professional staff have this role in their areas of expertise. They may encourage more review. The board ultimately must make the decision.

4. Decision Makers

In SVP this is the board in consultation with the steering committee and rabbi. In halakhic issues the rabbi would still be the final decision maker within the minhag of the congregation and denominational culture.

5. Executors

These are the people who must implement the plan. These are the volunteer and lay staff. In SVP the lead players will be the committee and task force chairs and their professional staff partners who develop action plans. Ultimately the board must monitor and track the performance of these groups.

Key Roles in SVP

The Board

The board retains its traditional authority to determine policy and to manage the financial issues of the congregation. It ultimately approves or declines proposals with policy or budget implications. The board also retains its authority over policy changes, including any changes that affect critical committees, such as the ritual committee (minyan) or the education committee. Team building in the planning process unleashes new ideas, but it doesn't eliminate traditional board authority boundaries.

The SVP process creates a practice field for current and future leaders to outline values and goals. The workshop designs are intentionally more democratic than the board's current practice. They provide a practice field where the spontaneous offering of an Eldad or a Medad can be accommodated.

The board is well represented in SVP but also learns from the perspectives of other stakeholders in the process. When the values, goals, and actions come before the board for action, they should be well received because many board leaders are part of the process. The board has been kept up to date and has blessed the model. It moves decision making to a more participatory approach because it has seen the benefits of this approach: new people, new ideas, and new energy.

The Steering Committee

As a result of the stakeholder workshops the planning team will get much larger. Just as the consultant has transitioned to give the steering committee more ownership, the steering committee must transition to let the stakeholders play a greater role. Some of the steering committee might like to provide an executive summary of its deliberations. Some would just like to tell the other stakeholders what they have learned. Just as the board has given the steering committee room to operate, so the steering committee has to strive to empower the stakeholders to do real work.

The Executive Director

The executive director should be a member of the steering committee. They should be the lead partners in gathering the internal data for the congregational profile briefing book. The executive director should provide leadership for all logistical planning, such as space requirements, registration for workshops, food requirements, and tools (e.g., flip charts, markers). The executive director should be active in suggesting stakeholders to participate in the process and in framing assignments for committees and task forces.

The Rabbi

The rabbis taught, "A teacher accompanies [the] students until the outskirts of the city" (*Sotah 46b*). In ancient days travel was dangerous. A teacher was challenged to care not just for the mind of the student but also for his spiritual and physical well-being. The SVP process is designed to inspire and raise up new leaders to partner with the rabbi, but these students need the rabbi's care as they do their work. The SVP stakeholders may come through different gates, but the rabbi needs to help escort all of them safely along the SVP way.

קְצוּנָה Today's stressful environment tends to keep clergy close to the managerial pole rather than the transformational pole of the leadership continuum.

Today's stressful environment tends to keep rabbis close to the managerial pole rather than the transformational pole of the leadership continuum. SVP tries to help the rabbi move toward the transformational pole by doing the following:

1. Recruiting a serious steering committee that is dedicated to partnering with him in fulfilling the synagogue's vision.
2. Giving the rabbi a better sense of where the congregation is so she can help weave her vision of the tradition and their needs together. As masters of the place (marah d'atra) they should provide clarity on religious boundaries for SVP.
3. Offering the opportunity to model "right" relationships with steering committee members. The rabbi can explore a partnership with the steering committee that might not be possible with the whole board.
4. Establishing the importance of values in determining how the planners and ultimately the congregation will work together. These values should challenge the mind-set of the "sovereign self" and reinforce more communal values.
5. Engaging select SVP leaders in a more in-depth review of key Jewish community values.
6. Providing the rabbi a chance to motivate key staff to address important task force and committee assignments.
7. Helping develop an articulate vision for the congregation.
8. Guiding the planners to align their emerging vision with the staff's vision.

In SVP the rabbi works closely with the leadership to interpret what they are learning from the process. This increases rabbinic leadership in terms of traditional, legitimate, and expert authority. Sometimes it takes a little extra support to cope with all of the learning coming from the process.

SVP tries to get more members into the kitchen to contribute to the meal—the congregation's plan. Part of this assertiveness training means that lay leaders begin to develop their opinions and arguments and to bring their recipes into the public realm.

I have had to assure anxious core leaders that the meal was not ready to be served and that it would be seasoned and adapted over time. The overall planning group has the skills to sort through most of the comments and find those elements that are the most relevant and constructive.

Half-Cooked Ideas

In one planning process, the rabbi became very frustrated as he listened in on various groups. I asked that the professional staff work in their own group, but the rabbi had decided to move about the room. He protested that many of the comments were not accurate. He entered into one of the break-out groups and began to argue that the ideas being suggested had been tried in the past. He objected to others' ideas as poorly conceived (I would call them "half cooked"). He clearly felt very uncomfortable and out of control. I explained that I could let him address all of the different issues that were being brought into the kitchen but that this would shut down the whole process of small group discussions. In my mind, meal preparation would grind to a halt.

Ironically, it had been the rabbi who had advocated for this process because he felt that the lay leaders were too passive. He wanted them to assert themselves and take ownership.

SVP CASE

In congregation after congregation the poorly thought out (half-cooked) argument or intemperate critique that appeared in early stages fades in importance.

Rabbis often feel they are carrying the congregation with less authority and more responsibility. They sometimes feel they are in the kitchen alone. Most will welcome a process that increases lay responsibility and accountability. It can be difficult for rabbis to increase the members' ownership and accountability if they don't let members struggle with congregational issues. As discussed in chapter 2, prospective leaders want to be empowered to do projects but also want staff support. While SVP encourages lay leaders to step forward, rabbis and other staff must escort them through SVP. They need to help get the right ingredients together and set up the kitchen. When the stakeholders are consulting and co-creating, they are going to make a few messes in the kitchen. The process requires that they mix things up a bit.

Rabbi and Professional Staff

In the team-building process there should be a clear understanding about what the staff's needs are. How can the various new volunteer planners help them meet those needs? How can the staff help focus and support some of the new energy that will be created? SVP requires a partnership between the staff and the planning team. As the consultant I will model this partnership by doing in-depth interviews with the staff to learn about their needs and what they are prepared to give. There are many opportunities for rabbis and other staff to bring their creativity to the SVP process. In the staff-driven congregation it may take multiple meetings to help clarify how the congregation's vision, the staff's vision, and the rabbi's vision will be aligned.

During the SVP process there is always pressure to cut the time commitments of workshops. Rabbis have been under the pressure of the clock for a lot longer than I have. Many just assume there is not enough time for more reflective learning or spiritual practice in leadership development. I encourage rabbis to be less reluctant to let some things go and more resolved to step forward to do some new things. Planning challenges rabbis to reallocate their time. There are few substitutes for the power of effective clergy leadership in helping a congregation step forward. Spiritually,

- Clergy can access the power of the traditional texts.
- Clergy are positioned to be present for sacred life cycle events.
- Clergy can focus us on transcendent issues.
- Clergy can help current leaders remember how their ancestors were called to serve.
- Clergy can raise expectations for covenantal kindness (ḥesed).
- Clergy model the spiritual disciplines leaders need.

Despite these opportunities many clergy find it hard to convene the conversations they need to have with leadership. SVP works to gather leaders and provide the rabbi the chance to step forward and get important issues on the synagogue leadership agenda.

Conclusion

This chapter has explored different types of authority and different roles in decision making. Synagogues are pluralistic. Members have a wide array of views about authority. Leaders must work to clarify the different roles people will play in decision making. Synagogues are loose affiliations, so individuals and groups may not know the rules. Synagogues also tend to be informal in writing down and communicating their decisions. In order to clarify authority and decision making the rationale and policies about organizational processes need to be written down and communicated on an ongoing basis.

In Workshop 3 (see chapter 15) I talk about the assignments given to task forces and teams. It will be important that the teams have the authority to do their work. They must leverage various forms of authority in order to part the seas of resistance.

Questions for Reflection

1. Look at your leaders. What kind of authority are they leveraging? How could they be more effective?
2. Review your decision-making process. Do the executive director, staff, board, and committees understand their roles in the process?
3. What role is your rabbi playing in congregational leadership today?
4. What roles and responsibilities need to be clarified?
5. In what area could you better support your clergy's authority and leadership?

7.

Congregational Readiness
for Change

Before God confers office on a man, he first tests him with a
little thing and only then promotes him to greatness.

—Shemot Rabbah 2:3

I am very enthusiastic about SVP's various tools and processes. So many of the leadership groups I see, however, are at a low level of energy—they are reluctant. Many have lost hope and heart. Many have long memories of failed projects and unresponsive members. They can tell you about the event they planned for 150 that only drew 20. It broke their hearts. In all of our teaching, motivating, and advocating for planning, you can fail to spend enough time in inquiry. You should not gloss over planners' concerns. They provide invaluable information about their readiness.

Our text above refers to the way God tested Moshe. He first observed how Moshe cared for his sheep in the wilderness. Then God trusted him to shepherd a nation. You need to make an honest assessment of your leadership. You need to see how they are doing the basics, the little things, before you ask them to embark on SVP, a very challenging process.

Evaluating Congregational Readiness

Inquiry

Before I agree to work with a planning team, I determine if the leadership is ready for the test. Congregations are different. Some are doing great and don't need to do developmental planning now. Others lack a readiness to plan. I have developed some characteristics of successful planning teams for leaders to consider. If a congregation does not have enough of these assets, they may need to set more modest goals. They may not be a candidate for serious planning. Even if they feel they are ready, many still struggle with key issues related to readiness. There are three key elements to sustain change: honest assessment of the present, hopeful vision of the future, and practical steps to move forward. Look for signs that these are present.

Look for signs of readiness for planning. Have a mental checklist: Do we have board approval? Is the rabbi on board? Do we have planning chairs? Do we have a budget? And so on. You may find that everything appears ready on the surface. One of the challenges is to try to understand the deeper readiness of the culture for change. All congregations have informal norms that they don't articulate. There are also deep unconscious (tacit) norms that they may not be aware of. The planning team must be humble about the ability of new plans to overcome the underlying DNA of the congregation. Planners need to check readiness but to expect surprises.

Motivation to Plan

An honest assessment of the present requires focus. Developing a vision of a desired future takes energy. If there are too many distractions, planners can lose focus. Let's look at some of the things that can affect readiness and focus. The elements of the SVP process work best when they are done sequentially and in full. Some congregations are able to execute the complete process in a pretty systematic fashion. Some have a well-developed volunteer culture; others are blessed with co-chairs with exceptional planning skills. Not all congregations are ready to plan at this level.

Most congregations do SVP because they feel that their leadership core is too thin. They also want to attract more support to their volunteer ranks. It takes a certain amount of leadership capacity to do SVP. Congregations that have little leadership on their executive committee find it difficult to get started. Who will recruit the steering committee? Who will recruit the parlor meeting participants? Who will recruit the stakeholders? Let's look at some of the factors to consider.

SVP Readiness Factors

1. The Rabbi Must Be Supportive, Enthusiastic, and Committed to Planning

While the administration and lay leadership play key roles, if the rabbi is not committed, it will be hard to sustain change. Programmatic initiatives that require professional staff to follow up may lose focus. Key members of the leadership supporting change may go unsupported or even be actively resisted. When the rabbi is not ready, it does not make sense to embark on visioning and planning. Lay leaders can certainly use the tools in this book for leadership development or transition planning, but the multi-year commitment for planning is too great without rabbinic support.

2. The Board Leadership Needs Committed President

SVP is a twelve-month to fifteen-month process. The ideas and initiatives that come forward in the planning need to be implemented over a twelve- or twenty-four-month period—or longer. This means the board president, both current and incoming, needs to be involved and committed.

3. There Must Be Urgency for Change

Some congregations are performing quite well. They may be in a great location with wonderful demographics for new members. They may have experienced and effective professional and lay leadership. The congregation has direction and is working effectively. These congregations may feel that their current governance and the leadership and management tools they have are quite adequate. They do not feel the need to mobilize co-planners or take the time to do SVP. They may simply want a small long-range planning committee to upgrade financial plans.

4. Key Lay Leaders Must Be Committed to Planning

There is seldom well-defined readiness for most synagogue leadership development programs. Even when I get a contract to come in, the leaders usually have an incomplete agreement. Some do not endorse the plan.

Others actively oppose the process. Still others are passive-aggressive. They will listen attentively but not agree to work on implementation. I try to review the plan with the core leadership and then ask for a meeting with the board. The entire leadership community needs to work through the issues. This models the kind of consensus-building skills needed in the process later.

5. There Needs to Be a Financial Commitment to Planning

Planning requires resources. Even if a congregation uses this book to self-guide their process, they will need to budget for meals, the preparation of materials, etc. Most congregations will want to hire some kind of outside facilitator to do the values and goals workshops (Workshops 1 and 2). This requires a planning budget. The process of getting some money in the next year's budget for planning will bring all of the other readiness issues into better focus. When the board has to vote on spending the money, they will dig deeper to explore their readiness.

In several cases SVP congregations were supported by grants. The funding was very helpful, but in some cases it gave an unrealistic view of their readiness. If the congregations are not investing any of their funds, they may not as invested in being ready to do the planning.

6. Planning Should Not Be Directly Competing with Other Major Projects

Congregations during SVP need to be focused. They cannot be distracted by another major congregation-wide project. If they are in the midst of doing a capital campaign or at the start of a building campaign, they may not be ready for SVP. Their focus needs to be on the other task. There is seldom enough energy to do both tasks. I once worked with a congregation in which a capital campaign was going on just before SVP began. The congregation had just gone through parlor meetings, interviews, and presentations as part of the capital campaign. They were drained. The capital campaign had its focus and drama. The financial goal was achieved and building plans begun. The work of the campaign had taken much of the energy needed to start up SVP.

In this kind of situation, I would suggest a short-term leadership development training rather than a whole congregation visioning plan.

You might reduce or eliminate the use of focus groups. You might accept a lower level of input from membership and might use a higher percentage of board members (up to 50 percent) if they are the ones most ready to work. If the congregation lacks the energy for a longer SVP process, I might reduce the workshop time.

7. Planning Requires Some Capacity for Creativity

Some congregations have little capacity for creative vision exercises. They are so resistant to change that they won't allow creative stakeholders room to brainstorm. They tend to interrupt brainstorming verbally or nonverbally. They discourage creative thinking in group sessions. Older established leaders remind new leaders that their ideas "have been tried before." They provide background information on why the culture won't respond to a proposed idea. I designed SVP to keep workshops fun, fast-paced, and engaging. I put a premium on creativity and collaborative learning to help overcome the reluctance of some stakeholders.

8. Planning Requires a Tolerance for Feedback

Some congregations are not used to getting feedback. They don't have much of a history of trust. It follows that these groups are often reluctant to empower new individuals or groups. Empowered groups will provide the leadership with the opportunity for new energy and creativity (as I noted above), but they will also provide some challenging feedback. They will ask questions and raise concerns.

In some processes I will make a special effort to focus on their strengths and explore the opportunities to build on these. I may design the questionnaires to focus on strengths or create an opening session that is more focused on building on strengths. I often use this approach when I am working with professional staff who feel isolated and harshly criticized. It does not help them to chronicle all the congregational problems. This can be overwhelming.

9. SVP Is Not for Congregations Facing Major Irrevocable Demographic Loss

Some areas are facing overwhelming demographic changes. The community may be aging. There are no students for school. Housing costs may have soared, and the congregation's neighborhoods are no longer affordable. Some areas have a changing socioeconomic mix; crime may be a factor. The old neighborhood may not seem safe. If the community is facing overwhelming demographic decline, they may lack the energy and hopefulness to recruit a large stakeholder group. Congregational redevelopment may be more appropriate than visioning (see Mann 1999). In redevelopment you don't focus on expanding all of the missions you are dreaming up. You begin to focus the congregation's limited resources on a few missions that make sense in this changing context.

10. Planners Need Conflict Management Skills

Potential SVP congregations should not be in the midst of a high-level conflict. It is too difficult to recruit participants when people are in warring camps. SVP requires a lot of energy. You have to sell others on the value of the planning and its value to the congregation. Planning is somewhat abstract. Congregations need to trust in the assumptions and processes of SVP. In a culture where trust is strained and conflicts are raging, it is hard to get people to trust you.

If you have a major conflict, it is important to delay SVP and work to acknowledge the conflicts and mediate the concerns of the various parties. After six months it may be possible to start some parts of SVP. Some congregations fail to fully describe this history of conflict in the pre-planning phase. It lies, like an iceberg, below the surface. Some leaders simply don't understand the full scope of what happened. Others may be driven to portray themselves, through revisionist history, in a more favorable light. At some point the community needs to begin to focus more on the future and less on the past. SVP can be a helpful bridge from the period of conflict to the period of promise.

Visioning stirs the congregational pot. Congregations need sufficient health to manage what bubbles up for parlor meetings and work groups.

Conclusion: Taking the Right Journey

Some congregations are not ready to do planning. Most can gain from a board retreat that helps clarify values and goals. Many could build on this with a series of leadership development workshops. Most could gain insight into their position, their identity, and their challenges and opportunities by doing parlor meetings. Congregations need to reflect on their readiness. Most can review this book and find some leadership development tasks they have energy and capacity for.

Questions for Reflection

1. How ready is your congregation for visioning and planning?
2. How ready are they for leadership development?
3. What would increase your team's readiness to plan?

8.
Understanding and Managing the Campaign

It is not your duty to complete the work but neither are you free to desist from it.

—Avot 2:2

Synagogue Visioning and Planning is about managing change. Planning leaders need to understand how they and their teams manage change. They need to find ways to communicate what they are learning about the planning journey. Each individual and team will experience change differently, but if you choose to work with this book, you will have begun the journey.

Recognition

According to Joseph Albo *awareness is the first step in personal teshuvah.* You must recognize where you have missed the mark ('al ḥet). Some leaders will pull back from their reflection and minimize their organizational problems. In consulting this is called the "flight to health." Just as the consultant is beginning to probe the problems, the client will often say that things are fine now and will try to stop the process. Just as the high holiday rituals are designed to heighten our awareness of our limited lifespan, so the planning process is designed to heighten our awareness of the need to address our mission now!

Leaders sometimes blame themselves for all of the things that have gone wrong in the congregation. Judaism values personal self-reflection and teshuvah. It encourages us to see where we have gone off the mark. Judaism encourages us to address communal issues as well.

The high holiday liturgy encourages us to speak publicly about our shortcomings (viduy). Judaism feels teshuvah is so important that we don't leave it just for individuals. We help support each other as a worshipping community. Synagogue leadership is too heavy a burden to carry alone. As leaders recognize where they have been off the mark it helps if they share their learning publicly. This models transparency and invites others to be more forthcoming. When it comes to organizational change, the congregation is too heavy to carry by oneself.

At the end of the planning process the community will have some shared values and goals. Just as you resolve to develop new personal practices during the high holidays, so leaders need to resolve to adopt new leadership practices. Goals should not be so easily achievable that they are not taken seriously. They should not be so unrealistic that they discourage effort. Resolve to address attainable goals by monitoring them and holding yourself accountable for action. Rabbi Tarfon says we must get over our resistance; we need to make a start!

Why Do Congregational Leaderships Resist Change?

Some Jews find they are not ready for the high holidays. They have not done the pre-work for teshuvah. Some congregational leaders find that they have not done the team building and planning necessary to address major changes. Congregational consultants talk about a congregational system in homeostasis. There is a "comfort zone" that the culture has established. In general, congregations tend to get stuck in that comfort zone. They often don't recognize that they are off the mark. Most congregational leaders are managers and not leaders. They help maintain the status quo.

Dr. Gil Rendle notes that "leaders who set things in motion make it hard for managers of the status quo to maintain stability" (1999, 64). Those managers may well not appreciate their limitations being brought to their attention. One of the challenges of leadership is to encourage new perspectives, even if these create some uneasiness. No one likes to admit their shortcomings, so the call for teshuvah, for change, can create resistance and conflict. Change leaders can become lightning rods for what Rendle calls "free-floating anxiety" (33). Leaders can find themselves out on a limb, where they are very vulnerable. SVP was designed to create a large group of co-planners so a few change leaders would not be identified as the problems. When the whole community affirms the Israelites' maps for the future on Mt. Ebal and Mt. Gerizim, it is hard to blame the message on a few leaders. Everyone has heard it.

All too often synagogue presidents become the focus of resistance. They never quite get a large enough group of people up on the mountain with them. In the face of this resistance many try to work even harder to make things happen and end up burning out. Many make a sudden exit after their presidential terms. They take with them valuable insights and experiences.

Understanding Fear and Loss

When you empower and energize new people, some new ideas and approaches are going to come to center stage. Existing leaders may not welcome all of these new co-creators. They will not have all of the traditional controls on the discussion. They cannot use Robert's Rules to call others out of order. New ideas are popping up on flip charts all around the room. Chaos indeed!

Most core leaders will argue that the congregation needs new members and the board needs new leaders. When the new people become leaders, there can be mixed feelings. Some existing members may feel as if they are losing control. New policies are being considered. New projects are being launched by new people. Existing leaders may feel that they are being pushed off the stage. They may have memories of a "golden age" of the congregation.

In the biblical narrative the people were given free will to express themselves. Some challenged God's plan and rejected entering the land. Some were ungrateful for God's redemption of them. They complained of lack of water and meat. Some didn't like God's chosen leader. Korah and his allies challenged Moses's leadership. When you have freedom, you can make a lot of noise. Oy! The community went through a lot of chaos before it regrouped to cross the river.

In the biblical narrative the people ultimately decided to follow Joshua and enter the land. They learned to engage with prophets and to support a monarchy. They built an army and priesthood. They built a Temple and a palace. They moved from being slaves to being a nation in this story. There were many bad kings and moral lapses; it was not a steady ascent to holiness. Similarly, in synagogue change one can see progress in one sector and regression in another.

Energetic, Tenacious Leadership

In order to undertake a visioning and planning process, leaders must maintain an above average level of energy. They must be able to face resistance to change and overcome it.

How do leaders develop the capacity to overcome resistance? We see some answers in the life of Isaac. Isaac was traumatized by his experiences, but he found energy from God. He had to settle in a difficult environment, but he was comforted by his faith. "Isaac dug anew the wells which had been dug in the days of his father Abraham and which the Philistines had stopped up after Abraham's death" (Genesis 26:18). He believed he would prevail and that God would bless his life on the land. This belief gave him the tenacity to settle the land.

We also see this tenacity in Moses. Even after he was punished for striking the stone (Numbers 20:12), he pulled himself together and went back to his leadership responsibilities. Even after God told him that he would not go into the land, Moses took up his responsibilities as a leader. He began to negotiate passage for his people with the king of Edom (Numbers 20:14-17).

Creating and Sustaining Momentum for Change

Peter Senge (1990) has described organizations as having reinforcing loops and balancing loops. In a reinforcement loop, projects gain momentum. They gain allies and resources. People talk about how things are "really flowing." In a balancing loop, projects slow down. People talk about how they are "stuck."

SVP tends to work on strengthening the reinforcement loops that lead to new practices and create momentum. As primarily volunteer organizations, synagogues are somewhat inefficient operations (as I have noted). The best projects can get bogged down in the congregational swamp. Given these patterns (balancing loops), sustained change processes are quite difficult and uncommon.

When boards do become discouraged and lose optimism about the future, they turn inward. It is not uncommon to hear lay leaders talk about the apathy of the congregation. They may bitterly describe projects where others failed to do their share. While this is understandable, it does not create the conditions for leadership development. The more desperate they become, the less joy they have in their work—the fewer possibilities they see for the future.

Some will try to make up for the lack of effort for others by doing a disproportionate amount of the work. This environment sometimes invites members with internal needs for authority and control to fill the vacuum. Some of the members, while well intended, do not have the skills or temperament to build teamwork. In this way deep cultural resistance and the general friction of synagogue life often contribute to some dysfunctional leadership. So what's the answer?

I have noted that change can move forward in one area and slip back in another. Even the most promising planning work can be derailed by a change in presidents, a change in the professional staff, some external factor, or conflict with the rabbi. The readiness of a congregation for change can accelerate or decelerate. For this reason most planning processes need to be flexible. Leaders need to be resilient like Isaac. They need to be willing to re-dig those wells throughout the planning and implementation process.

SVP: The Campaign

SVP understands that planners can go through difficult stages. Each step is important, and leaders must maintain the momentum of the group through the process. Harvard professor and management consultant John Kotter argues that planning leaders must address the following change management elements to maintain the momentum for change (1999). We will now consider how the various phases of the SVP process help maintain momentum for change.

1. Establish a Sense of Urgency

SVP clarifies the critical issues that need to be addressed in the data gathering phase. When you agree to hold parlor meetings and gather data, you are confirming that you want to understand key issues. You are moving away from an attitude of denial. (Recall that we explored the implications of changes in the environment in chapter 5, "Gathering Data: Understanding the Land.")

Leaders must explain that the work of planning requires an above average effort. It takes energy to overcome the tendency for avoidance and denial. One of the greatest barriers to the change process is the limited amount of energy that is available for planning. One congregational leader asked me, "How can you argue for such an intense process while pointing out that the declining amount of volunteer discretionary time is the major environmental change factor impacting congregational life?" I agree: it is an apparent contradiction. But most business turnarounds require that the leaders make a major investment in energy to take the organization to the next level. It is not realistic to expect that the average leadership team will always sustain this level of effort, but in order to build an infrastructure of data, values, and goals it requires a significant up-front investment. The teams must agree to work at a higher level for a while.

2. Form a Powerful Guiding Coalition

In SVP I meet with the rabbi and the executive committee. I interview senior staff to get their input. I recruit and train the steering committee. When a steering committee of eight to twelve people has been put together and thirty-five to fifty-eight other planners have been recruited, a powerful guiding coalition will have been created. These stakeholders represent different segments of the community, so they create a community "buzz" of energy. The model is designed to manage as many as seventy stakeholders. (Remember the significance of seventy, representing a holistic community, as discussed in the preface.)

This is not the average planning group. It has a symbolic power when it emerges from the congregational scene. Others in the community sense that "something is happening." Traditional gatekeepers who have been able to avoid certain conversations (the balancing loops) find that the guiding coalition is less likely to be sidelined. The group is hungry to understand the whole story, to see the full range of what is possible.

3. Create a Vision of the Future

SVP creates a values statement in Workshop 1. This provides shared values for the work throughout the process. Many people ask me why we don't start the process by working on a new mission statement. I do give the steering committee, as part of the training, a worksheet to analyze their current mission statement if they have one. Most leadership groups do not have enough shared meaning about the congregational environment and system to write a mission statement or charter task forces. They need to come together as a team.

4. Communicate the Vision

SVP encourages scenarios about the future. You will share environmental trends, congregational data, and members' wants and needs with the congregation. When this works well, I have seen groups leave behind old conflicts and enjoy imagining a shared future together. In visioning exercises groups have created skits about what the religious school will be like in five years and set them to show tunes. The tradition says that joyfulness

Reluctant Recruiters

In one congregation the steering committee lacked the energy for stakeholders recruitment. When one of the leaders was turned down, the pessimism spread to the next. Instead of finishing the recruitment in ninety days, they spent six months. They continued to make excuses and delay the start of the work. I needed to understand that they were a congregation of young families and they were all too busy to volunteer. There were bar mitsvahs, school programs, cultural events that all had priority over our work. There were few Calebs or Joshuas to confirm that this work and this moment needed an above average response. The air was filled with a fearful report: "This project is too hard for us." Where were the leaders to affirm that the mission would be blessed? No one stepped forward to reestablish leadership. The lack of leadership in the congregation played out in the planning task. The time for the workshop approached, and there were about thirty confirmations.

In another congregation with similar demographics the steering committee tried a range of approaches. I received an e-mail asking if I could manage a larger group—ninety-three had signed up!

SVP CASE

helps one create a hopeful vision. Planners find that they are enjoying working with their team, and this joy lets loose wellsprings of creativity.

Opponents of planning often focus on the negative. I try to instill in leaders the principle that while there are many elements of the synagogue they cannot control, they can try to control their attitudes. Attitude matters!

The SVP process creates an opportunity. Some seize the day and unleash new energy. Others may bring old fears to their new work.

5. Empower Others to Act on the Vision

SVP convenes brainstorming sessions. A diverse group of voices is heard. Small group discussions put an emphasis on participation. These "whole system" sessions communicate that "all ideas matter." Workshops demonstrate the belief in the dignity of all participants. People are challenged to resist being too judgmental. Many boards are dominated by a few strong personalities. When the facilitator breaks down these old hierarchical organizational walls, a lot of new energy flows.

Before Workshop 3 you will begin to focus on the task force delegation and management plan. You will want to get more buy-in for the implementation of the plan. In order to get a widening awareness of SVP work, you may want to hold a community meeting. After receiving congregational input, you will revise your interim values statements and interim goals. You will then seek board approval so that these agreements can be passed on to committees and task forces. Each committee and task force will get a copy of the values and goals as well as a specific charge to provide them with direction. This empowers them to step forward.

6. Plan Short-Term Wins

SVP creates a "wish list" from all committees and staff so that planners are aware of volunteer opportunities. One of the central needs identified by most congregations is for better volunteer management. SVP shows planners the potential talents and gifts of members. It elicits ideas and projects. This outpouring of creativity encourages congregations to find a better way of identifying volunteer interest and monitoring how these are put to work in the congregation. This creates urgency for the development of volunteer management systems that can institutionalize a spirit of welcoming. SVP encourages the use of membership profiles so that you have the chance to immediately match members' talents and interests with emerging congregational needs and opportunities.

SVP hopes to create short-term wins by recognizing these prospects and by deploying their talent. Some ideas that come from early parlor meetings are immediately "fast tracked" and referred to current committees for action. Some teams create a fast-track process to assign ideas that come out of the parlor meetings to committees rather than wait for the creation of task forces in Workshop 3. (For an example of a fast-track idea, see p. 147.) The board will be asked to track these initiatives and ensure a response from a committee.

7. Consolidate Improvements

SVP creates a key initiatives tracking process after Workshop 3 to ensure follow-up. Each strategy in SVP has SMART objectives: that is, objectives that are specific, measurable, attainable, relevant, and time-bound (see p. 118). These goals will address key values and visions in your plan.

Consolidating improvements requires that you keep focused on implementing your values and objectives. It requires that you track your work against key strategies. You also need to encourage officers and chairs to do a self-assessment (ḥeshbon nefesh) about their work. How are they progressing? All of these processes help the planners consolidate improvements and encourage more change. (See the table on p. 120.)

8. Institutionalize New Approaches

SVP attempts to connect committees and task forces to the synagogue's values and visions. When staff or leaders communicate to the congregation, I encourage them to tie these communications to the congregation's values and goals. SVP leaders look for "teachable moments" to reinforce the values and goals they have identified and developed.

Judaism values the practice of repetition and reinforcement. These values are built into the Jewish calendar. We don't celebrate Pesach every three years; we do it every year. The Jewish calendar seizes the teachable moment of the holidays to repeat the essential values we need to remember. What are your synagogue leadership traditions? What is reinforced?

The principle process for institutionalizing and anchoring change in SVP is through the development of an SVP communications plan and an SVP synagogue board development process.

Examples of SMART Objectives

Goal	Specific	Measurable	Relevant	Time-Bound
1. Increase the depth of engagement in worship and the number of participants.	Offer Shabbat learners minyan.	Offer it monthly; goal for average attendance is thirty.	Ties to strategy and values statement.	Begin by November 1, 2007.
2. Build the capacity of the synagogue's leadership. Improve skills of current and prospective leaders.	The board, staff, and nominating committee will recommend candidates for leadership development.	We will recruit twelve to fifteen members. We will conduct at least three two-hour workshops.	Ties to value that we are all teachers and students. Steering committee members will help teach the class. We will get staff involved and recruit some of the promising stakeholders from SVP.	Begin by December 1, 2007; end by May 1, 2008.
3. Make improvements in physical plant to ensure we can continue to meet our needs in the next ten years.	Create committee to review preschool's needs. Get architects' suggestions for expanding the preschool.	Committee will interview at least two architects.	Ties to strategy of targeting young families with preschool children.	Review estimates by December 1, 2007.
4. Build on identity as a family-oriented congregation. Target families with preschool children.	Create open houses for prospects. Offer several family Shabbats to reach out to new families.	Offer second preschool open house. Raise money for outreach Shabbat.	Ties to strategy of targeting young families with preschool children. Addresses outreach goal.	Second open house by May 1, 2008.

Anchoring Values: Synagogue Board Development (SBD)

1. Relates to synagogue board development. The SVP SBD shows how committees and task forces can focus their energy on the goals.
2. Helps members to better understand clergy and lay leaders. SBD classes are taught by the clergy and lay leaders. The teachers model emerging congregational values.
3. Teaches leaders new skills that help them manage committees and task forces.
4. Provides board members with a practice field to try out their new skills. In the SBD workshop all board members review how to run a meeting, make a recommendation for policy or programs, and organize committees. New leaders see that these lessons were not abstract intellectual exercise but that the new knowledge can be applied to real congregational work.
5. Ensures clear responsibility for the recruitment and program development of the leadership development workshops.

Communicating the Vision: Communications Plan

The steering committee must take the lead in communicating the work of SVP. The following are some of the kinds of communications that are helpful:

1. Congregational Introduction Letter: This letter lets the congregation know that a steering committee has been chosen to work on a long-range plan.
2. Recruitment Letter: This letter announces that parlor meetings will be held for different segments of the congregation (new members, empty nesters, etc.). It also invites the general membership to participate in some all-purpose meetings.
3. Workshop News: The rabbi and leaders should talk about the Values and Goals in Process Statements via e-mail, mailed newsletters, and pulpit speeches. They should invite feedback.
4. Fast-Track Ideas: Practical ideas will be generated out of the parlor meetings and workshops. Some of these can provide short-term opportunities for action. Since SVP is a multi-year process, any short-term opportunities need to be acted on. When new things are tried, they should be communicated. Program successes should be celebrated. For example, short-

term successes can be featured on the synagogue's bulletin boards and Web site; the members who are driving those successes should be recognized publicly.

5. SVP Leadership Profiles: SVP leaders are making a major impact. I encourage board members to interview SVP stakeholders about their personal interests and congregational Jewish journey.

6. Town Meetings: Not all communities have the volunteer energy for the old-fashioned New England town meeting. Some communities have offered these with little response. Other have brought in more than a hundred people and have had a rich combination of information exchange and feedback. Leaders will have to assess the community's level of interest.

Conclusion

Teshuvah for individual and community change starts with recognition. You must do something new to address the challenges of your current environment. It will take more than just a good idea: there must be a visceral sense of urgency. By stepping forward to give voice to new plans you will gain momentum. Leaders working together with the congregation can maintain the momentum for change and make progress toward achieving their vision. They can resolve to develop a new leadership practice.

Questions for Reflection

1. Have you seen projects lose momentum? What happened?
2. Think of a successful project that you participated in. What helped keep the team focused and energized?

Part 3

'Avodah:
Putting Ideas of Planning
into Action

Everyone whose deeds are more than his wisdom,
his wisdom endures; and everyone whose wisdom is
more than his deeds, his wisdom does not endure.
—*Avot* 3:12

SVP is about taking the leap to action. Leaders may not have all of the answers. They may not be sure they are the most gifted leaders. They may not be sure this is the best time. At some point, planning leaders agree to step forward and make a start. Like Joshua, they know that the future of the Jewish people cannot be achieved by waiting in the wilderness of Paran. They have to step into the waters of the river Jordan.

9.

Getting Started:
The Steering Committee Prepares
to Build Community

Rab Johannan said, "The builders—these are the disciples of the wise—who throughout their days are occupied with building up the world."

—b. Shabbat 119a

How do you get started building your team? How do you plan to plan? It all starts with the steering committee. They agree to coordinate the process and to take the lead in reflecting on the learning. While SVP is a very democratic and collaborative process, the steering committee leaders have a greater responsibility than the other members They must put in more hours. They must also make decisions and guide the work of the project.

I mentioned in chapter 1 the text from Trumah that describes the building of the mishkan, the desert tabernacle. In this story, every Israelite gift was welcome, but there was an intermediary who managed this project, Bezalel, the master craftsman. Bezalel had the requisite talents and skills. He had the vision, inspired by God, for the project. So too, the steering committee, needs to help organize all of the data that is generated by the process.

It is a significant challenge to recruit the right group of planners. Potential leaders will be willing to do some extraordinary things if they feel the project is going to make a difference and if their special talents are going to be put to good use. This is the major selling point of SVP. It is a process with enormous potential, and it creates extraordinary opportunities for lay leadership.

The Steering Committee's Tasks

The first step is to recruit co-chairs for the SVP steering committee. These co-chairs will work with the consultant and the rabbi to recruit ten to twelve additional planners. The steering committee plays a central role in the planning and visioning model. You will have the highest expectations for them. They are challenged to do many important leadership tasks:

- Recruit leaders and volunteers
- Train leaders and volunteers
- Identify important data
- Help define values
- Help create consensus goals
- Help make assignments to task forces and committees
- Work with the board to put assumptions and priorities into a five-year plan
- Manage conflict
- Manage lay-staff differences

You will want to recruit steering committee members with leadership talents. Throughout the planning process you will do planning tasks and reflect on these tasks. In the training session the committee will learn about the process and how to use the new techniques introduced throughout the process.

Relationships: Critical Building Blocks

One of the key process steps is for the chairs to build relationships with the steering committee members. In order to build a leadership team you must help the leaders build relationships with each other. As you learned in chapter 1, people usually step forward because the right person asked them. They stay on the team because they respect their teammates. They maintain their membership because their friends are at the shul. Relationships are a critical building block.

Why do you need to spend time learning about your partners? The tradition says that developing teammates requires an investment. We see this in the development of Joshua and Moses's relationship. "And the LORD answered Moses, 'Single out Joshua son of Nun, an inspired man, and lay your hand upon him'" (Numbers 27:18).

You'll be asked to invest in your teammates, to get to know them better. I encourage leaders to fill out their membership profiles in advance so that each team member can have profiles of all their partners. You will come to understand your differences and your special gifts for community building. The tradition values an appreciation of differences.

> He used to recount their praise, R Eliezar Ben Hyrcannus is a plastered cistern that does not lose a drop. R Joshua Ben Hananiah, happy is he that bore him. R Jose the Priest is a pious man, R Simeon Ben Nethanel is one who fears sin, and Rabbi Eleazar Ben Arakh is like a spring that gathers force. (*Avot* 11)

In this text we learn that the rabbinic community is blessed with different personalities. One has a great memory (plastered cistern), while another rabbi has great energy—his mind gushes and gathers force. Leadership teams need those who have great attention to detail as well as those who have creative energy for innovation and imagination.

Teams on the Run

Most synagogue teams I have encountered present a major challenge for teamwork because they are seldom willing to spend the time in team building. You will need to ensure that there is a place at the table for everyone invited to the steering committee.

> Ben Azzai said, "You will be called by your name, you will be seated in your place, and you will be given what is properly yours." (*Exodus Rabbah 8:2*)

Most planning leaders are task-oriented. If they are going to do SVP, most are looking to achieve some bottom-line results: more leaders, more members, more contributions, more engagement, etc. Throughout the SVP process, exercises will require planners to take time to build relationships and common ground. This makes it more likely the team will stick together.

SVP slows down the group's tendency to want to "solve the problem" by having participants do more reflecting and connecting to maintain their team. In the steering committee training members describe and reflect on their Jewish journeys. In the norms and values workshop participants reflect on their views of the culture. In the goals workshop they reflect on their congregation's history. In Workshop 3 they create a vision for team before they move to action planning.

Consultants Jerry Garfield and Ken Stanton offer several suggestions for what they call "teams on the run" (2005). I believe the key idea from Garfield and Stanton is to have leaders describe how the team will work together.

When you recruit the steering committee, you need to let them understand what the expectations of the team are. You will review the following:

1. Proposed outcomes of SVP
2. Their roles and responsibilities
3. Composition and personal characteristics
4. The overall scope of the project: the work plan

1. Proposed Outcomes

SVP seeks to develop leadership and focus them on shared values and goals.

2. Roles and Responsibilities

The Steering Committee has the following responsibilities. We encourage every prospective member to review task and time commitments:

STEERING COMMITTEE TASKS	HOURS
Phase One: Three Months	
Attend 1 steering committee training session	3 hours
Attend 1–2 follow-up sessions to ensure recruitment	2 hours
Attend 1 home meeting	2 hours
Attend 1 debrief session	2 hours
Phase Two: Four Months	
Attend norms and values workshop	3 hours
Debrief values workshop; plan Workshop 2	2 hours
Attend strategies and goals workshop	3 hours
Debrief strategies and goals workshop; plan Workshop 3	2 hours
Attend steering committee/board meeting	1 hour
to discuss assignments to committees and task forces	
Attend action planning Workshop 3	3 hours

Phase Three: Six Months

Town meeting (optional)	2 hours
Board and steering committee meeting on assumptions and priorities	1 hour

Phase Four: Ongoing Implementation

3. Composition and Characteristics

All the steering committee members will fill out the Congregational Membership Profile (see Resource 2 in the Appendix). This includes information about their background, occupation, skills, and interests, especially specific interests in different elements of congregational life. These profiles are reviewed by the chairs and the consultant so that they are aware of the gifts that members will bring. This process also helps clarify if the team is missing any key pieces. You are putting together a team on the run, but you want to slow down to see who is coming. You will also follow this process when you form the committees and task forces.

The steering committee should be composed of ten to twelve people plus the rabbi and executive director.

- Three or four should be from the executive committee and/or be experienced board members.
- Four or five should be people with significant process skills from their work experience. They should have a passion for planning and see SVP as a great opportunity. (Examples of these are curriculum designers, human resource planners, business planners, consultants, project managers, and people with significant nonprofit governance experience.)
- Three or four should be people who represent key constituencies: empty nesters, religious school parents, preschool parents, worship leaders, fundraisers.

All should have some planning or project skills. No one should be put on the steering committee just because they represent a segment or need new leader orientation. They must be skilled and committed. And, of course, the rabbi and the executive director should be additional members.

The planning process takes nine to twelve months for the SVP component and another six to twelve months for implementation. Planners need to be willing to make a significant time commitment. Some chairs

The SVP Work Plan

Step	Participants	Activities	Model Dates (month)	Outcome(s)
Pre-planning meetings	Rabbi, president, planning chairs, executive director	Identify critical strategic issues; explore SVP process	1	Prepare to present to board
Board presentation	Rabbi, executive director, board	Get board agreement for work	2	Approve contract or plan
Steering committee workshop	Rabbi, president, chairs	Review SVP process; prepare for parlor meetings and recruitment	3	Set next meeting within two weeks
Steering committee follow-up meeting	Steering committee	Write congregational letter; define affinity groups; assign recruiters; review team profiles re: backgrounds and skills	3.5	Create steering committee contacts and profiles sheet; congregational letter describes process, team, next steps (all-purpose parlor meetings)
Conduct parlor meetings	Steering committee	Recruit congregants; hold meetings	3.5	
Debrief parlor meetings	Steering committee	Review debriefs from parlor meetings	5.5	Debrief summaries, emerging themes
Workshop 1: Values	Steering committee, stakeholders	Do values map; identify aspirations	6	Interim values statements
Debrief Workshop 1	Steering committee	Discuss and write values statements	6.5	Publish interim values statements

Step	Participants	Activities	Model Dates (month)	Outcome(s)
Workshop 2: Strategies and Goals	Steering committee, stakeholders	Do time line, and reflect on past; review SVP briefing book, and gather observations; identify data needed	7	Interim goals
Debrief Worship 2	Steering committee	Discuss and write goal statements	7.5	Publish interim goal statements
Steering committee, board presentation	Steering committee, board	Get feedback and approval of goals and assignments to work groups	8	Approval to present; to community
Town meeting	Community	Present goals and values statements; get feedback	9	Go forward with goals and values
Form committees and task forces; make assignments	Steering committee, board	Create teams to address goals and values	10	Publish committee and task force groups
Workshop 3: Action Planning	Steering committee, committees, task forces, staff, stakeholders	Develop specific action steps, accountability, and time lines; create short vision of area	11	Publish updates of action plans; create short vision for each area
Task force follow-up meetings	Steering committee, or implementation committee, committees, task forces	Continue work	TBD	Publish updates
Committee/ task force priorities	Steering committee, board	Provide assumptions for plan	TBD	
Final plan	Steering committee, board	Write final plan	TBD	Final plan

have made the mistake of recruiting new people to get them motivated to be more involved. Some of these recruits simply were not used to the rigors of nonprofit leadership or the complexity of planning. They faded too soon. Even if they have not been active in the synagogue, they are viable if they have demonstrated their commitment and talents for other organizations (Jewish community center, school board, professional association, etc.). SVP is an opportunity to recruit new talent, but it must be talent with a track record from corporate or nonprofit leadership. They must be proactive. All steering committee members will be assigned some recruitment for parlor meetings and stakeholder groups.

It is important that steering committee members have the following general attributes:

- Be team players
- Not be super advocates of a single issue
- Focus on the overall needs of the congregation
- Be fair-minded
- Be interested in learning, curious
- Be open-minded, emotionally mature

4. Scope of Project

The steering committee receives a work plan that allows them to see all of the steps in the process (p.130–31).

The Importance of Teamwork

SVP is an exercise in teamwork. The steering committee is challenged to work as a team and model teamwork for others. SVP provides them with some tools to get to know each other better so that they can be welcoming and bring a heightened sense of engagement with other stakeholders and members generally.

Questions for Reflection

1. Think about a successful team that you were on. What made it successful?
2. What kinds of things help a team get off to a good start?

10.
Recruiting for Parlor Meetings and Stakeholder Groups

All of the words of Torah need one another, for what one word closes another opens.

—Tanhuma Hukat 52

Now that the steering committee is ready to run the parlor meetings, they will need to recruit participants for the planning process. From these participants and other lists they will recruit SVP stakeholders. Parlor meeting participants agree to come and share their thoughts for about two hours. This will produce some data on the congregation. Stakeholders will be selected to represent the nine congregational segments that the leadership chooses to represent the diversity of the community (new members, long-standing members, etc.). The stakeholders agree to go to three workshops.

It is important to note that not all parlor meeting participants will agree to be stakeholders. Some people who come to a parlor meeting and show interest are potential prospects to be stakeholders. Some of those who come feel they have done all they are prepared to do. They have little interest in future involvement. Some members may be great candidates to be stakeholders but are not able to attend the parlor meeting.

Use the same tracking forms that helped you recruit for parlor meetings to keep up with stakeholder groups. You don't have to reinvent the wheel.

Recruitment is hard work that takes hope and heart. Many congregations are suffering from very low engagement; perhaps only 10 percent of the members are highly engaged. Many of these dedicated core members have been burning out. Now you will be asking this core group to take on a major task. They have to recruit people for both parlor meetings and the planning workshops!

The steering committee will be recruiting people to gather data and looking for people to participate as stakeholders in this process. Many would be willing to come to a Sunday retreat themselves, but the task of soliciting others and dealing with all of their different demands is daunting. Why go to all of this trouble?

Why so much emphasis on stakeholders? It is helpful when core leaders are blended in with more peripheral members. It changes the conversation. It provides new insights. It disrupts old norms and unproductive practices. The steering committee may need to be reminded that all of the different synagogue stakeholders, like words of Torah, need each other.

Parlor Meeting Recruitment

After the steering committee training session, the committee must meet to manage the next steps in the process. There is considerable logistical work to do now. They will need to send a congregational letter to communicate to the congregation that parlor meetings are planned and participants are being sought. Some members will sign up, but most will need to be solicited. Why is solicitation necessary? I find that groups really put a lot of energy into the invitation letter to attend parlor meetings. They rewrite and rewrite it. I often inquire if they find that people respond to letters to attend a gala or to give to annual campaigns. They immediately note that most of their success comes from phone calls or face-to-face meetings.

Today's members are overwhelmed by junk mail. The direct mail letter is simply background. While it may put the congregation on notice, it seldom produces many participants. The recruitment letter does provide a good script to help the steering committee recruit participants. The letter describes the key aims of the SVP process and announces that parlor meetings will be held. This helps ensure that anyone who wants to participate in the process has a pretty good opportunity to do so. Ultimately SVP participants, like most leadership prospects, are recruited the old-fashioned way—one person-to-person encounter at a time.

Synagogue boards ask me, "How can you suggest that we recruit seventy people to plan? We have worked with you to review our environment, and we find that the people we would be targeting are very secular, have less discretionary time, and don't feel they need to come to synagogue to feel Jewish. Aren't you being awfully inconsistent here?"

Judaism has adapted to the challenges of different eras. After the destruction of the Temple the sages left Jerusalem and went to Yavneh and built a Rabbinic Judaism to replace the Temple cults. With all of its adaptations contemporary Judaism has a strong core of fundamental values. Every morning observant Jews recite modeh ani, a prayer of thankfulness that states, "The beginning of all wisdom is fear (awe) of God." We have to be thankful for what God has given us. We need to keep God's vision of a holy life in front of us.

I may not always be successful in asking leaders to put in more hours to create a sacred community. God is certainly in a position to challenge today's Jews, as he challenged Jonah, to face the community and ask for more commitment. God challenged Moses to lead the people out of Egypt. God challenged Joshua to lead the people into the promised land. What is God challenging today's leaders to do? My Christian colleagues call this experience of being challenged "the call." SVP was designed to gather leaders together so that they might find a congregational calling and their own personal call within this vision.

I give basically the same recruitment task to all SVP teams. Many steering committees complain about how hard it is to get ten to twelve people to come to their home for parlor meetings. After ninety days they are still whining. In one of these "reluctant" congregations they were only able to recruit thirty-five of the seventy stakeholders. One of the twelve steering committee leaders was able to recruit almost 33 percent of the total. Why? *Tenacity.* Another congregation had to recruit seventy stakeholders in only thirty days. They recruited ninety individuals and never once whined. The difference? *Attitude!*

קְדּיּמָה What is God challenging today's leaders to do?

Targeting Individuals

In my experience you can include almost everyone who really wants to participate. But you have the right to recruit more vigorously certain kinds of talents that you need. You want people who have shown some talent for congregational life and/or shown talents in other organizations and causes. The steering committee will look over the congregation and brainstorm prospects.

You are also trying to approximate nine balanced stakeholder groups. With this in mind you will want to recruit a mix of different segments of the congregation. If you use get twenty responses for the empty nester segment, this would become an oversubscribed group. Keep an eye on your categories, and look at the lists as they fill up. Where are you oversubscribed? Where do you need help?

The rabbi and the entire professional staff are part of the solution. Whom do they know? Who might be interested? They should review membership lists, benefactor lists, school parent lists, etc. These lists can jog memories. Brainstorming surfaces some wonderful assets. It's worth it. You can do it!

Sources of parlor meeting recruits and stakeholders include:

- Contacts from steering committee members
- Contacts from staff
- Those who respond to congregational letter
- Those who show interest in parlor meetings

Tracking the Recruitment

I suggest the steering committee chairs create a tracking form that lists the nine groups and includes those who have confirmed their participation and those who are prospects.

Consider these key questions while tracking recruitment efforts:

- Are we on schedule to recruit stakeholders so we can start the first workshop?
- Have we checked for duplications? We want to avoid having the same person contacted by two solicitors.
- Can other steering committee members suggest names for undersubscribed groups?

Resistance to Recruiting

Some congregations are not fully ready for SVP. Some congregations do not have a well-developed volunteer culture. Participants may embrace the idea of planning but not be at all prepared for the work of planning. When it comes time to recruit people to go to focus groups or to become stakeholders, some recruiters face the following challenges:

1. They can't complete their calls.
2. They lack sufficient energy and enthusiasm to be effective solicitors.
3. They don't keep their planning leaders informed, so there are lots of surprises.
4. They confront a lack of commitment on the other side.

Recruitment Motivated by Urgency

Most people do not like to solicit. Most people will tell you that the major reason they came to a volunteer program was because the right person asked them. SVP asks leaders to step forward to do the thing they know is pivotal in volunteer recruitment: to dial that number.

I have noted that change requires a sense of urgency, a hopeful vision of the future, and a practical plan. If there is no urgency, there will be no pre-planning meetings. SVP tries to reinforce this emerging urgency. It highlights the importance of the ritual of calling others. SVP provides a step-by-step process to turn that call into an engaged volunteer experience for the good of the synagogue. If the prospects step forward to a parlor meeting or a stakeholders workshop, something practical will emerge.

Questions for Reflection

1. How did you get recruited as a volunteer?
2. Have you ever successfully recruited another person? Why were you successful?
3. If you were coaching a new solicitor, what would you tell him or her?

11.

Conducting and Interpreting Parlor Meetings

I have endowed him [Bezalel] with a divine spirit of skill, ability, and knowledge.

—Exodus 31:2

The SVP process is not just about creating a plan. It is about developing leadership. The steering committee has worked with the consultant to review the different parlor meeting questions. They have explored how to recruit members to different homes and different dates. They have developed some segments of the membership to gather in affinity groups. One of the things that leaders do is convene important conversations. One way the steering committee does this is by conducting parlor meetings.

קדימה "We created a process that we will turn to time and again for getting to know our members, and in doing so we trained our leadership in an important skill."

—Rabbi Joshua Davidson, Temple Beth El, Northern Westchester

Leaders also make meaning out of diverse pieces of information. Leaders know that a team can pick up more of the messages than a few individuals, so the steering committee debriefing meetings are of critical importance for leaders to use their skill, ability, and knowledge.

SVP uses a combination of very spontaneous and more deliberative approaches. The parlor meetings and large workshops are more on the spontaneous end of the spectrum. The steering committee debriefs are more careful and analytical. What are people saying? What does this all mean? How are we seeing this information as a team?

Conducting Parlor Meetings

The following is a model agenda for conducting a parlor meeting. I have included a model questionnaire. Each congregation must adapt this to fit its needs. Please consider what you would like to know as you summarize the reports.

I have a bias. I want to see how strengths can be connected to opportunities. I want to see how suggestions can be yoked with people willing to step forward.

Principles

- Focus on *strengths and opportunities.*
- Survey *broad areas* but look for *specific priorities.*
- Connect their *comments* to possible *commitments.*
- Steering committee reviews membership profiles for talents, interests to create a *volunteer profile.*
- Send thank you notes to all. Call on most *promising and passionate* first. They are potential stakeholders for the workshops.
- Parlor meetings allow people to *share what they write* on their questionnaires and to listen to others. They provide a place for each member to be heard. That's is why these forums are valued more than mail-in surveys. Note: Some congregations do choose to supplement this effort by mailing questionnaires to all members.
- All communications are *confidential, but not private.* We will not disclose any person's name or share a story that is only about them. The only readers of your group's questionnaire will be the steering committee parlor meeting facilitator and me, since we have been tasked to write reports:
  - the steering committee facilitator is charged with writing up a summary debrief of the meeting;
  - I am tasked with the responsibility of weaving all these parlor meeting debrief summaries into a dominant themes report.

Some leadership teams, while not committed to the whole workshop model, have used the SVP parlor meeting process simply as a way to get a feel for the pulse of their congregations.

Parlor meetings can sometimes be difficult to recruit for. Some congregations have developed a culture of distrust and apathy. This affects the attitude of would-be solicitors. The fact is, when people go to parlor meetings, they almost always enjoy them. When we review debriefs, they almost uniformly report that the experience was rewarding for participants, hosts, and facilitators alike.

Conducting Parlor Meetings

Temple _____ Steering Committee Training Session
Introductions
Membership Profiles
- Name
- Important Jewish "stepping stone"
- Gifts (skill, passion) you'd like to bring to process

Introduction: Synagogue Visioning and Planning
- The journey
- The role of the steering committee, rabbi, staff, board, etc.
- What are your goals for the process (use the template below)?

Your Goals, or Desired Outcomes	Synagogue Visioning and Planning Steps

Parlor Meeting Training Principles
Simulation: Conducting a Parlor Meeting Process
Review Debrief Process
Next Steps: Assignments
- Develop segment groups for parlor meetings
- Assign captains for each group, and recruit hosts

Parlor Meeting Recruitment Tracking Worksheet

Group	Group Captains	Name	Parlor	Workshop 1 March 1	Workshop 2 April 1	Workshop 3 May 15
New Members	Mike	Betty Thal	Yes	Yes	No	Yes
Long-Standing Members	Barb	Dan Field	Yes	Yes	Yes	Yes

- Write congregational letter to announce the process and parlors.
- Make assignments to staff and lay leaders for the briefing book.
- Set next meeting within two weeks.

Close

Model Questionnaire

(Please review and adapt.)

Name _____   Years of Membership _____

Attitudes about Congregation:

I. Strengths: What do we have passion about?
What do we excel at?
1.
2.
3.

II. Weaknesses: What could be improved?
1.
2.
3.

III. Opportunities: What forces may be affecting us? What are some opportunities for the future?

1.
2.
3.

IV. Threats: What forces may be impacting us? What are some future concerns?

1.
2.
3.

V. Synagogue Satisfaction

Based on your experiences, how would you rate the following elements of synagogue life? These are adapted to your congregation. (See critical issues.) If you have no experience as a user or leader you may write "NA."

Programs	1 Very Satisfied	2 Satisfied	3 Not Satisfied	4 Very Unsatisfied
Religious School				
Preschool				
Beney Mitsvah Process				
Post BM-HS-Youth Activities				
Worship Services				
Social opportunities—Adults				

Family Education				
Outreach— New Members				
Administrative Staff-Support				
Fundraising				
Lay Leadership Development				
Community Involvement				
Affinity Groups— Havurot				
Facility	**1 Very Satisfied**	**2 Satisfied**	**3 Not Satisfied**	**4 Very Unsatisfied**
Location				
Parking				
Sanctuary				
Office				
Social Hall				
School				
Maintenance				

VI. Priorities

Take one area from the above list that is most important to you.
1. What would you suggest the leadership do?
2. What role would you like to play?

VII. New Programs

1. What is the most important unmet need that you see?
2. What specifically would you suggest that temple leaders do?

VII. Synagogue's Goals

What should the synagogue's three most important goals be?
1.
2.
3.

Host's Role: Personal Debrief

After the parlor meeting you attended and/or facilitated, you will want to fill out the Personal Debrief form (see page 256, part of Resource 3 in the Appendix). This will help you remember the evening's events much better. It will also help you describe your observation to others. Many talented members have trouble finding the words to characterize their observations about the congregation; the words are simply not accessible.

My Role as Consultant

The steering committee hosts are responsible for writing up the data from your group. I will read all of the debrief summaries to get a clear picture of the overall community. I will prepare a draft of what I have identified as the dominant themes. I will review the program satisfaction data and other data, and use my notes to coach the steering committee in writing their final version of the dominant themes report.

Steering Committee Processing of Debriefs

All of this individual personal debrief work begins to really pay dividends when you begin to learn from others during meetings.

Organizing Data

All Personal Debrief sheets (see Resource 3) from the parlor meetings should be given to the planning chairs and copied for the facilitator. The summaries will be part of the SVP briefing book. The steering committee should keep a record of all meeting summaries and all specific volunteer suggestions by name. The steering committee will send me a copy of all the debrief summaries from each parlor meeting and the home meeting facilitator's debrief for that session.

Facilitator/Host Presentations

At the steering committee debrief meeting the group should listen to the reports of all parlor meeting facilitators/hosts. They should ask a few questions after each presentation. This process increases the breadth of understanding of the entire steering committee. They are learning to see the congregation from different segments and through the eyes of different leaders.

Dominant Themes

After the steering committee has reviewed the parlor meeting debriefs, they may find it is helpful to identify the dominant themes they are hearing from the meetings. The process of defining dominant themes is helpful to the steering committee. It helps clarify what they are learning. It helps them integrate their learning and prepare for the stakeholders phase of the process. I usually prepare a draft of a dominant themes report to guide this discussion.

Here is an example of a dominant theme: Most members recognize the need for membership growth. They feel the congregation needs the membership revenue and the energy of new members. Some are concerned that the current facilities cannot handle this growth.

Fast-Track Process

The team should review suggestions that have come out of the parlor meetings. Some are very general, such as "do more social events." This can wait for future action planning. Some may be very specific: "let's try having an earlier family Shabbat dinner." This suggestion may be tried now. It doesn't need to wait for task forces to report in six months. The steering committee might review the fast-track list from parlor groups and decide to fast-track several items. If the leadership agrees to implement an idea it can make a great bulletin article—SVP stories build momentum.

Fast-Track Candidates

The following is a partial list of real ideas that were generated from one congregation's parlor meetings. I have divided these into short-term and long-term projects. I have also identified some as priority items to fast track.

- One parent suggested we "benchmark other synagogue nursery schools and religious schools to see where we might offer exclusive courses or activities." It would be helpful to do this research in order to know what possible gaps or duplications in programs and services there are that we might consider, and also it would help nursery marketing efforts.
- Create a marketing plan with activities to tell people about the congregation.
- Use high holidays as opportunities to market the synagogue to new members and guests; in the two months before, advertise and push for people to try us out. Give a credit to guests based on amount paid for their seats if they join based on their experience at services.

SVP CASE

SVP CASE

Short-Term (one to six months):

- Organizing religious school plays, chorus (already created), music events
- Change time to allow children to eat earlier during family services
- Generate ideas for events for younger members even outside the synagogue

Long-Term and Short-Term Goals

Long-term goals are complex and will take more time to start. They also have strategic elements that will be informed by the strategic planning process. You don't want to rush to alter your Internet identity when one of your SVP goals is to clarify your identity. On the other hand, a short-term task might be to find someone who will work on this project later or join as a stakeholder. Leaders must be able to differentiate between easy short-term goals that can be fast-tracked and the long-term goals that need deliberation.

Celebrating Results of Parlor Meetings

To show that you are serious about tracking and supporting your members' gifts and suggestions, you will assess them and determine whether they are short-term or long-term goals; you then publish the documents for all stakeholders at Workshop 1. This celebrates the work of the parlor meetings and builds a bridge to future work. It also stimulates the thinking of the members in the workshop. They see the kinds of things their fellow members are thinking about. The ideas are cross-fertilized.

Questions for Reflection

1. What are benefits of debriefing the parlor meetings as a team?
2. If you had to list the dominant themes in your congregation, what would they be?

Part 4

'Omets Lev: The Courage to Engage

Be strong and resolute.
—Deuteronomy 31:23

Who is a hero? He who controls his passions.
—*Avot* 4:1

This section describes the three large stakeholder workshops. It takes a great deal of courage to accept the responsibility for recruiting forty to sixty people for planning. The steering committee will have their doubts. Solicitors will feel the sting of rejection. Some will challenge the leadership's decision. Planning leaders need to be strong. They must harness their enthusiasm so that it can sustain them through the ups and downs of planning. They must also manage their frustrations when they encounter others' lack of commitment. They must manage their own fear of failure. They must control their feelings when their pet issues are discussed in new ways. It takes courage and patience to engage the community.

12.
Overview of Strategic Workshops: Developing Strategic Direction

Rab Judah said: "A man should always gather words of Torah in the form of general principles and bring then forth as specific details, for if he gathers them as specific details they will so weary him that he will find himself helpless."

—Sifre Deuteronomy 306

One of the key elements in the SVP process is the large stakeholder workshops. The steering committee and from forty to sixty stakeholders will be involved, and people need to know their part in these workshops of engagement. When Joshua crossed the Jordan, much of his leadership was devoted to assigning the different tribes their places in the land. The congregation is made up of various groups, and we need to assign them their places in the planning room.

The shofar (ram's horn) was used to warn of enemy attacks, so it is part of the tool chest of leadership. The shofar is used in high holiday services to awaken the sinner to the error of his ways. In the SVP workshops stakeholders need to "wake up" and look beyond their personal views of the synagogue and engage in the exploration of the diverse needs of the whole congregation.

You will amass a large, diverse multitude to plan. You will create important leadership tasks for the stakeholders to experience together. They are to bear witness to an important consensus-building discussion. They are to create strategic agreements (mission, values, goals, objectives, and actions) that demand attention. You will create a large group to shout out to the community that this is not business as usual. You want to get their attention.

151

If you immerse members in details of action planning before they understand the broader principles, many will be overwhelmed. If you try to decide, for example, how many rooms to add to the preschool or how to adapt the Shabbat service before you have reflected on your broader values and goals, you may take the wrong path. Shared values and goals help create guiding principles that keep people stepping forward—together.

Communicating Identity

Synagogue leaders will often ask, "Why do we need to talk about missions, values, and our identity? We all know what we do. We do services. We run a school. We have life cycle events. We are affiliated with a denomination. What's the big deal about identity? We are just a shul."

The language of brands may seem too corporate for many synagogue folks. A brand is marketing terminology for an identity. Congregations are not accustomed to talking about their culture and their identity. For strategic purposes it can sometimes be helpful to borrow some ideas from the world of branding to better clarify the messages you are sending to your current members and prospective members.

If you are a gourmet chef, your training and passion involve a commitment to excellence. You may not want to run a hamburger restaurant. The market may want hamburgers, but that is not your purpose. Judaism is different from other religions, and our tradition suggests that the Jewish people were challenged for a special mission. A congregation that is devoted to traditional worship and study may not want to meet the needs of families that just want to get a bar mitsvah with the least amount of student preparation or parental involvement. Yes, there may be demand, but that may not fit the synagogue's purpose. The synagogue, however, may decide to maintain a traditional liturgy (steady in purpose) but to do extraordinary things to help less skilled members develop their Hebrew skills (flexible in strategy). Synagogues need to be steady in purpose but flexible in strategy. The traditional congregation, for example, might decide to offer some extra help to support students who have weak Hebrew skills. This is a compromise of strategy—not purpose.

קידום **If you immerse members in details of action planning before they understand the broader principles, many will be overwhelmed.**

Chapter 4 described the task of identifying data about the congregation's best prospects. When leaders look at the different segments they might serve, they need to ask the following strategic questions:

1. Should we adapt our programs and services to better meet their needs?
2. How big is the gap between what these groups want and our self-assessment of our strengths and our mission (see chapter 4)?
3. What kinds of changes in our capacities are necessary to do this?
4. If we can't or don't choose to meet their needs, can we find other target groups that we might be a better match for?
5. If our best prospects do not make up a large enough population to sustain us, are we prepared to downsize or move?
6. If we determine that, in fact, there is a good fit between their needs and our capacities, how can we focus on increasing their awareness of our synagogue? The challenge then is not just the product; it is getting prospects to know us better.

Mission Statements: Who Are We?

At this early stage in the SVP process, you will just be beginning to reflect on you congregation. You will review the current mission statement. If you don't have one you will do drafts in rough bullet form. We do not recommend you spend time wordsmithing this so early in the process. I remember hearing a presentation by Sheldon Harnick, the lyricist of *Fiddler on the Roof.* He confided that the song "Tradition," which starts the musical, was not written until the end of the project. Harnick explained that Jerome Robbins would constantly ask the writers, "'What is this play about?' After months of reflection on the whole play it became clear it was about people trying to maintain their way of life in the midst of change." Out of these conversations the introductory song "Tradition" was born. While it came late, who would debate the outcome? In SVP the stakeholders look at all of the facts and emotions, dreams and plans and then revisit the mission language when they are ready.

What do we want to be? Mission statements help organizations communicate their identity and purpose. The word "mission" comes from the Latin word *mittere*, to throw or send out. The mission statement gives "the fundamental reason for the organization's existence" (Senge 1990, 303). A mission allows the community to get some idea of what you stand for. Most congregations have some type of mission statements, but most of these state the obvious:

- We offer life cycle events.
- We provide religious education.
- We celebrate holidays.
- We offer religious services.

Some of the terms that do clarify identity might be based on geography or denomination. Mission statements can also take us deeper into some of the values and culture of the congregation.

- We have a denominational affiliation (Reform, Conservative, Orthodox, Reconstruction, etc.)
- We serve a certain geographic area (the greater Albany community, etc.).
- We are egalitarian.
- We are traditional.
- We are focused on outreach to the unaffiliated.
- We are inclusive! No one will be denied access to programs for financial considerations. (No one will be turned away because they lack the financial resources, we do not charge for high holiday tickets, etc.)
- We are dedicated to tikun olam: we offer a soup kitchen at the congregation on Tuesday and Thursday.

Prospects will gravitate to specific programs that bring your mission into focus. If you say you offer a soup kitchen on site, some people will assume you are deeply committed to "hands-on" social action. They might imagine a whole community of socially conscious members and programs. They know some congregations are fearful to have poor people in their facility. If you say you don't charge for HH tickets prospects may draw a distinction between your congregation and those that even have a pricing structure based on the location of your seats. If you don't have assigned seating they may infer other values. This policy becomes like a strong branch of a tree. It creates a general outline of congregational values. People then infer other qualities to the organization based on this outline. They may assume you are less hierarchical, more democratic, or more welcoming. They sketch in other attributes, like leaves, on to these branches. The outline of the tree is filled in by their imagination.

The steering committee should review the current mission statement. Does it answer the questions below? What is missing? If they do not have a mission statement, they can start by answering the questions below (adapted from *The Strategic Board*, by Mark Light). (They may want to look at some other congregational statements. Most are available on their Web sites.) They will be able to revisit this interim statement after the second workshop.

1. Who are the owners? For example: Jewish members of all ages in the [geographic] area
2. Who are the customers? For example: members, staff, and community partners
3. What is the outcome? For example, develop committed, knowledgeable, and caring Jews dedicated to the building of our beyt midrash, beyt tefilah, and beyt kneset.
4. What is the reputation we want to have? For example, a community that is knowledgeable, warm, welcoming, caring, inclusive, and relevant to the lives of our members and dedicated to tikun olam, support of Judaism, and Klal Yisrael.

Finally, you'll want to create a summary. For example: We help members engage in meaningful Jewish worship, study, and community within the tradition of [Orthodox, Reform, etc.] Judaism. We provide kindergarten through twelfth grade religious school, worship services, adult study, social programs, and life cycle events.

Leaders should simply do this review in outline form. Don't waste your energy trying to carefully articulate a mission statement until you have listened to the stakeholders in Workshops 1 and 2.

Strategic Direction: Values, Priorities, Goals, Objectives, and Actions

The word "strategy" comes from the Greek word *strategos*, which means the art of the general. It is involved in issues of allocation of focus and resources. The word "goal" comes from the old English word *golen*, which means to hinder. A goal creates focus. It limits our range of considerations. Tactics are the methods used to achieve a goal. They involve objectives that can be measured and tracked on a schedule. They also involve the individual steps that are required to meet this measurable outcome. Strategic direction provides maps to give guidance to us on our journey and tactics provide specific action plans to keep us stepping forward.

The steering committee will identify strategic issues in their early meetings then recommend these strategic issues to be considered in Workshop 2. They have focused on these issues based on their review of the congregational data, the parlor meetings, and their discussions. In Workshop 2 the stakeholders will share their reflections of these strategic issues and better define what they would like to do in these areas.

Steady in Purpose and Flexible in Strategy

As mentioned earlier, congregations need to be steady in purpose but flexible in strategy. Many congregations talk about their commitment to the three houses of the synagogue, beyt tefilah, beyt midrash, and beyt kneset. A synagogue may be faithful to these missions but choose to make a greater effort to reach out to younger families with a nursery school. In contrast one congregation I attended in downtown Chicago has as its mission to be a community for adults. There is no religious school.

Some congregations may feel there is a great unmet need. They may feel the congregation needs to change in demographic mix; it is aging. Another congregation with a very large group of people in their fifties and sixties may feel that an expanded adult education program makes sense. Their members will have more time to participate at this stage of their lives. Both are related to the overall purpose. Each congregation needs to consider where it needs to invest more emphasis now. That is the strategic question!

The president of United Synagogue of Conservative Judaism, Dr. Ray Goldstein, in his message on the organization's Web site, communicates the movement's commitment to fundamental values and its openness to new strategies (2006)—showing steadiness in purpose and flexibility in strategy:

Steady in Purpose
The Conservative movement and the synagogues that form United Synagogue are a halakhic entity that separates itself from the

other major strands of Judaism by recognizing a pluralistic, evolving halakha. We do not apologize about our stance—instead, we sing its praises. We have beliefs that are intellectually honest and halakhically authentic. Our halakha sets boundaries, which form the walls of a tent.

Flexible in Strategy

It is a tent large enough to house the pluralism that is a hallmark of our movement; . . . large enough to cover, protect, and value the authenticity of egalitarian and non-egalitarian minyanim.

Dr. Goldstein suggests the movement be steady about the movement's stance but flexible in finding ways to house the pluralism that is its hallmark. Conservative leaders need to know how to put these values into action. This is a challenge.

Allocating Resources to Reach Strategic Goals

One of my Alban colleagues worked with a congregation that wanted to reach out to a very diverse and changing community. He asked leaders to write down on a large sheet of newsprint all of their current programs. The participants filled up the paper with their programs. He then asked them to identify those that were addressing new members or new segments. Very few programs addressed those groups. The congregation clearly was not allocating resources commensurate with the importance they formally placed on new members.

SVP CASE

It is not uncommon for a congregation to have a core value, say outreach. When we look at their priorities we may find they are investing little time or money on this value.

Nonprofit organizations must learn to prune their existing programs, according to expert Peter Drucker. Some of the old programs must be moved aside to make room for new initiatives that are more important now.

Strategic Stepping Stones:
The Case of the Welcoming Congregation

Let's look at some of the strategic stepping stones of our planning journey. We will list the statement and provide an example of it in action. In order to do this let's take the case of a congregation that had welcoming as a part of its mission statement. Leaders wanted to use the planning process to build on this.

1. Mission Statement

"A warm welcoming congregation serving the _____ area."

2. Jewish Values and Vision Statement

Example: The Jewish value of hakhnasat orḥim

"We seek to welcome guests as Abraham did. He opened up the flaps of his tent to include strangers at his table. The desert environment was a dangerous place. He took the risk to welcome others. He personally attended to their needs and provided his best food and drink for them."

3. Situation Analysis: Congregational Profile Briefing Book

They might look at their membership history. They might review the reasons people gave for why they joined or the reasons they provided in their exit interviews on why they left.

4. List of Strategic-Critical Issues

Welcoming, worship participation, fundraising, adult education

5. Strategic Goals and Priorities

Priority Goal: Outreach

"[Name of congregation] will strive to become more welcoming and connected to the [name of local community/geographic area/etc.]. It will reach out to current and unaffiliated members and create policies and an annual calendar of events targeted to attract them." (See examples of other strategic goal statements in Resource 5 in the Appendix.)

6. Strategic Direction for Working Groups—
Recommendations to the Board

"Create a welcoming task force to report to the VP of Membership."

7. SMART (Specific, Measurable, Attainable, Relevant, and Time-bound) Objectives

Example: Planned Welcoming Events

"The welcoming task force will conduct four community Shabbats targeting the unaffiliated from October 2006 to May 2007. We will focus on welcoming and minimize formal membership recruitment techniques." The chair will be Saul Lewis.

SMART objectives put our Strategic Goals into focus. At the end of Workshop 2 we ask each goal work group to develop one SMART objective to bring the goal into focus.

8. Action Plans: Stepping Stones Keep us Moving

Example: Shabbat Outreach Subcommittee

Actions	Who	When
Recruit an outreach subcommittee	Saul	Nov. 1
Create event chairs for each outreach Shabbat	Jack, Sue, Barb, Beth	Jan. 1
Raise $ to cover costs of dinners; consider sponsors	Committee	March 1
Coordinate calendar with executive director	Saul	Ongoing
Develop internal and external communications plan	Barb	March

Putting Plans into Action

One community valued being warm, welcoming, caring, and inclusive, but when the leaders reviewed their programs, they found they were not doing very much to demonstrate those values. They had the language in their mission statement, but they had not really focused their energy on what it would mean to drive this value. For example, board members would usually choose not to wear their name tags at the oneg Shabbat. This is what strategic direction is about. If something is a core value or a strategic critical issue for the congregation, then their goals, objectives, and actions (wearing name tags)—their stepping stones—need to be aligned to make it happen. This takes intentional planning. When Joshua crosses the Jordan, he takes the stones from the river bed to build a monument to the covenant in the new land. On that monument he inscribes the law. He thus ritualizes that every stepping stone on the journey should be focused on fulfilling the people's mission—a Torah based-community in the land of Israel.

Steering Committee Work and Welcome

The steering committee members clearly have leadership roles in SVP. They are challenged to perform tasks and also to role model the values of the congregation. They are asked to welcome a cross section of members—the stakeholders. Some of these they know well; others they may not know. Some of the stakeholders may share their views on key issues. Others may bring different perspectives and priorities. It is not enough to just recruit a diverse group. The steering committee needs to welcome these members with enthusiasm, warmth, and joy. Change consultant Peter Block argues that leaders need to role model the changes they wish the organization to adopt. Our ancient tradition also emphasized that our attitudes mattered.

> Shammai said, "Make your Torah a fixed practice, say little and do much, and receive all [people] with a cheerful countenance." (*Avot* 1:15)

The steering committee will likely have a strong sense of their team's mission, but they must work hard to genuinely welcome the different input of others. SVP is designed to be fun. Greet your stakeholders with a cheerful countenance!

The Steering Committee Works to Prepare the Meal

I work with the steering committee to recruit the stakeholders and help facilitate the workshops. The committee members are active participants in the workshops. They also must debrief what is happening in the workshops and make meaning out of them. The values statements and the goals that the steering committee generates are more than just a summary of all of the notes from the discussion tables. If all they do is function as recorders, they will not fully evolve into a leadership group.

The steering committee must develop an understanding about the critical values that need to be articulated. They must be able to identify which goals are the most important to do now. After Workshop 2, I challenge the steering committee to write a one-page vision of what the congregation will look like in five years. This model requires a great deal of discernment from the steering committee. One leader spoke eloquently of the challenge, saying that all of the ideas from the stakeholders "taken alone are just a shopping list. The groups gave us the ingredients for the meal they would like to see. It is our responsibility to cook them" (Lisa Belkin, Temple Beth Abraham, Tarrytown, New York).

Multiple Paths:
Different Recipes for Workshops

Leaders have to decide how to use the SVP ingredients. Learning to prepare this meal is a team effort. SVP is less a step-by-step recipe and more like a cupboard of ingredients. Leaders can use these ingredients in different recipes.

1. Do it in full: They can do SVP in full. They can create a steering committee, do parlor meetings, create a briefing book, and do the three workshops outlined in the next three chapters.
2. Speed up or stretch out: Some have tried to accelerate the process to nine months, and others have been happy to move more deliberatively over twenty-four months.
3. Some have just chosen to focus less on the large stakeholder workshops. They may combine the values and goals into one Sunday, or Saturday night and Sunday morning.

Some Congregations Want More Control

Some congregations (particularly larger ones) may want more control over who goes to each workgroup. They may feel they are doing well and simply want to explore developmental change, that is, What is next for us? The steering committee will look for new talent from the parlor meetings and the values workshop. They will decide who is invited to each committee or task force. This is particularly well suited for large, established, staff-driven congregations with high-functioning committees. The process uses dispersed authority in parlor meetings and the values workshop to create energy, and then it moves back toward more concentrated staff and board authority in Workshops 2 and 3, for defining goals and objectives and in implementation. In this model the town meeting follows Workshop 2. The whole congregation is invited to review the dominant themes that have arisen, the values that have been developed, and the goals in process. They can provide feedback before more detailed action planning is done.

Some Eliminate Workshop 3
and Let Work Groups Move at Their Own Pace

Some congregations buy into the overall model, but they choose not to do Workshop 3 as a whole-group exercise. They like the idea of monitoring the progress of all of the committees and task forces, but they feel it is just too hard to schedule and recruit for a third large workshop. They manage goal implementation outside of the SVP workshop process.

Some Swap the Goals Workshop
for the Values Workshop

A congregation might have recently done a values workshop. In this case the first large workshop experience might be the goals workshop.

The workshop stage is dedicated to creating common ground. It develops shared values and goals. It clarifies what assignments need to be made to implement these values and goals. It helps provide insight for the final mission statement and creates a picture of the synagogue of the future: a vision statement. These shared documents will help provide direction to committees and task forces in Workshop 3 and beyond.

Questions for Reflection

1. What is your purpose? What are you committed to?
2. Who are your best prospects? Why would they be attracted to your congregation?
3. What strategies are required now to meet the needs of your prospects and your current members?

13.

Values:
How Will We Work Together?

WORKSHOP 1

Rabbi Elazaber Sharma taught: The dignity of your student should be as precious to you as your own; the dignity of your colleagues should be as dear to you as your reverence for your teacher. The reverence for your teacher should be as great to you as your reverence for God.

—Pirqe Avot 4:11

The importance of life is a theme throughout the tradition. How do we teach our children to value life? We teach them day by day to value the importance of every individual. Charity begins at home. We learn at our families' tables and then bring this learning to the world. We need to carry these Jewish values with us. When we discuss the challenge of helping synagogue leaders create shared Jewish values, we must realize that we are working in an environment where most members are not accustomed to calling on these values to guide their life decisions.

Dr. Bethamie Horowitz interviewed more than 1,500 people throughout the New York area. She was able to put them into seven categories (2000, 29–31). She asked them to assess the following statement in terms of how much they agreed or disagreed with it: "When faced with an important life decision, I look to Judaism for guidance." Of Orthodox respondents, 80 percent completely agreed. Of the intensely engaged non-Orthodox, 20 percent completely agreed. In none of the other five groups did more than 10 percent completely agree with the statement.

My experience supports her findings. Most leaders do not know how to access their Judaism when they try to lead. They may know a little or a lot, but their ability to use the tradition in their leadership is underdeveloped. Many rabbis also struggle to use their deep knowledge of Judaism. They may know a lot of information, but finding ways to engage the reluctant is hard. Finding forums to engage leaders spiritually when they are looking at their watches and hoping for an "efficient" meeting can be frustrating.

In my consulting practice with synagogues, I have noticed that congregational leaders often recognize the need to create more of a sense of a "spiritual home" in their communities, but they have a hard time talking about what God is calling on them to do in this place. Instead they often apply tools of management that come from the business world. This is the language that most congregational leaders are more comfortable with. For most leaders their corporate or nonprofit experience is their "default setting." Under pressure they will go to what they know.

They are comfortable gathering data because they know this is an important marketing skill. What is the connection between the parlor meetings and the values workshop? The parlor meeting may look like a marketing exercise, but it includes several core values.

In Workshop 1 on values and norms you will answer questions like: What has worked well? How do we want to build on this as we work together? What assumptions do we have about the congregational culture? What kind of culture would we like to aspire to? You will need to resist the temptation to use this workshop to describe new programs that you want. Instead, remember that you are seeking principles to guide your work together. One of the values that supports SVP is the idea that everyone deeply respects the personal values and insights of each stakeholder and that all are prepared to learn from others. There are many sacred texts that describe how we should respect our fellow human beings. It is also possible to bring sacred values to such seemingly secular tasks as running a parlor meeting.

Parlor Meetings: Value the Individual

The parlor meetings set the stage for Workshop 1 because they role model the value that each person is in the image of God (betselem elohim). One does not need to do research to participate in Workshop 1. You do need to bring a desire to share your years of congregational experience and Jewish living.

Organizational consultants sometime speak of participants' life experiences as the "intuitive wisdom" in the room. As a marketer, I have seen this demonstrated in new product brainstorming groups, and I have experienced the power of this in congregational work. There is a rich vein of understanding to be mined. When stakeholders gather in a workshop community of mutual respect, there will be moments of holiness. The stakeholders will develop some values in process, which will provide the raw material for a more refined values statement in the future.

Briefing Book: Increasing Empowerment

As the stakeholders are leaving Workshop 1, they are given the briefing book for Workshop 2. This book will have membership trend data, school enrollment, an organizational chart, pie charts on the sources and uses of funds, and other community data. It is not often highly scientific data from a statistical point or corporate marketing point of view.

The SVP process works to create helpful, user-friendly marketing and management information. In almost all cases it is more data than 90 percent of the planners have ever been exposed to. The data will help the stakeholders develop shared facts and work to get on the same page.

Empowerment also suggests a greater level of accountability. Stakeholders will need to do their homework. They will write down at least two observations from the data and identify at least one piece of data they would like to know more about. The distribution of the briefing book ritualizes a transition in the SVP choreography: moving from internal personal reflections about values to an external focus on facts. You will see the summaries from a large number of parlor meetings and find that you are better able to understand the needs of their members. Study these facts and identify the facts you still need. You will be able to identify some general goals, but you will also become cognizant about the work that must be done in the future to make proper decisions (better data, financial implications, prioritizations, etc.). You come to understand that these are just goals in process.

Steps to Creating a Values Statement

Leaders need to help congregations create values statements and educate them on implementing those values. When values are put into action, they can inspire leaders. SVP leaders are learning how to listen better. Part of the leadership challenge is to learn to focus and pay attention. One of the ways God could see Moses' potential for leadership was by watching his encounter with the burning bush. Moses was in a terrifying place, but he kept his cool. He paid attention and noticed that the bush was not consumed.

Leaders often find themselves in anxious positions. They are worried about how the congregation will perform under their watch. It is just at these times that it is so important for leaders to make the extra effort to be patient and pay attention to their culture. SVP is constantly calling (sounding the shofar) for higher levels of reflection, attention, and focus.

In the parlor meetings you listened to small groups who share some common ground. You met with empty nesters and religious school parents. Now you will put them all together. Leaders need to see how the story changes when they have assembled some of the divergent elements of the congregation .

One exercise I assign during Workshop 1 has participants describe how they create synagogue life; that is, they are asked to describe their norms, behaviors, and practices. As in any brainstorming exercise there is no debate, and a typical group can think of fifty to sixty descriptions in fifteen to twenty minutes, from which they can draw a short list and identify priorities. We then ask the stakeholders what values have supported them over the years when they were at their best. A list builds.

The planners then vote on the behaviors that they think are most important. The groups are thus encouraged to focus on the most important behaviors as they move into discussion groups.

The group separates into smaller discussions to define more clearly what their congregation's current norms and practices are and what participants hope they become. They may choose a strength to build on or a challenge to address. A strength might be that "our adult education program is growing." They might go on to describe how they aspire to train more adults to teach in the school, be bar mitsvah tutors, etc.

Challenge Behavior: The ushers are not friendly.

Value/Aspiration: The ushers should be friendly. They should hand members the prayer book, opened to the appropriate page.

Finally, after the smaller groups have identified some aspirations for the congregation, they are asked to make the connection between these ideas and Jewish tradition. What texts speak to these ideas? What rituals do we have that celebrate these goals? What events from Jewish history resonate with these aspirations? Thus, the participants might explore the value of welcoming and find support for this in the Torah.

Jewish Tradition: Even though the desert was a dangerous environment, Abraham welcomed his guests and fed them. It should not be so difficult to walk across the room and greet new members after services.

Another group might identify "managing the diversity of learners" (of varying ages, skills, and observances) as a value to be put into action:

Current Behavior: There are "introduction to Judaism" classes, but few advanced classes. Few lay leaders function as teachers.

Value/*Aspiration*: Offer a range of programs that would appeal to different segments. Encourage those members with gifts in teaching to help support new programs.

Jewish Tradition: In the Passover Seder we are told the story of the four sons. One is wise and another does not even know how to ask the question. Jewish tradition challenges us to meet each person where they are.

Real-Life Experiences and Values

Typically leaders have only been exposed to a brief scriptural text discussion or a dvar Torah. Many fail to make the connection between ancient texts and that night's agenda. They have pressing immediate concerns that dominate their attention. They have anxiety. The norms and values workshop takes as a starting place their real problems and concerns. When you start with their aspirations on their terms, you get more energy.

They are then more ready to search for guidance from the past. Some colleagues have challenged my model. They wanted me to insist on study first. Given the low level of Torah literacy I have encountered, I have sought, in this SVP experimental model, to engage people where they are and talk in terms of their congregational aspirations.

Rabbi Marc Margulies has been most helpful by reminding me that the hallowed Jewish values that are taught today came to us out of a real-life context. This wisdom came in response to the nitty-gritty pressing problems of that day. These problems created energy for the sages. The people needed leadership; they called for a ruling. When our stakeholders start with their own experiences, they are recreating the conditions that energized the rabbis and were later given form in our texts.

Whether you study the traditional values and reflect on the congregation's context or start with context and reflect on traditional values, you must make this important connection if you are going to transform the board from a nonprofit management board to a leadership community based in Jewish values. If you undergo these processes, you will see new approaches. Just as focusing on a congregation's operational details (roof, catering, parking lot, etc.) can generate more ideas about operational issues, focusing on values will show you ways to build and find consensus around those values. You can build a reinforcing loop by cultivating a values-focused leadership.

Values Education as a Core Leadership Strategy

I strongly encourage the rabbi to take the raw material from the values workshop and help the steering committee explore the texts and traditions that speak to these communal aspirations. I offer several resources for studying values. One good resource on values is *A Guide to Jewish Practice* by Rabbi David Teutsch (2003). I offer an exercise to explore values from Dr. Isa Aron. The bibliography offers various books that will also help enrich this discussion.

The texts can build on the work of the planners. It can also shape new reflections. The workshop is designed as a springboard for a steering committee values conversation, not as the final arbiter of congregational values. If the rabbi and the steering committee bring low energy to this task, the values statements may simply reflect secular, consumer, and American preferences for product changes.

"Values in Action": Implementation

Once values have been identified, they need to be integrated into all of your committees and task forces. These values need to be practiced if they are to permeate your gatherings. Each year the leadership should identify a few sessions where they can dedicate thirty minutes of a board meeting to explore a key value. Every major committee presentation should include a list of the values. The religious school can make these values a topic for a month's study. The children can be asked to talk to their parents about these values. Students from the religious school might be asked to interview board members about the role that values play in their leadership. Children's questions can sometimes change how leadership thinks. I can attest to this as a one-time seventh grade teacher.

In order to ensure that implementation occurs, I recommend comprehensive orientation training sessions to help leaders align committee objectives with these congregational values.

By making these connections, leaders will see that many mundane managerial tasks can be imbued with moments of Jewish spirituality. While leaders may find it difficult to speak about their congregations' vision and values, through the effort of developing values and training others, they will begin to put these values into action. They will gain new skills and new attitudes about the sacred community they are building.

WORKSHOP 1: Values
AGENDA

Introductions
- Chairs

Overview of SVP Process
Theme: Stepping Forward: Bringing Our Gifts,
Welcoming the Gifts of Others
Review the SVP Stepping Stones Map

> *Tell the Israelite people to bring Me gifts; you shall*
> *accept gifts for Me from every person whose heart*
> *so moves him.*   —Exodus 25:2

> *See, I have singled out by name Bezalel son of Uri son*
> *of Hur, of the tribe of Judah. I have endowed him with a*
> *divine spirit of skill, ability, and knowledge in every kind*
> *of craft.*   —Exodus 31:2-3

Group Brainstorm: Community Visual Map
Facilitator Leads
All of the stakeholders are asked to get up from their tables and stand before a large six-foot high by twelve-foot wide piece of paper. They are asked the following questions and invited to brainstorm their

responses. There is no debate. We encourage the group to avoid any side conversations or editorials. We will write down all of their comments about their culture.

Questions about Culture
- What is working well? Example: We are hamish, unpretentious.
- What could be strengthened? Example: New members sometimes feel like outsiders.

Values List

We then ask them to reflect on their comments. These reflections will be listed on a separate piece of paper called "Our Values."

Reflections about Values
- What values have supported you when you were at your best? Example: Welcoming, openness, or a commitment to social justice.

Vote

Each person can vote with four stickers for the comments they think are most critical to discuss today. The facilitator will add up the votes while people return to their seats. The facilitator will suggest some groupings for the stakeholders to consider. They might group the following:

Issues Group: Welcoming (19 votes)

Observations/Comments Voting Stickers Received
We are hamish 10
Greet new members Shabbat 4
We wear name tags 3
We call everyone for high holidays 2

Each group of stakeholders will then choose an issue, like welcoming, to discuss in their stakeholder segment discussion group.

Stakeholder Discussion Groups   35 minutes

- Appoint a scribe to make notes.
- Facilitator will read the comments that got the most votes.
- All stakeholder groups review the observations and comments that were reported out. They decide as stakeholders for the one most important issue *for their group.* They may choose a different issue than the top issues reported if they want.
- They split their flip-chart paper in two parts. On the left they put the issue under the heading "Doing Today"; then they discuss how they would like to see their congregational practice change or develop under the heading "Hope to Do" on the right.
- They name the value that best describes what they want to bring to the service of their future. They can look at the list of values the group brainstormed or choose a different one.
- They look at how this value has been historically understood in the Jewish tradition. (See Model Worksheet: Values.)
- Finally, groups describe the behavior that they would expect to observe if their value became the accepted value of the congregation. (See Model Worksheet: Values.)

Break

Report Out

Each group has 3–4 minutes to report on their value.

Future Assignments

- Assignment to Steering Committee: Members of the steering committee will type up the flip chart sheets. They will then hold a meeting to debrief the worksheets and to weave them into a values and (or) vision statement.
- **Assignment to Stakeholders:** Stakeholders will provide feedback on the summaries, which will be sent out to all of them—electronically if possible.

Close

MODEL WORKSHEET: Values

1. Chosen Value: Welcoming

Members aren't always greeted. Some enter the sanctuary and don't know what page the service is on.

2. Aspirations

Doing Now

Don't have ushers greet worshippers

Want to Do

Have ushers greet,
   provide prayer books and note
   page number.
Meet people where they are in
   knowledge and observance-
   learner's minyan.
Help seniors out of cars if needed.

3. Reflect on Jewish Values

- From "Our Values" list: welcoming, hamish, caring, family
- Quote a specific mitsvah or Jewish value. Informally describe a value you know about even if you are not sure of its textual source.
- Be creative in extending this principle to contemporary situations. See Rabbi Joseph Telushkin's discussion in *The Book of Jewish Values* (2000) about the Torah's attitude about safety ("Build a parapet around the roof," Deuteronomy 22:8). Help seniors get out of their cars in the winter.
- See Telushkin on hospitality. He argues that Jewish law requires that "one should accompany one's guests into the street" (Telushkin 2000, 184).
- The rabbis taught that "a teacher should escort the student as far as the outskirts of the city (*Sotah 46b*). Consider all of our members needs as they enter and leave.

4. Identify a Behavior to Monitor

If this value were in place in our congregation we would see:

- Ushers would show people what page the service was on.

Conclusion

The values workshop helps the diverse stakes to come together as a team. It suggests that individuals can work more effectively if they agree about guiding principles and values. It asks leaders to think about their current culture and to explore their hopes for it. It invites leaders of various levels of knowledge to ask questions about what the tradition might have to say about their leadership task.

Questions for Reflection

1. Why do you need to understand Jewish culture?
2. Why do shared values help you be a team?
3. How can you put congregational values into action?
4. How would you communicate your leadership values?

14.
Strategic Goals: Where Should We Focus?

WORKSHOP 2

For a lack of vision a people lose restraint.

—Proverbs 29:18

A people without direction will go in every direction. Leaders thus must ask, "What direction should we go?" Judaism is a religion of hope and optimism. The first Jew, Abraham, hears God's call and picks up all his possessions and leaves Haran. The story of Abraham is a central pillar of the faith. Abraham's way is not the way for most. When we feel inspired, few of us will choose to leave our families, our jobs, or our communities. Dr. Arnold Eisen, Chancellor of the Jewish Theological Seminary, wrote about the way of Abraham.

> Most Jews in America come to the Torah from afar. They were not raised on the story of Abraham leaving his homeland and the house of his father for a land that God would show him. In many cases American Jews must literally leave their own parents' home in order to encounter Abraham for the first time, and must certainly depart their parents' culture—that of secular America—in order to cross the river into observance of the covenant that he first entered. (Eisen 1997, 3)

It is hard for us to take a fresh look at our mission or budget. We have come to assume that what we do is "in stone" and that new ideas from new lands won't work. We have history. We have friends and relatives. Few groups are starting 100 percent new. Their synagogues are full of memorial plaques honoring loved ones. The hallways show pictures of their children at bar mitsvahs and confirmations. The rooms are full of memories. It is much easier to make changes in a new congregation or in a homogenous one. Most congregations are old and heterogeneous. They have an existing story. How do we honor that past history and still have the courage to move forward?

Moses gave the spies this challenge. They were asked to find the words to describe the road ahead for the people. Their report had to balance the real dangers that they would encounter (foresight) and respect for the people's capabilities (their strength, God's help, the Torah, etc.). The spies were so fearful of the road ahead that they terrified themselves and the people. We all know congregational leaders who are so anxious that they can't provide a vision of hope.

Leaders need to be willing to sit with new people from new neighborhoods. They need to get up from the board table and move the chairs around. They need to have different conversations. Abraham challenges us to be willing to leave "our parents' house"—to be open to some new ways of being together.

The SVP process starts by asking the steering committee what they think the strategic issues are. You will keep these in mind when you interview the staff and when you consider what data you need. Keep this list as a work in process because you need to see how the larger planning group will identify the congregational leadership priorities. Later, before the first workshop, you will ask what are the dominant themes they see from this planning work. You will help planners focus on the challenge of picking up and moving to the new place (Abraham's job).

Strategic Goals in Process

In Workshop 2 you will discuss the question "What direction should we go?" This is the central theme of what I call the leadership plan. When you distributed the briefing books, you asked the planners to review past reports and congregational trends, factors, and forces. You have asked them to review their members' attitudes, wants, and needs.

For the SVP process to be successful leaders must have a good foundation in congregational facts. Too often I see leaders arguing about the implications of facts but have never agreed what those facts are. My role in the data gathering phase is to be a champion for the gathering of facts. I encourage leaders to suspend judgment and maintain an open mind—to be reflective. They are encouraged to read the briefing book before they speak.

In Workshop 2 you look at congregational history within the context of the community. The planners think about their congregation's history using a time line. They invite stakeholders to consider the congregation during different eras.

At the end of Workshop 2 you begin to ask what strategies you might want to take. How would you like to intentionally bring forward the best of your congregation's past (themes from time line, testimonies). What story do you want to tell the congregation that will allow them to move forward?

Remember that the stakeholders enter the process far behind the steering committee. They lack the cohesiveness, the experience, and the understanding of the steering committee. There are inherent limitations in doing a large system workshop on goals. Can the group work through all of the details around these goals? Can they prioritize them in any way that would be credible for the board during later reviews? Clearly, this can's happen in one night. A lot more work needs to be done, so the goals that are being developed are called "goals in process."

Shared History: Time Line

Synagogues are "both/and" places. They honor the past and the present. One walks into buildings and sees memorial plaques that recall past generations. The lighting is often somber and dim. When we open the prayer book, we honor a rabbinic liturgy and language that has resonated for over two thousand years. We are inspired by tradition and moved by memory. When we say the 'amidah, we invoke the blessing received by our forefathers and foremothers ('avot ve'mahot). We are nurtured by historic practices. We thus have mixed feelings about change.

The synagogue is also a place where we take traditional values and use them to address the issues of the day and the challenges of the future. But a leadership focused solely on nostalgia is in trouble. We adapt Abraham's approach because we are dedicated to bringing the best of our past to the service of our future. Workshop 2 begins by honoring the past.

Planners will construct a time line of the congregation. What were the key events in the history of the congregation and the Jewish people? Three or four people will talk for about three minutes each about an era of synagogue life. This is an enjoyable exercise for planners. They get to decorate the time line with pictures of beloved rabbis and historic facilities. They note key events—the opening of the preschool, the first mitsvah day.

They are reminded of key milestones in the congregation's history. They can be nostalgic about the past and curious about the future. They reflect on the passing of leaders. These leaders witnessed the challenges of capital campaigns or the conflict around certain decisions. For the older, more experienced members, SVP may be a time of reflection. For newer members it may function as a history lesson. They often know little of the congregational history. They certainly don't know how older members feel about this history. For the entire planning group the time line is an educational process.

The awareness of congregational history may vary. Some know more. Most know less. We can be relatively sure that little has been shared together. These individuals have probably never stood in front of this time line narrative before. Now they are at Sinai together! They will start to address common questions about the last thirty or so years. What was happening in their life? What was happening in the Jewish world? What was happening in the congregation? These synagogue questions are different, argues Rabbi Randall Konigsburg of the Temple of Aaron. "Our conversation is richer, our relationships are different, our aspirations are elevated when we gather inside the synagogue walls."

The time line exercise assumes that you can learn from your past and be inspired by it. If God is really going to be a stakeholder, then you also need to ask, "What is God calling us to do at this point in our history?"

You will use the time line to explore how decisions were made. Workshop 2 reviews the outcomes of those leadership decisions. All the planners are given an SVP briefing book of key historical congregational facts so that they all have the same shared facts. They need to understand where they are before they are asked to affirm where they want to go. If people have a different view, they can share it. Your facilitator will note it. A few individuals could hijack the process. There will be times for debate later in the process.

Inviting God to Be a Stakeholder

When you get focused on leadership development, planning, or board best practices, you can begin to take on the language of secular work.

Of course, you are doing this work for a religious purpose, but it is easy to forget one of your main partners in this work: God. Are you a little embarrassed? Well, don't be. I have as much of a problem putting God in the center of my Jewish communal service practice as the next person. The only difference in my practice is that I know it is an important question. I know it is meant to be struggled with. Elie Wiesel has said that a Jew can be angry with God but he can't ignore God.

Too often we try to ignore God. When you are working with the time line, you are reflecting on the mission of generations of our fellow Jews. What were they called to do in their time? How did they feel God was speaking to them in their time? What were those great moments where God, as one leader said, "grabs you by the scruff of the neck" and challenges you to address the issues of your day?

Abraham certainly knew what this call was like. He knew how it felt to be grabbed. The first Jew got up and left his native land. He left all that was comfortable and familiar because he felt something lacking. He looked deep into his soul and asked, "Is there nothing more than this life?" He was moved by hope for something more. God made a covenant with Abraham and promised that Abraham's seed would become a great nation. Yes, God chose him, but Abraham still had to have the capacity to believe, to be inspired. Some SVP leaders come out of these synagogue conversations with much greater focus—we are now getting their attention.

The first part of the 'amidah, the central Jewish prayer, speaks about God's love of our ancestors. Our mission will be blessed because God looks with favor on the descendents of the matriarchs and patriarchs. God is predisposed to look for our goodness because of those who went before us. While our personal histories, as I have shared, are often a mixed bag, we still can be hopeful of God's blessing. Our ancestors were not perfect. They were full of flaws. They were often in despair. We say the 'amidah because the covenant was made with flawed people like us. We say the 'amidah because their lives were made noble by their commitment to have a relationship with God. They did not stop asking, "What does God want us to do here?"

We are not operating our congregations in a vacuum. We are part of a long history of Jewish communities in search of meaning. We are trying to bring the best of our past to the service of the future. Those names on the memorial plaques are not meant to be just nostalgic old stuff. We stare at the dignified bronze names. We see the dates. The bronze glows in the yartseit lights. What light goes off in our minds? As congregational students, how are we to be instructed by these artifacts that surround us? Are they silent? I believe, like a still small voice, we should ask this question, "How will you build the best community with the time you have?"

As the facilitator I have brought a tool chest from my business, teaching, and consulting experience, from Alban congregational research, and from the best practices of many Jewish organizations I have observed. My clients may see me as an expert, but in truth I am not always certain how things will evolve. I came to this work through an unlikely set of circumstance. Most of my stakeholders have never done this type of work before. We have tried to structure a healthy and helpful congregational conversation, but I don't control the outcome. I have been witness to some wonderful moments. I come to this work with the conviction that when people gather to do Jewish work in good faith, God is a fellow stakeholder.

Exploring Strategic Areas

The steering committee will by now have identified six to eight critical strategic issues to explore based on the dominant themes that emerged from the parlor meetings and the values workshops. This is a leadership task. The steering committee must frame the work of the larger group. The stakeholders will review their briefing books, reflect on their congregational history and experience, and search their hearts. This process should bring their gifts to the goal development process.

The planners have many intuitive skills that are not purely analytic. They have more collective insight than just a set of facts. There are divine sparks in the room. The sometimes chaotic sharing of observations and requests for more information helps draw from deep wells of intuitive understanding. Unlike in formal corporate strategic planning, you are trying to blend facts with the spiritual and emotional intuition of planners. This can be a spiritually transformational process. It helps a broad cross section of people—many who do not normally look with a strategic lens—make meaning of these facts. When this works, the planning group experiences resonance.

Resonance suggests that the historicity of the story is not as important as the question of whether or not it rings true. When the story rings true it enables the listener to generate new ways of thinking and acting that embraces—or even advances—the truth the story represents. (Denning 2001, 29–39)

The Community Billboard: Posting Observations

The congregational briefing book has a variety of internal congregational facts and external environment facts. Each workshop participant is asked to write down at least two observations about the congregational facts on sticky notes. They are also asked to identify at least one piece of data that they would like to have, using a sticky note of a different color.

In earlier steering committee discussions with the leadership, from six to eight critical strategic issues have been identified. You can list these issues (worship, religious school) across a fifty-foot expanse of butcher paper, which becomes a community billboard. Participants post their observations and requests for information under the appropriate strategic topics. There is a column marked "other" for all items that don't necessarily fit into one of the major categories. When all of the stakeholders are working from the same briefing book, with the shared values from Workshop 1, conversations can gain resonance. Here are some examples of postings:

External Facts
- Jews are moving to many different neighborhoods. There is no Jewish center for the town.
- The cost of housing has skyrocketed. Young families are moving further out.
- We are attracting more professional and fewer business people to the area.
- The Jewish population is aging.

Internal Facts
- Dues are 45 percent of revenue.
- Membership has averaged 5 percent growth for five years.
- The greatest school expense is personnel costs.
- 20 percent of members pay less than their scheduled dues charges.

Key Issues, Observations, and Data Needed

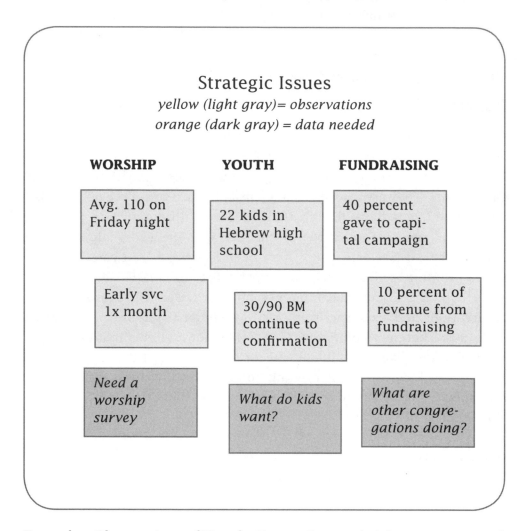

Examples: Observations of Trends, Forces, Factors (sticky notes mounted on a wall)

Group Work

Once the community billboard is completed, take the goal sheets down and bring them to each break-out session on that strategic issue. You will no longer ask the stakeholders to sit as segments, as you did in the values workshop. Stakeholders vote with their feet: they go where their interests are. When people go with their passions, you are much more likely to get the benefit of their special gifts.

Ask each group to appoint a scribe. They review the postings with the group and invite them to describe where the congregation is relative to the goal areas—"Doing Today." They are invited to suggest where the congregation might go—"Plan to Do."

All tables are asked to follow the same process.

1. List all observations on the left side of the newsprint under "Current Situation."
2. Describe initiatives they would like to see to address these observations under "Future Plans."
3. Turn these initiatives into one general strategic goal statement.
4. Provide one SMART objective that would address the general goal.
5. Ensure that all notes are typed up and distributed.

Shared Goals

It is important to develop strategic goals publicly. When leaders shape goals within a public discourse, there is a greater potential for clarity. Let's look at a strategic goal on finance and facility: "provide a long-term plan to develop and sustain our facility to shelter our mission and members." The goal statements at this stage are called "goals in process" because they need to be subjected to many rounds of conversation.

A strategic goal is an overarching goal—not a specific measurable task. One example of a strategic goal in process is: "Annual fundraising efforts will be coordinated to tell a compelling story and increase the number and value of contributions."

We will work with supporting objectives in Workshop 3. Supporting objectives are more specific. They are measurable and trackable. One example of a supporting objective is: "We will create a fundraising committee in the next three months to ensure coordination and consistent communications. The committee will coordinate all fundraising efforts of the congregation (youth, brotherhood, sisterhood, donor dinners, plaques, contributions, special campaigns, etc.)." See the examples of goal statements in Resource 5 (in the Appendix).

The goals that come out of these break-out groups are in process: there will be a great deal more discussion about them over the next several months. The workshop shapes these goals, but the steering committee, the staff, and the board will be encouraged to refine and publish them.

The steering committee and the board discuss the values and goals statements. Once they have approved them, they need to assign their goals to committees and task forces. You are encouraged to hold a town meeting for your congregation to discuss the SVP work in process. This discussion will provide fresh insights about the goals.

In Workshop 3 groups will address these goals as task forces and committees. They may choose to reshape these goals as they continue their work. You will ask them to honor the strategic topics but to help shape them as you go.

MODEL WORKSHEET: Fundraising T-Chart

Current Situation	Future Plans
Most of our money comes from dues.	Do a fundraiser with religious school families.
We get a lot of fees from school.	Help members understand our financial picture better.
We have many young families who have to pay school fees and dues.	Launch a campaign to "burn" the mortgage.
We still have a mortgage on the building.	
Fundraising has grown by X percent.	
Jewish attitudes to giving are changing.	

Closing Reflections

You will close the meeting with some reflections on the day. You may simply invite those who are willing to share their experiences. What observations have they made? What insights have they gained? In some groups, time permitting, you may go deeper. You may invite participants to share what things they are proud of in terms of the congregation. They may also be encouraged to share if there are things that they regret about the congregation.

WORKSHOP 2: Strategic Goals
AGENDA

Introduction

Review Results from Workshop 1: Norms and Values

Read value statements; request feedback.

Time Line Stories   20 minutes

People are encouraged to review the time line when they come in. Have some markers near the time line and post this message: "Please review the time line. Feel free to note an experience that was important in your life, in the congregation, or in the general Jewish community."

Have three members with good knowledge talk about some of the key periods and events (start up, first building, decision to move, changes in school, changes in leadership, etc.). Encourage them to have a written outline and to speak for a maximum of 3 minutes. You may wish to videotape these speakers.

Group Reflection

- What are major changes that have occurred in this congregation? (Consider the founding era, the glory days, our current era.)
- What issues has the congregation wrestled with?
- What were some of the outcomes of these challenges?
- What values supported us?

Review Briefing Book   30 minutes

- Share community data, congregational internal data, dominant themes from parlor meetings.
- Everyone will be encouraged to write down the following on sticky notes:
    1. One idea about additional data they would like to know
    2. Two implications from the briefing book exercise

Whole Group:
Place Notes under Goal Headings

Put up to eight major goals on the wall. Each goal will be assigned two sheets of paper. One will be labeled "All Other."

Break

Get some food, and join a goal discussion.

Goal Discussion Group: 35 minutes
Current Situation versus
"What We Should Plan to Do"

- Each table will have a goal written on a table easel (see below).
- People go to the table they are interested in.
- They will then use the comments from sticky notes to start their discussion of the goal.

Each goal discussion group creates a double T on the flip chart and describes the current situation and what they think the leaders should do.

Goal Discussion Group

Goal: Facility Planning

Scribe	**Members' Sign-in**
Current Situation	**Future Plans**
Comments: Observations about Current Situation	**Comments: Observations about What We Should Do**
Social hall too small; large membership growth affects school; small endowment; old building	We need to remodel foyer. We need a long-range plan. We need better lighting in hallways.

Comments:

Information We Need

What was cost of roof? What would it cost to add two classrooms? Are other schools expanding? Would our members have more events here if social hall was different?

Other Comments

The group should finish by putting their key ideas into a goal statement. They should also write one supporting objective that brings the goal into focus. For example: *Supporting Objective:* The facility committee will review all of the initiatives from the planning process in terms of facility needs. They will also look at all of the assumptions about growth for the next ten years. They will create a short-term and long-term facility plan and report by August 1, 2007.

Report   45 minutes

Individual Reflections

Close: Next Steps

Outcomes of the Strategic Goals Workshop

Goals give the planners a team focus. The briefing book gives them a sense of shared meaning about their environment. The planners are encouraged to interact with this data and choose key implications to reflect on. When a leadership community has shared goals, it helps them get on the same page. The goals workshop energizes the groups by helping them reflect on the past and create direction for the future. The steering committee will now take these goals and supporting objectives and develop an SVP recommendation to the board to charter committees and task forces to address the strategic issues.

Questions for Reflection

1. Why are goals important for your leadership?
2. How do we translate goals into action?
3. How could you communicate goals to the whole organization?

15.

From Vision to Action Planning: Who Will Do What?

Why do you act alone, while all the people stand about you from morning until evening?

—Exodus 18:14

The delegation and management plan requires that you put your values into action. In the previous chapter we looked at how the spies handled their assignment. Not well! The story of the spies is not a story of successful delegation. Just because they failed, it does not follow that leaders must do everything themselves. We have to know when it is time to call on others. SVP sounds the shofar to the steering committee, the stakeholders, and many community participants. It announces that now is the time to step forward. Yes, leaders need to empower and delegate, but followers need to step up and do their part. Leaders and followers are in a relationship: they affect each other.

We can see leadership values in action in Parashat Yitro (Exodus 18). Moses was facing burnout when Jethro, his Midianite father-in-law, provided the classic piece of advice for management: Delegate! Moses was told to appoint officers—upstanding, trustworthy people—or he would "surely wear [himself] out" (Exodus 18:17). Jethro told him, "You shall also seek out from among all the people capable men who fear God, trustworthy men who spurn ill-gotten gain. Set these over them as chiefs of thousands, hundreds, fifties, and tens" (Exodus 18:21).

Moses was a visionary. He witnessed extraordinary things. He experienced God's presence (as a burning bush). He saw God's power (deliver-

189

ance from Egypt). He heard God's voice (thunder from the mountain). He understood the importance of the mission. One cannot, however, live on vision alone. One has to help others to help you—to help the mission. Jethro, Moses' father-in-law, was not even an Israelite—he was a Midianite. He was somewhat outside the tribe, and so he could look with a different lens. He saw the need for others to help implement the plan. This allowed him to make his practical suggestions.

Leaders need to set realistic goals that still stretch their potential and strive to achieve them. This will have a dramatic effect on both performance and community building. When a person fulfills his or her given word, the sages are pleased with that person (*Shev 10:9*). In order to increase a commitment to accountability you need to encourage "buy in." We need to provide a clear charge, adequate support, and a realistic goal.

A Clear Charge for Action Planning Groups

At this point in the SVP process you have gathered data and developed values, priorities, and goals in the process. The steering committee is now challenged to summarize their learning and write a short one- to two-page vision of the congregation in five years. With a draft of their values, goals, and vision they are ready to make recommendations about assignments for current committees, new committees, and task forces. These assignments will provide an outline for the delegation and the accountability plan. This is a critical planning moment. The steering committee needs to ensure it has support for their overall direction from the rabbi, the board, and the community before it assembles the groups for action planning.

Rabbi's Support

The rabbi has to be committed. The rabbi is a member of the steering committee. He or she attends all the workshops and is usually the principal wordsmith of the values statements and a key strategist in determining goals. The rabbi has usually been an active recruiter for task forces and committees (see chapter 9). The rabbi needs to confirm his or her support for these statements before others are asked to do their work.

I also work with the rabbi to facilitate a staff meeting to get additional input from the entire program staff.

Board Support for Recommendations

There are certain boundaries that need to be respected. One of these is the ultimate authority of the board. Many of the board members are part of the steering committee and the stakeholder groups; however, you will not have more than 35 percent of the planners from the board, so the board is not fully represented. Given this, it is important that the fully constituted board be given an opportunity to bless the work of the planners. They need to approve the charge to working groups.

Community Support: Town Meeting

The insights and opinions of the general membership also need to be heard. You have made an effort to do this with the parlor meetings. Obviously not all of them can participate. Most would not choose to make the time commitment to be a part of the entire planning process. While not as engaged as the planners, they still have important input. The town meeting provides them with a forum to be heard.

The community meeting discussion groups are facilitated by SVP leaders. The strategic goals in process (usually six to eight) are placed on flip chart paper and posted around the room. There is a steering committee facilitator for each group. The members start by asking questions as opposed to rendering judgments. This is a technique drawn from Torah text study classes. You want to get members out of the habit of responding too quickly with judgments. After they have discussed the questions, they can make some concrete suggestions for possible programs and initiatives. These notes are then typed up by the steering committee and distributed as new information.

The town meeting has several goals:

1. To allow the community to hear an overview of SVP work to date.
2. To give the SVP leaders a chance to practice making presentations on their work.
3. To present the goals in process.

4. To provide the congregation an opportunity to respond to the strategic goals in process.
5. To let congregants go to a discussion group about the goal that they have the most interest in.
6. To tap the concrete suggestions that congregants have about how to drive these goals.

In some communities people are unlikely to attend an open meeting. Some cultures have less engaged members. Some members may have more hectic schedules or more difficult traffic and commuting lifestyles. To elicit a response from those who do not attend the town meeting, you may wish to post key materials on a Web site and seek feedback. In some communities you might get sixty to one hundred people to attend. This presents a wonderful opportunity to extend the engagement.

Accountability

Workshops 2 and 3 lay the foundation for accountability. Without shared goals it is hard to expect people to perform consistently. Workshop 2 helps create overall goals. Workshop 3 makes specific assignments to people. If you want accountability you need to make sure you have "ownership." You have worked to increase ownership throughout SVP, but now you must get more formal support from the board and community.

Why is accountability so important? We need to be accountable to ourselves, the community, and ultimately to God. The traditional Jewish practice of tsedakah is a developmental value. When a person has been living in a town for only a few months, there is a lower expectation about his or her commitment to the community. The longer he or she is a "citizen," the more of the community's obligations the person is expected to share.

> One who settles in a community for thirty days becomes obligated to contribute to charity together with other members of the community. . . . One who settles for nine months becomes obligated to contribute to the burial fund of burying the communal poor. (Zevit, *Offerings of the Heart*, 2005)

SVP understands that many members have been living in the congregational town for a long time without fully accepting their share of the community's concerns. Research and experience confirm that there are many members of the congregation who do not want to be more engaged in program or leadership at any given time. Leaders often send bulletins and flyers to groups that are not really receptive. Occasional pep talks (sermons, letters, etc.) often don't change their practice. As we noted, the Torah says that we must not hide ourselves from community's needs. We are challenged to stop our journey to help someone who is in distress. Even when we see an adversary on the road, we are to treat him or her with the respect we have for all human beings. Leaders have the challenge to engage others. The Midrash argues that when we are shoulder to shoulder on a task we see each other differently. Our attitudes are changed. SVP has a lot of members working shoulder to shoulder in parlor meetings and workshops so that there is a greater sense of accountability for the needs of the community.

Accountability versus Entitlement

Americans have been empowered to demand customer service. As Michael Hammer writes in *The Agenda* (2001), we live in a culture where the customer is king. In such a culture advocating for one's consumer rights is considered a skill. Companies are constantly under pressure to create the "new and improved." It is not surprising that Jewish communal observers have noted that congregants often bring this attitude to their approach to synagogue membership. Synagogues must manage the needs of consumers, but they depend on dedicated leadership from members. In a volunteer organization with hundreds of members and only a few staff, how can the mission succeed if everyone is standing with their hands in their pockets waiting to be served?

Jewish history has a long tradition of complaining. The whole narrative in the desert is a series of complaints ("We were better off in Egypt!"). It was not easy for Moses to lead his people. The American cultural tendency toward individualism and entitlement can create a powerful force for complaint and criticism. I have observed a "culture of criticism" that dominates some boards. What can help keep this in check? Accountability. When leaders are held accountable for their part of the solution, they often transfer their energy from complaining to providing. When you are accountable for your committee or task force, you also gain some humility for how hard it is to get things done in a volunteer community. Accountability reinforces a commitment to performance and real humility—essential leadership qualities.

Handoff: Steering Committee to Implementation Committee

Steering committees are encouraged to stay together for at least four months (see work plan) after the end of Workshop 3. This allows them to support the early meetings of the task forces and committees. Some groups will choose to continue for the next twelve to twenty-four months. In other cases the steering committee members may decide they no longer want this responsibility. They are tired. They may feel they have fulfilled their responsibility to the process. In fact, they have done what we asked of them in the steering committee job description. Part of a good accountability system is an honest description of the work for volunteers. If they want to step down, we need to honor this, but we need others to agree to step up.

One option is simply to assign this to the board to implement. I prefer that the steering committee form a smaller implementation team to monitor progress on initiatives. This group of four to six people is made up of dedicated officers, members of the steering committee, and a few senior leaders such as past presidents or long-range planning chairs.

Why Are These Handoffs So Important?

Handoffs are one way we ritualize our accountability to each other. The handoff says, "I acknowledge that this issue is my concern, not just someone else's." In our parlor meetings you ask members to critique different aspects of the congregation. You ask for their opinions about the strengths, weaknesses, opportunities, and threats. They share their level of satisfaction with different aspects of the congregation. Then you shift the focus, asking them what the leadership should do. You want a concrete suggestion about what might be helpful as opposed to just a critique. You then ask what they are prepared to do. Congregational change is thus not just the leaders' responsibility—it is theirs. From the very beginning of SVP you have been trying to signal that accountability must be shared. The large group of seventy stakeholders signals that the board does not own the whole problem. The nine tables of stakeholders suggests that the rabbi's study does not carry the full weight of the community. Now you are ready to raise the bar by giving real work to real people.

There will be forces of resistance to the emerging plan. The delegation plan sets the foundation for good accountability. Just as Joshua asks the people to commit to a new covenant after they cross the Jordan, so the steering committee asks the stakeholders to recommit to the covenant, to move from visionaries to doers and builders. You are getting ready to enter the land—the land of action. If planners become overconfident, they may try to skip some of the SVP processes. This can be a serious error because there are significant factors that can work against successful implementation.

Task Forces/New Committees

The steering committee should appoint a chair and one staff person (if available) for each task force. If a goal is referred to an existing committee, the current leaders will manage it. A total of no more than twelve others should be chosen for each task force. This will hopefully ensure at least eight per meeting. Members should be chosen from among the following:

- Those stakeholders who participated in the action planning workshop exercises.
- Others in the community you feel would be most helpful.
- Representatives of existing committees.

Reviewing Profiles

You will review the membership profiles of all the people assigned to a task. You will want to understand their skills and interests and also identify what skills you may need to round out the group. Look at those stakeholders who attended specific break-out sessions in the goal-setting or action planning workshop. You will know if they have demonstrated an interest in the religious school or fundraising by their efforts in these workshops. You can then create a team folder and a contacts list.

Late Joiners

The steering committee will recruit and encourage most stakeholders to go to certain groups. I have found it helpful to publicize that the task forces are forming and to invite the membership to come to Workshop 3. In reality only a few will show up, but I have been pleasantly surprised by some of those who have decided to jump in at the action planning stage.

Encourage the steering committee to talk to the unassigned stakeholders before they just go to a group.

Why Task Forces Rather than Committees?

Sometimes I will encourage the development of a task force rather than a standing committee to manage an issue for a while. If we do opt for the task force, we will clarify its relationships with standing committees. We will define its purposes and get board approval for the task force. In general, we use task forces for the following reasons:

- We have a large diverse group of stakeholders who have developed energy for an issue.
- The issue crosses over the boundaries of different committees.
- Committees often have well-established approaches to issues. Task forces are designed to maintain the creativity of the visioning workshops. Task forces can keep certain kinds of developmental conversations going longer.
- Committees can become very managerial. Task forces encourage more strategic thinking.

On the other hand, task forces take a great deal of energy. Sometimes the issue can best be managed by an existing committee if the above issues are not significant challenges. Some committees are performing at a very high level and are very well suited for the challenge.

Implementation Details

The task forces and/or committees must then develop the following implementation parameters:

1. Clarify the goal in process they are focusing on.
2. Create a short vision statement in bullet form about what this area of congregational life would look like in five years.
3. Develop supporting objectives and actions for the goal.
   - Responsibility: a list of people to be responsible
   - Coordination, Liaisons: other committees or leaders who must be communicated with
   - A time line for each action
   - An estimate of cost

This action planning stage will last for six to twelve months. It is very important that the task forces be monitored. Momentum is easy to lose.

The Fundraising Task Force That Wasn't Fun

One congregation created a great deal of energy through Workshops 1 and 2. They had not had a strong lay leadership culture; normally initiatives were staff driven. They were excited. When it came to picking task force chairs, they found that they were losing energy. A great deal of creativity was encouraged around the fundraising task, but the chair who was chosen was not a fundraiser, and the staff person assigned was not able to overcome parochial issues in the various fundraising groups.

SVP CASE

The recommendations and assumptions that come from the committees and task forces need to be given to the finance committee and developed into a final plan. If the steering committee can maintain their energy and commitment, they can help the board by staying on and leading this process.

If the steering committee is tired, it makes sense to make this handoff after Workshop 3. If it is done, it should be communicated to the congregation, and the steering committee members should be thanked for their service. I encourage the congregation to celebrate the conclusion of Workshop 3. One congregation held a dinner for 150 people to thank SVP participants.

Implementation requires a plan and should be addressed before the stakeholders begin Workshop 3. You should approach Workshop 3 with a vision of increasing accountability. You have identified your values and goals. You have assigned people to do essential work. You are now ready to put these values and goals into action.

Shifting to the Future

In Workshop 3 the shift to the future is continued, and the focus is on a vision for each task force and committee. I encourage leaders to begin to create the future story.

WORKSHOP 3: Visions and Action Planning
AGENDA

Introduction

Review Values and Goals

While we are waiting for everyone to come in, the group is encouraged to review the following documents posted on walls:

- values statement
- strategies and goals statements
- steering committee vision statement (1 page)

Committee and Task Forces Formed

Most members have been asked to go to specific groups. Unassigned members will work with the steering committee leadership to find the most appropriate work group.

Group Assignment   60 minutes

1. Introduce all members (1 minute each)
2. Fill out the Task Force and Committee Charter Form.
3. Develop a vision for your committee or task force:
     - If your group was extremely effective in improving your area of congregational life (leadership, worship, etc.), what would the congregation look like in five years? Pretend that you are a reporter who is observing the community five years from now. What are youth doing? What is the board doing? What are people learning? How are they worshipping?
     - Provide a sketch for your area of focus. Write this up in bullet form. Do not wordsmith.
4. Develop some specific ideas that might bring this vision into reality.

Groups Report   60–75 minutes

Note: Some use creative ways to present (skits, etc.). Some groups choose to videotape all presentations. Some take photos of the workshop.

Close   10 minutes

Outcomes of Workshop 3: Expanding the Circle of Ownership

Our sages taught, "a community is too heavy for any one person to carry alone (*Deuteronomy Rabbah* 1:10). It is too heavy for the core leadership to carry alone. SVP tries to expand the circle of ownership so that people balance their criticism of leaders with their commitment to provide ideas and efforts. It seeks to shift the conversation from entitlement to accountability. Some will be willing to go to parlor meetings. Some will be willing to attend some workshops. When it comes to committee and task force work, you will need to assess the participants to determine who is really prepared to take the handoff and continue the journey.

Questions for Reflection

1. Why are handoffs so important?
2. Why is it necessary to hold a joint steering committee and board meeting on assignments?
3. How should the values and goals statements shape committee/task force work?
4. Why should we start with a committee/task force vision first?

16.

The Accountability Plan: Transparent Planning Invites Healthy Feedback

You shall surely rebuke your neighbor, and incur no guilt because of him.

—Leviticus 19:18

Judaism believes in the importance of a shared mission. We began this book with a reflection on the parable of the spies. They failed to live up to God's expectations and were held accountable and their community was also held accountable. Judaism believes in feedback because learning to give and receive feedback is a capacity that makes teshuvah possible for individuals and groups. In this chapter we will look at how leaders create a leadership culture that is transparent about its assumptions, values, and goals and accountable to track their progress on important goals and objectives.

We are not asked to "rebuke" our neighbor just because of our own personal agendas. We give feedback because we have communal values and goals that we need to honor. Leaders are committed to do SVP to build community consensus around key facts, trends and forces, values and strategic goals. Now we ask them to clarify their priorities and implement their plans—to be accountable.

Accountability: Transparent Decision Making

If we are going to have a more transparent feedback environment we need to become more transparent about our decision-making process. How do we decide how to prioritize the various initiatives that come out of planning. In chapter 2 we talked about the different gifts that members bring. We reflected on the fact that many business people try to bring their business tool kit directly to the service of the synagogue and sometimes fail to see how the multiple gifts of others must be woven into a shared language. There are times, however, when we really need the gifts of business language and logic.

Handoff to the Finance Committee

"If there is no meal, there is no Torah, if there is no Torah, there is no meal" (*Avot* 3:21). The task forces will not all complete their work at the same time. One group may have the modest goal of scheduling one or two new social functions. Another may have a complex facility task. What questions should they consider? At some point all of these SVP hopes and initiatives need to be placed within the structure of a business plan. The planning leaders need to give the Finance Committee a set of assumptions about revenues and expenses so that they can do their job and put these plans into the language of business budgets. We cannot effectively implement our synagogue values, visions, and goals without a financial road map—without resources there is little Torah.

The following are some questions planning leaders should be prepared to answer.

1. Can We Increase Revenue?

When leaders are evaluating a plan to increase revenue, they must ask a series of questions. Let's take the case of a congregation that wanted to expand their preschool.

If they increase the preschool, will new members come? They can look at their waiting lists and at the demand at other centers. Does their waiting list tell the whole story? Are people discouraged from considering them because they have heard about the waiting list? Is the population of children ages two to five growing? Are current competitors about to expand their services? Are new competitive programs being planned? There are many unknowns in estimating demand.

If there is a waiting list and they can increase their capacity, they have a good prospect of benefiting from this demand. New students, however, do not always show up at once. If students can't afford the full tuition, how will demand be affected by the scholarship policy?

Leaders must make best estimates of future membership, school enrollment, and program attendance. These are hard to predict. If leaders become immobilized over making estimates on major issues, they may pay more attention to smaller tactical issues. Finance needs to understand the big assumptions.

2. Can We Reduce Risks?

Sometimes we need to invest money without the hope of a cost benefit. I had a case where there was a hazardous drop-off near the playground. They needed a fence. Many congregations ignore hazards if they don't seem an immediate risk. They don't see the return on investment of fixing them. I have seen cases where there was hazardous wiring, lack of security, poor financial controls, poorly lit walkways, inadequate snow removal, and other situations that could lead to grave risks. Leaders must make investments to avoid harming a member. Failing to act raises some legal liability issues. Reducing risk is not just a business issue, it is a values issue.

3. Can We Enhance a Core Value?

There are many situations in which congregational leaders need to invest resources in areas with no immediate payback. If we believe that every child is in the image of God (betselem elohim), then we will find various approaches to teach Torah to them. A school might need to recruit a teacher who can work with students with learning differences or train existing teachers. This initiative would not immediately change the business plan of the congregation. It might increase the credibility of the leadership community by demonstrating that their actions are aligned with their values.

4. Can We Address an Unmet Need?

In some cases, there may not be an obvious income stream attached to an initiative. In other cases, you may be simply enhancing your membership or addressing a core congregational value. One could argue that a youth program might be justified simply to provide more continuity for older teens. One might argue that this activity helps maintain the family membership after the beney mitsvah, post-religious school period. Often leaders will have to make these investments without a clear sense of return. Members leave for many reasons, and exit interviews are usually sketchy. It may not be clear how much an incremental effort to develop youth programs will yield in terms of retention so leaders may have to make these investments without a clear sense of return.

5. Can We Reduce Costs?

A cost-benefit analysis is a relatively simple technique for deciding whether to make a change. Add up the value of the benefits of a course of action, and subtract the costs associated with it. Costs and benefits may be one-time or ongoing. You need to estimate the payback period. This is the time it takes for the benefits of a change to repay its costs. The percent of the investment that is returned each year is the return on investment.

Investments to reduce costs depend on accurate estimates of the investments and the stream of cost savings. Planners often get excited about cost savings because they can see how the return on investment works. Investing in new programs to increase demand (such as the pre-school, as discussed above) seem often less certain because estimating demand is somewhat less concrete than reviewing current costs.

6. Can We Identify Short-Term and Long-Term Benefits?

You may also want to look at different actions in term of their short-term or long-term benefit, or return on investment. You may think that aging baby boomers will want new and different kinds of adult education. In the recent study (Sales 2004), this was not a highly rated need. Should you invest in this today to take advantage of opportunities to meet the needs of these future empty nesters?

The research on members in their early thirties is that they have particular needs. They want to connect with other young couples. Should the leadership invest in developing a young adult congregation? Should they allocate key staff time to this even though it may take three to five years to realize the benefit? It may seem to make sense as a long-term strategy. Many of the boards making these decisions are not very representative of this age group. How do you get them to consider the emerging needs of this group? Part of SVP is to assess whether you are investing in growth opportunities or patching up old programs that are past their prime. Because of how managerial most boards are, it is much more likely for them to seek to patch up an old program than to invest in new ones.

On the other hand it is difficult if all of the initiatives are long term. Leaders can be discouraged if they don't see steady progress. It is important that leaders do enough things to keep short-term gains flowing. In SVP we look for ideas that can be put into action. We call them fast-track ideas. We may see them in a parlor meeting or in an early workshop. We would not rush to judgment on a major long-term decision, but some ideas are low risk and low cost. Why not give them a try now?

7. Can We Consider Multiple Options?

Grid Analysis is a useful technique to use for making a decision. It is most effective where you have a number of good alternatives and many factors to take into account. Listing benefits and weighing them is a core marketing task. The weighted benefits approach provides a formal tool for doing this kind of analysis.

Framing Decisions:
Developing Scenarios, Exploring Implications

In some congregations the planning group develops several scenarios in order to visualize the implications of each goal. This has been particularly helpful in considering decisions to build or move. They use all of the data from the SVP process. They consider the various initiatives. They then ask what kind of structure they will need to hold these missions. The facilities task force develops a profile of several choices, and then the planners engage in dialogue about the pros and cons of each path.

The implication question can be a useful tool here. This approach comes from a very helpful book on sales called SPIN Selling (SPIN stands for "Situation, Problem, Implications, Needs Fulfillment"; Rackham 1988). When decision makers contemplate the implications of an initiative, they sort through their own thoughts. When they emerge, they may be more sympathetic for the need for action. As one veteran salesperson once told me, "The seller doesn't sell—the buyer buys." I suggest you invite your board to consider these questions; you may get more buy-in. Review each objective in terms of the questions in the table on the following page.

Implication Questions

Implication Questions	**Leadership Responses**
If we made the investments in time and money that are called for, how positive an impact would it have on our critical needs and values?	
If we did not make the investments in time and money that are called for, how negative an impact would it have on our critical needs and values?	

It can be helpful to provide planners with a narrative for their plans. You could use the implication questions in a Bibliodrama of the parable of the spies. You might ask one of the reluctant leaders what life would be like if they all stayed in the wilderness of Paran. What is the implication for that choice?

Once we have leaders asking great implication questions we can encourage them to ask a needs fulfillment question. What would it be like if we could unite our people and walk with the ark and the presence of God into the new land? What would it be like if we could motivate a whole range of committees and task forces to work together with shared purpose and renewed energy (ruaḥ)?

Steering Committee Accountability:
Final Recommendations

The steering committee is responsible to lead the joint meeting of the board and the steering committee. In this meeting they propose a recommended set of charges to committees and task forces.

In some groups the steering committee will be dismissed and an implementation or governance committee, or the executive committee, will take over. A leadership group must take responsibility for gathering up the learning from the next six to twelve months and prepare some final recommendations.

Board Accountability:
Initiative Tracking Process

The board needs to hold the steering committee responsible to make recommendations. Then the board needs to role model accountability by tracking the most important goals and objectives at its meetings.

One helpful tool is the initiative tracker. The leadership identifies some of the most important goals and puts down the estimated completion date. The tracker is reviewed by the executive committee and staff throughout the year so that leaders can see how they are tracking toward their milestones. Note that the tracker simply provides concrete observations. It does not blame anyone for what has happened. It simply presents the facts.

קדימה **In my experience the dominant condition in synagogues is that people are prone to avoidance.**

How do we avoid embarrassing board members with incomplete work? I suggest you only review this quarterly with the board and focus on milestones completed. Do not criticize "incomplete work" publicly but affirm groups that have "stepped forward" and affirm accountability!

In some cases the steering committee or an implementation committee, rather than the executive committee, will take the responsibility to monitor and report progress on the plan. They touch base with groups and help them step forward. They try to integrate their efforts. They champion communications on progress. They celebrate success!

Feedback

As the teams go to work in Workshop 3 leaders will observe their performance and their teamwork. Over time it will be important to have conversations with committee chairs. How do we do this? In my experience the dominant condition in synagogues is that people are prone to avoidance.

Accountability conversations are hard to start because there are few job descriptions for committees and few written goals. Leaders are afraid to confront others because they are not sure how. They are also concerned about alienating the volunteers they have worked so hard to recruit.

In synagogues the president will be challenged to give formal feedback to paid staff and less formal feedback to volunteer staff (officers, chairs etc.). How should the President and other leaders think about these relationships? As I mentioned in chapter 2, the synagogue is not purely a business but it does need the wise use of some business tools. Let's look at two approaches to congregational relationships developed by the Alban Institute's Susan Beaumont.

Supervision and Feedback: Employment Relationships versus Covenantal Relationships

Supervision Relationships*

	Covenantal Relationships (Benevolence)	Employment Relationships (Utilitarian)
Nature of the Psychological Contract	The entity with the greater power looks out for the best interest of those with lesser power.	Collectively, we pursue a course of action that produces the greatest "pleasure over pain" for the greatest number of people.
Focus	Mutual need, Mutual promise; Mutual relationship	Supply and demand; Maximize bottom line; Outcomes
Values	Submission; Protecting the "least of these;" The pursuit of justice, righteousness, and mercy	Acceptance; Fairness; Equity
Objective of the Relationship	Fulfillment of a promise	Fulfillment of a contract
Outcomes Sought	Restored community; Right relationship; A blessed future	Career satisfaction; Monetary reward; Professional growth; Job security
Staff Members Are	Ministry participants; Pastoral care recipients	Resources to be employed

*A version of this chart appears on page 27 in *When Moses Meets Aaron* (see p.267)."

	Covenantal Relationships (Benevolence)	Employment Relationships (Utilitarian)
Accountability requires	Clearly stating expectations; Honoring the covenant; Reconciliation when the covenant is broken	Clearly stating expectations; Honoring the conditions of the contract; Mediation when the contract is broken
What failure looks like	Isolation; Broken relationship	Unemployment; Terminated relationship

The business model seeks to have a contractual relationship with associates based on utility—the maximum benefit to all. The covenantal model seeks to develop mutual need, commitments, and relationships.

Giving Feedback: Covenantal Caring Conversations

I believe that building healthy relationships is one of the desired outcomes of the synagogue's core mission. Nonprofit consultant Peter Drucker once commented that for nonprofits the process is a part of the product. Once we understand this we can see how synagogue feedback needs to strive to be somewhat above the letter of the law. I am not suggesting, nor is tradition demanding, that we ignore poor performance. The tradition asks us to give feedback in the least negative way so that we can maintain our relationships.

A Relationship-Building Process

The tradition values covenantal caring. This is more than a feeling of love or affection. It is the fundamental honor and respect that we owe another human being by virtue of God's creative power. God made humankind in God's image (betselem elohim), so we are bound by our covenant with God to honor our fellow human beings.

If one believes that the other person was created in the image of God, it is easier to imagine that they seek to be ministry participants. They have fundamental needs to serve the community that go beyond money, benefits, and career aspirations. Just as you feel part of a larger purpose, so might they. It also suggests that we have needs for relationships that are not just based on such business factors as supply and demand, return on investment, or short-term goals. Betselem elohim suggests one of our organizational goals is to develop and maintain relationships.

Learning the Hard Way

Because I have taken Jewish studies classes I am aware of some of the key values in our tradition. I also have learned about these as a father (three teenage sons at one time!) and husband, a son and a friend through sometimes painful trial and error. As a synagogue consultant I have had the relatively special experience of changing roles and experiencing new relationships. As a lay leader I gave suggestions or even direction to Jewish communal staff. As a consultant I am often treated by the lay leadership of the organization as the staff or worse "the help." Most often I am treated with respect—but not always. I have been exposed to some (blessedly few) uncaring volunteer and professional leaders over the years. I have arrived in towns where little was done to facilitate my stay or my work. I have been minimized and attacked. These often unexpected responses hurt. I have had my share of sleepless nights. I keep a pack of antacids in my briefcase next to my masking tape and markers.

I have taken the time to reflect on these painful experiences. If congregational conversations have caused me so much pain, as thick-skinned as I am, how does it feel to be a Jewish professional worker who is called to synagogue service to teach children, to lead the congregation in prayer, or to pastor to people's needs? How does it feel to be an overscheduled member and try to bring one's volunteer gifts to the congregation and feel ignored or minimized? It became clear to me that synagogues need congregational conversations that are worthy of their mission.

Covenantal Caring Conversations

How do we foster good relationships while providing honest feedback? First, we try to avoid doing harm. We are not to shame a person in public but speak gently in private first. We are to respect ourselves. Improper humility encourages us to think of ourselves as weak and powerless (grasshoppers). The covenantal caring conversation is based on having respectful relationships with others. Covenantal caring is not servitude. Rabbi Hillel's famous words speak of the need to find a balance between your needs and those of others: "If I am not for myself who will be for me? If I am only for myself what am I?" (*Avot* 1:14). These words require that we share our feelings with others when things don't seem to be working properly. The Torah encourages us to "reprove" our neighbor when we feel they are off the mark. In the same parasha it also asks us to love our neighbor as ourselves. We are to be empathetic and compassionate. The tradition thus encourages leaders to provide feedback but to do this in the most compassionate, caring, and respectful way. We are not empty handed. We can carry our reflections on Jewish values from Workshop 1.

How might these values shape our accountability conversation?

- Humility: I am "but dust and ashes," says Abraham (Genesis 18:27). When we are humble, we are much less likely to move carelessly without getting input from others. Humility makes us slower to judge.
- Respect for all: "Let the honor of your friend be as precious to you as your own" (*Avot* 2:15). When we respect someone, we see that person in full. We pay attention. Everyone has their strengths and weaknesses. Everyone, according to the tradition, has their day. When we respect others, we tend to render a more balanced view of them.
- Good manners: "If there is no Torah, there are no manners" (*Avot* 3:21). Good manners (derekh 'erets) help reduce the focus on our personal agenda and individual needs. If I am constantly thinking about the needs of others, I am less likely to do something insensitive. Good manners build a foundation for trust. They help lubricate the synagogue system.
- Self-respect: Since we are made in the image of God, we deserve respect. "And God created the human being in God's own image (betselem elohim)." While we are challenged to put ourselves in others' shoes, we are not asked to ignore our own legitimate needs, feelings, and wants. We have the right to stand up for ourselves.
- Self-control: "Who is strong? He who subdues his evil impulse, as it is said, He that is slow to anger is better than the mighty and he who rules his spirit than he who takes a city" (*Avot* 4:1). Many of our values require judgment. They are not black-and-white. Leaders need to take the time to patiently explain their decision-making processes. Leaders should take time to let others know their assumptions and values. When members give criticism leaders need to try to see this as information.

One quality that helps us make better decisions is to learn to control our emotions—particularly anger and defensiveness.

Leaders may be afraid to confront others because of lack of skills in this area. Often their frustration bubbles up in anger directed at volunteers. It may erupt during contract negotiations with professional staff. To reduce the risks of such explosions leaders need to find a way to engage in the right conversations at the right time. Having these kinds of conversations in private protects the dignity of both people while being true to the individuals' needs and those of the community. SVP has been an exercise in trying to help planners hold the right conversation. Healthy congregational conversations help keep conflict manageable.

How do you encourage accountability without adding to the culture of criticism that one finds in so many congregations? How do you give helpful feedback without alienating the volunteers? How do you give feedback to dedicated staff who work long hours to help build the community? How do you avoid such unhealthy practices as blaming, generalizing, and labeling?

It is not enough to know some Jewish values. You also need the "how-to" in order to put them into practice. I suggest leaders start at the top and learn to give helpful feedback. Dr. Marshall Rosenberg developed the concept of nonviolent communication. He suggests that we can make our concerns known to others but in a nonjudgmental way. He suggests that in nonviolent communication we describe to others:

- The concrete actions we are observing that are affecting our well-being
- How we are feeling in relation to what we are observing
- The needs, values, desires, etc., that are creating our feelings
- The concrete actions we request in order to enrich our lives (Rosenberg 1999)

Effective Feedback for Staff and Volunteers

There are times when leaders must gather information in order to provide a formal evaluation of a volunteer or paid staff person. Reviews may be summative, looking back and assessing what has happened in the past. What goals were met? What competencies were exhibited? Other reviews focus more on a formative approach, seeking to clarify opportunities for improvement in the future. They will try to reframe incidents and turn them into "learning opportunities."

Good feedback helps people to reflect on their performance throughout the year so that they are in a process of continuous improvement. When it comes time for their reviews, there are fewer surprises. When they look to the future with a formative plan, they do so with greater hope.

Sue's Last-Minute Call List (Tuesday afternoon)

Observations: Sue, I noticed that you made a request to our receptionist, Barb, on Tuesday afternoon for the office to do one hundred phone calls to recruit for our community Shabbat dinner this Friday.

Feelings: I am grateful for your hard work and dedication. I am, however, concerned about your request. Two staff members told me that they were confused about what to do.

Needs: I have been working with the whole staff team and our officers to provide more advance notice on all requests. The board felt we needed to reduce our deficit so we have one less person in the office vs. last year. Our budget makes the assumption that better planning can help the staff stage their work and reduce costs.

Request: I would like to request that you review your concerns with the executive director on Wednesday morning so that we can see if there are some immediate things that can be done for this Friday. Perhaps you could suggest a short list, maybe ten to fifteen names, of some of the members who have regularly attended. I would also like you to consider working with the committee to suggest some long-term approaches that might help create more consistent attendance at these dinners.

SVP CASE

It is the goal of a covenantal caring leadership to encourage people to tell leaders what is on their minds so that leaders can give them helpful feedback. This kind of leadership seeks to move more issues into the public arena.

If you build an environment of trust and become more skilled in giving feedback, it will be a lot easier for Sue and everyone else to receive feedback.

There are some concerns and motivations that we can't discern unless the other leader discloses them. Sue can't know how the president feels unless he shares his feelings and needs. Synagogue leaders need to learn to hold themselves accountable to manage difficult conversations and to learn new skills in giving effective feedback.

The SVP process has gone to great lengths to define major areas of focus: values, strategies, and goals. The president is empowered to speak to Sue on behalf of the planning and leadership community. Without his sharing what is known to him (disclosing his values for teamwork and prioritization of resources), valuable information for Sue is hidden or avoided. The covenantal caring conversation is good management. It is also a foundational process for building a covenantal community. The covenantal leader believes that Sue needs and wants to better understand the leader's values and hopes. The covenantal leader is optimistic about this relationship and the power of congregations to convene these covenantal conversations.

Self-Assessment

One vehicle for encouraging paid and volunteer staff to disclose their thoughts and feelings is the self-assessment. When you ask someone to assess himself or herself, you help the person organize his or her feelings and needs. That person is then in a much better position to identify things that are working well in addition to considering things that might be strengthened. Let's look at a simple template for a volunteer or paid staff self-assessment. It builds on some of the work done by the Reform and Conservative movement in developing helpful feedback processes.

Committee Leader Self-Assessment
1. What goals did you set for the year?
2. What resources did you identify and request?
3. What difficulties or barriers did you face?
4. What can you do to overcome these barriers or difficulties?
5. What can the synagogue board do to help you overcome these barriers or difficulties?
6. What are some accomplishments that stand out in your mind?

7. What are some skills, talents, or areas of knowledge did you demonstrate?
8. What is the most important thing you learned this year?
9. How have you grown Jewishly through these experiences?

The self-assessment encourages disclosure between key officers and chairs. With the benefit of the chairs' self-assessment, the officers can also share their feelings and needs and explore some requests that might help the synagogue fulfill its mission. This process could be used with a wide range of volunteers but it must be role modeled at the top. Start there.

Using Covenantal Caring Conversations with Yourself

Answer the questions above to do your own self-assessment. Then go back and look at the words, tone, and feelings you used to describe your performance. Were you overly judgmental in your self-assessment? Go back and talk to yourself about your observations, feelings, and needs. Then make a request of yourself. How did this conversation feel? When we are too critical of ourselves, we put a stumbling block before our ability to do an honest self-assessment (ḥeshbon nefesh). We may become so critical that we just shut down. This doesn't help create passionate Jews or leaders.

Conclusion: Better Communication, More Effective Teamwork

We have explored board accountability. We have reviewed language that helps leaders be more transparent about assumptions and factors that shape their decisions. SVP seeks to encourage accountability by ensuring groups to accept responsibility for working together to implement their goals and visions. SVP encourages covenantal caring conversations because these will lead to healthier relationships and more effective teams.

When I was young, I used to play with what we called Chinese handcuffs back then. When you pull on them, they get tighter and tighter. They cut off circulation. Only when you relax the handcuffs do they become more pliable. Covenantal caring conversations (social hall, board room, or parking lot) help leaders have real communications without cutting off the other person's circulation. As people move forward from avoidance to engagement, they will find that the old handcuffs loosen and they can step forward into healthy and accountable teams.

Questions for Reflection

1. Why is it important to hold a joint steering committee and board meeting on assignments?
2. How do you track goals? How could this be improved?
3. How can you start having some more intentional covenantal caring conversations between officers and chairs?

PART 5

Hoḥma:
Lessons Learned

The teaching of the LORD is perfect,
　　renewing life;
　　the decrees of the LORD are enduring,
　　making the simple wise;
The precepts of the LORD are just,
　　rejoicing the heart;
　　the instruction of the LORD is lucid,
　　making the eyes light up.
　　　　　　　—Psalm 19:8-9

In this section I review some of the lessons learned from congregational planning. By working together we discovered multiple approaches, multiple paths, for different communities. By working faithfully we gained a hopeful vision and, I think, some wisdom.

I share some of the things that worked well and that need more work. By being open to feedback I try to see criticism as new information that can illuminate—"light up"—the road ahead.

17.

Leadership Lessons: Unleashing Congregational Energy

Ben Zoma said, "Who is wise? One who learns from all people."

—Avot 4:1

Synagogue Visioning and Planning is a work in progress. It began with some workshop experiments in 2003–2004. In 2004 I began to consolidate some of what I had learned and to formalize these tools. In these three years I have been as much a student as a teacher. I have borrowed from many writers from the world of synagogues, education, consulting, sociology, management, and marketing. I strongly believe as a matter of faith that I can learn from many different people. For me Torah is a living tradition, and it gains new meaning as serious Jews weave its ancient truth with their current realities. I came late to Torah texts. I have a vivid memory of my struggles to engage the texts, the tefilah, and the traditions. I believe the Torah lives and breathes as we turn it—and it turns us. I'm still turning.

Even as I write this last chapter, my desk is covered with stacks of open books. I am constantly being challenged by new ideas. There is a legal pad by my bed and sticky notes all over my monitor. I ask for congregations to raise their energy level. I try to model energetic leadership. I also encourage planning disciplines. I would like to say that I have come to demonstrate a new level of self-discipline, but actually it was

219

my editor who called and gently but firmly said, "Stop writing! It's a first book. It's time to go to press."

I am proud to acknowledge several influences, as it is written, "Whoever reports a saying in the name of its originator brings the world to redemption" (*Avot* 6:6). I have been guided by my colleagues at Alban and in the synagogue world. I took the initiative to put myself in a position to learn from others. I have drawn some major lessons from this planning work, but I have also come to realize that there are multiple paths for different congregations, contexts, and times. I encourage leaders to come away from this chapter with an appreciation for the diversity of congregations (multiple paths) and the potential of the planning (hopeful steps).

At the end of this process I started mining my files for lessons learned. When I added up the list, I had eighteen. The number eighteen stands for life (l'hayyim). Coincidence, you ask? I don't know if I have fully described congregations, but I feel as if I have fully lived with them. I do not know if I have fully honored the work of my colleagues, but I know their ideas have brought my work to life. I am not sure if I have "written the book" I dreamed of, but I am proud to have captured some of the things leaders hope for.

I also need to acknowledge all that I have learned from congregations. I have worked to disguise most case studies. Most represent composite sketches of several congregations. I cannot cite them by page number, but they have stepped forward on to these pages. I feel I have had the opportunity to bring my life experience to great projects and wonderful people. By stepping forward I helped meet synagogue life halfway. A core group of congregations have used most of the elements of the model since 2004, and another ten have used significant elements of the workshops for leadership development. When I stepped forward, others stepped toward me. These leaders were talented and successful. They had to open themselves to some of my ideas and exercises. At times I challenged the existing leadership. Some may have seen me as a rival at times. It is said that "no man loves a rival in his craft, but a sage loves a rival" (*Genesis Rabbah 32:2*). I appreciate the courage it took for leaders to let an outsider have a significant role in their leadership. I have learned that

קדימה I encourage leaders to come away from this chapter with an appreciation for the diversity of congregations (multiple paths) and the potential of the strategies (hopeful steps).

one of the things that limits the use of congregational mentors, coaches, consultants, and resources is fear. Leaders are afraid of what others will find. They are afraid they will be judged harshly—asked why they haven't ever developed goals for the year, etc. This fear is particularly true of congregations facing demographic decline. They are often in a state of denial. The first step for these leaders, according to Jim Collins (2005), is to face the "hard truths." I appreciate the courage of leaders who entered workshops that committed them to engage some hard truths!

A Vision of Congregational Learning

Here I offer some lessons that need to be urgently considered, some hopeful steps, and some practical advice about multiple paths of planning. I offer eighteen lessons about congregational leadership, and planning. In cases where I have suggested multiple paths, I have noted some of these. In each case I will also leave you with a hopeful step for the future.

1. Synagogue leadership development is about expanding the size and vision of the core leadership.

Synagogue leadership can get set in its ways. They can get in the habit of looking inward—talking to the same core leaders. They can get stuck reworking the same missions. Leaders need to go deeper to explore their relationships with their teammates. They need to look outward to learn from others (congregational visits, denomination resources, etc.) They need to see the gifts of their neighbors. Leon Puttler of Kehillat Israel in Lansing noted the following while debriefing: "I was excited to see some new people step forward to lead these work groups. We have many talented members. It's great that some of them are adopting leadership roles within our community."

The theory of servant leadership is that leaders are judged by how they develop others. Model leaders are very clear about the hard truths of expanding the core, but they are confident that if they create a disciplined learning community, they can attract and motivate great talent. They realize that in order to help prospects step forward, they need to create a project that is important, takes advantage of prospects' gifts, can be fun, and would achieve some worthwhile results (be successful).

Hopeful Steps

Whether SVP is used to create a detailed plan or to develop some board agreements, these tools attract new people and ideas. The process of looking makes it easier to look outward, inward, and around to tomorrow.

2. SVP creates a choreography in which prospects and solicitors can step forward onto the leadership stage and say, "Here I am."

Core leaders have often lamented the consumer attitude of peripheral members. SVP leaders try to work understand consumers better. They gather data; they try to be empathetic marketers. They watch members in services and at events. They listen to them in parlor meetings and workshops. They try to avoid simply running a customer service desk. SVP helps leadership from going negative by always coupling the consumer's right to shared input with their membership obligation to be part of the solution—to reframe consumer issues from complaint to collaboration.

You want members to share their views, but as part of the team—not outside it. You want them to say, like Abraham, "Here I am" ("Heneni").

SVP goals gain more momentum because there is already a group of people ready to work on them and some support from the wider stakeholder community. Congregations have many goals. Some are formal; most are informal. You know you will have services on Friday even if the board has not passed a recent motion. Strategic goals, however, have urgency because they are something that needs to be addressed now. We have learned that combining the goal idea and the people to work on it helps create urgency for action.

Consumers give input by . . .	As members they are asked . . .	SVP leaders respond by . . .
Suggesting changes.	To go to a parlor meeting.	Welcoming them, organizing a listening session.
Providing feedback on congregational questionnaires.	What they would like to do about their most important suggestion.	Carefully identifying the members' concerns and recruiting those with skills and motivation to work on certain projects.

Consumers give input by . . .	As members they are asked . . .	SVP leaders respond by . . .
Asking what will be done with data.	To participate in three large stakeholder workshops.	Organizing effective, relevant, and fun workshops.
Demanding that their voices be heard in planning.	To engage the diverse voices of other stakeholders.	Creating a safe place that respects difference.
Asking questions about implementation.	To join one of the committees and task force in Workshop 3.	Making wise assignments. Giving each team clear and helpful direction. Clarifying the roles of lay chairs and staff leaders.

Hopeful Steps

Like the rituals in Leviticus there is an underlying hopefulness that you can learn by doing. Prospects learn that SVP synagogue leaders will work hard to get to know them by encouraging them to step forward in parlor meetings and workshops. Leaders learn that they can actually do this team-building work. Both are changed in the process.

3. Steering committees learn that soliciting new leaders takes courage ('omets lev)— it puts their credibility on the line.

The steering committee develops a hopeful vision of a future leadership that is larger and more engaged. They have a list of practical steps. At some point they have to go out and recruit members to go to parlor meetings. SVP starts with some risk taking. Lech-Lecha (Go Forward on the Way) leaders have to move beyond their comfort level.

Multiple Paths

Not all solicitors are equal. It is sometimes necessary to develop a range of options for those with less energy for recruitment. In some cases we had fewer parlor meetings (total of fifty interviews). In some cases there is a smaller stakeholder group (thirty to forty people). In one case where parlor meetings floundered, stakeholders filled out the questionnaire at the first workshop to ensure some data is available.

4. Parlor meetings are purposeful:
they gather both paper and people.

The parlor meeting is an important SVP ritual. Parlor meetings are usually successful. SVP identifies new leaders and inspires old ones. The parlor meetings help the steering committee identify people with the motivation to plan. The publicity about the planning process excites and energizes some fresh faces. Some more seasoned leaders choose to come back into the leadership circle to participate. Parlor meetings are an important source of data. They help clarify critical issues. They also are a source for recruits for the planning process.

Parlor meetings demonstrate the leadership's commitment to gathering information about members' needs and wants. They create a buzz—favorable word of mouth for the process. Alban Institute research has argued that creating this word of mouth is an essential element in making leadership more attractive to current and future prospects. Parlor meetings are usually a hit!

Multiple Paths

Some congregations do not want to do parlor meetings. They may have done them in recent years. They may have just completed a survey. They want to use the three workshops for their board and the long-range planning committee. Many large, successful congregations have this view. Since they are in the stability stage of their life cycles, they are less interested in welcoming new planners or revisioning. I have found that I can help these groups plan, but they are less able to overcome deep cultural issues without input from the larger planning community.

Hopeful Steps

Parlor meetings reach from 40 to 120 people. Probably 50 percent of these go on to be stakeholders. Even those who don't go on to join the workshops have a positive experience because their voices are heard.

5. SVP creates a practice field to increase
the leadership team's capacity.

Let's be realistic: SVP is not a intensive corporate management training program. Large corporations can spend thousands of dollars per person to develop leaders. They usually pull from a select group of prospects who have the dedication to invest time and money to spend a week in training. They can recruit well beyond the walls of the synagogue. These trainees will return to organizations that have high expectations for them. They will often receive incentives (reward and punishment) to motivate them to use new skills.

SVP's focus is the leadership team—the community. It works with a cross section of volunteers—"the willing"—with a limited number of volunteer hours. The strategy is to work with people who may not be natural leaders in their work or community life. SVP gives them a taste of strategic work and exposes them to some core leadership tasks. It invites them to do some learning in a fairly safe and collaborative environment.

The SVP work plan requires that they pace themselves for the twelve-month journey. Tools and skills are provided to help the steering committee members get to know each other. It is often assumed that just because they work on a committee or the board that they understood each other's skills and interests. SVP provides the opportunity for them to test these new tools and disciplines in real synagogue situations: a practice field, a leadership learner's minyan.

The Practice Field

Skill Needed	Skill Learned	Skill Practiced
Forming a team	Understanding each other's background, skills, and interests; clarifying roles and responsibilities	Creating leadership profile, creating shared steering committee goals, critical issues, team expectations
Gathering data	Developing a congregational profile briefing book	Using the briefing book to develop implications for actions in Workshops 2 and 3
Running listening sessions	Conducting structured group interviews	Conducting parlor meetings
Debriefing congregational input	Debriefing the steering committee	Writing up parlor meeting observations

Skill Needed	Skill Learned	Skill Practiced
Developing shared meaning	Writing the dominant themes report	Reviewing dominant themes with the steering committee and stakeholders
Developing shared values	Creating values statement	Presenting the values statement to the congregation and using it as a guide in other workshops; integrating it into congregational life (sermons, hallways, Web site, school, etc.)
Developing a communications plan	Developing a communications calendar that helps build interest, engagement, and credibility.	Learning to update the congregation about the overall plan, parlor meetings, stakeholder sessions, emerging plans, the town meeting, the annual meeting, SVP stories, and SVP people
Providing a charge to committees	Developing direction for committees and task forces; working with a team charter	Developing the charters and getting board approval; recruiting leaders to join existing committees and new committees

6. Leadership changes (turning; teshuvah) take time.

Transformation is seldom a realistic planning goal. There are transformative moments, and there are transformative experiences for some individuals. Given the synagogue culture, the promise of transformed congregations seems like an awfully big claim for most of the planning I have experienced. Judaism encourages us to be careful what we vow! One of the challenges I face is managing my own enthusiasm. While I have a passion for SVP, I try to help leaders find a realistic path. That is why we speak of "multiple paths."

Synagogue agreements are fragile. Groups can go through planning and six months later get some unexpected news. A major donor may take back a gift. A building project comes in over budget. A key staff person decides to leave. One leader may have a health crisis. Sometimes it's a hurricane that rattles everyone. A membership estimate doesn't come in as planned. A conflict emerges that distracts the leadership. Planning seeks to bring to the surface some of these issues while the stakeholders are gathered, but there are no guarantees that life will follow the plan. Progress in one area can be neutralized somewhere else. Most congregations do not move in a linear pattern. Like our biblical ancestors we often take two steps forward and one step back.

Many of the congregations I work with feel somewhat "stuck." They are not very confident about their potential for change. It is important to set realistic goals and to celebrate their success. In some of the early projects planners made the mistake of being too ambitious. As a leader, I tend to focus on strategy and somewhat less on team building and morale. All of us need to learn to run with our strengths and try to strengthen undeveloped areas. I have learned that if goals are too much of a stretch they can get people stretched out of shape. Leaders can end up reinforcing the narrative of frustration: "Nothing gets done here." Celebrations ritualize that we can build new leadership one small successful action item at a time.

Celebrating Messages about Mitsvahs and Milestones

Mitsvahs and Milestones	Celebratory Message	Celebration Event
Start up steering committee	Leaders have "stepped up" to look at future	Bulletin article
Finish parlor meetings	Congregational invitation to brunch to honor participants	Congregational Kiddush lunch in honor of participants with service honors

Mitsvahs and Milestones	Celebratory Message	Celebration Event
Complete draft of values statement	Include in bulletin; insert in prayer service	Make it topic of a sermon Frame stories in foyer
Complete draft of goals statement	Offer congregational meeting led by representatives of board and steering committee.	Congregational meeting with great food, allowing members to share feedback and even join certain work groups; end with singing!
Key committees report progress	Honor whole committee—let them present to the board as a team	Do profiles of the committees, posting pictures, key action items, and testimonials about their work in the foyer

Hopeful Steps

What is possible is a gradual growth in leadership capacity. Leadership teams can learn some new skills. Individual leaders can gain confidence and adopt these tools to make a difference. Congregations can get unstuck and step forward to the next stage of their life cycles. They can celebrate their success and build energy for future work.

7. Leaders learn to work with the Jewish calendar.

As I became more literate about Jewish living, I became more in sync with the Jewish calendar. I came to appreciate its seasons. There are times when SVP is in sync with the calendar. One congregation had major news to report by the May annual meeting. Another was able to tell some visioning stories during the high holidays. Momentum is often challenged by the three weeks' hiatus around Passover or the three weeks around the high holidays or summer vacation. All the congregations I have worked with experienced a loss of momentum over the summer. They had to get back on the phone in the fall and re-dig those wells.

Leaders can work on keeping up communications in the summer, but they need to be realistic about the need to reengage in the fall. Task forces might be formed in May but not be able to meet consistently until September. Future SVP congregations will be better served if task forces start up by February so that they have at least three months to work before summer, or they should begin in the fall.

As you manage the synagogue calendar, you will become more focused on the need for a twelve-month board plan. If the board feels they need to complete a whole list of board improvement goals overnight, it feeds the narrative of hopelessness. The twelve-month board members have time to create opportunities for team building, key issue reviews, and so on.

Hopeful Steps

Leaders can learn to work with the synagogue calendar to anticipate the stops and starts that are inherent in planning. They can develop a twelve-month board plan that identifies several key issues that will be addressed during the year. If a problem arises that dominates the next few meetings, it need not prevent the leadership from refocusing on key goals.

8. Leaders can help teammates grab hold of leadership.

I have explained the need for more disciplined handoffs between the steering committee and the stakeholders, between leaders and followers, and between current boards and future boards. The kind of team building discussed for the steering committee (chapter 9) is an important ritual that boards need to embrace.

In order to maintain leadership learning it is important that congregations ensure more continuity from one board to the next. In order to achieve this, nomination and bylaws committees should consider ways to create such continuity. They need to balance presidential appointments to the executive committee and some leaders who are following a ladder of succession. There also needs to be continuity of ideas. Leaders should emphasize the importance of the briefing book and the written goals, values, and committee plans so that you can demonstrate that you value the past work of others. SVP learning must have some continuity of leadership to make certain that the planning traditions are passed on.

Planning processes brings key organizational issues into focus. SVP is focused on identifying and engaging leaders and the importance of volunteer management. New volunteers need to be trained and matched up with the right work. Committees and task forces need to be properly chartered and led. Groups need timely data and access to resources. Chairs need to get feedback on their progress. All of this takes administrative leadership. If congregations are to go from good to great, they need more disciplined practices. These may take several years and will not usually be demonstrated in any assessment you do of SVP at the twelve-month mark.

How Governance Finally Got Going

One congregation was having a tough governance issue. They wanted to reduce the size of the board. They also wanted to get more consistent commitments from the board. The board had tried to change the situation on several occasions. The large coalition kept this issue alive. Ultimately they agreed to set more challenging standards. Several members who had poor attendance records agreed to resign. Others who did not want to meet the criteria of serving on a committee agreed to step down. These vacancies allowed new members to take the stage. It took the authority of the larger group to empower this governance committee to do its work.

SVP CASE

SVP is intentionally designed to motivate the board to create a governance committee and to support the development of a leadership development program, which we call Synagogue Board Development (SBD).

Synagogue Board Development

SVP Insight	SBD Task	SBD Opportunity
Leaders are not on the same page	Create a twelve-month team-building plan throughout the leadership year	Do an annual retreat to develop better relationships, more trust, and shared values

SVP Insight	SBD Task	SBD Opportunity
Leaders don't have shared facts	Keep congregational profile up to date	Spend time orienting members about key facts; connect the facts to key board topics throughout the year
Leaders don't reflect on their processes	Do SBD board self-assessment	Develop a twelve-month board agenda
Leaders don't have shared goals	Develop SMART goals for the year	Build a culture of accountability
Leaders don't know how to give or receive feedback	Create self-assessment for chairs; create dialogue process between chairs and officers	Encourage healthy leadership conversations

Multiple Paths

SVP was originally designed as a short leadership development process. I was not hired to guide the implementation. I chose to limit my role because I felt the original model empowered the congregational leaders. It also reduced the cost of the consultation. I have changed my mind about this in recent years. I have concluded that providing support for implementation is critical. Today I would rather cut some elements of the program to fit the budget in order to include this support. I now offer ongoing teleconferences for task forces and committees. This book will allow planning congregations to do more of this as a self-guided process. In this book I spend a lot more time describing committee chartering, initiative tracking, budgeting, and accountability (chapters 15 and 16) than I did in the field in 2003–2004.

9. Synagogue strategists need to be sensitive to size.

SVP can be adapted to meet the needs of congregations of different sizes. Large congregations are often staff-driven because they can afford many highly skilled staff and because their members tend to expect a high level of professionalism and performance. The staff are held accountable for high levels of performance and execution. Lay leaders may bring creative ideas. Some may choose to work "shoulder to shoulder" with staff, but in the end the staff will often be held accountable for their performance. In such a culture lay leaders' follow-through on their assignments may be inconsistent. Staff may be fearful to let lay folks make mistakes. In such a culture some staff may decide it is easier just to do it with their paid professional team.

The way organizations are designed determines the results they will produce. A staff-driven culture will end up making staff-driven changes. The large multigenerational congregation is usually not designed to make significant or sudden changes. Large congregations need to address shared values and goals, but they need to do so with more careful attention to staff's visions and core leaders' concerns. Planning work must be appropriate to its context.

Multiple Paths

In large congregations SVP needs to get more direction from the professional staff up front. Parlor meetings work well in large congregations. The values exercise can be helpful. In large congregations much more care needs to be taken in working with the steering committee on debriefing data and preparing a charge to task forces and committees. Through the staff interviews and staff meetings planners should have an idea of the staff's vision and some of their wish list. This vision needs to be incorporated in the charge to committees and task forces. Leaders need to make sure that staff are given the most important assignments.

In such cultures I would be willing to skip the goal-setting process and move directly from shared values to committee and task force assignments. The goals workshop is effective for clarifying direction and seeing who wants to work on key assignments. If the culture is staff-driven, the whole dynamic of people "voting with their feet" may be ephemeral. There will be too much fanfare in group setting and not enough energy in implementation.

Large, older, multigenerational congregations have more entrenched core leaders. There is the board, then the executive committee, and then an inner circle of past presidents and trustees. They all want the congregation to grow, mature, and prosper, but they are reluctant to allow new people to reshape too much of the culture. In some cases it is simply not realistic or desirable to empower a large stakeholder group. It is better to do parlor meetings, gather data, and empower the steering committee to make recommendations.

Smaller congregations, by definition, are often more managerial because the volunteers need to be very hands-on to keep the place running. With smaller congregations SVP must be downsized as necessary to create attainable goals. They shouldn't have an assignment they can't realistically perform. That could weaken their confidence.

10. Creating the briefing book builds consensus and trust.

The SVP briefing book development models many important leadership skills. It teaches leaders to look at the external and internal environment and to establish what is important to learn. It encourages them to draw implications about these facts and their context. This is very productive. When all the stakeholders are empowered with the same data, it creates more trust. You can observe this increased trust in the increased capacity of the diverse stakeholders to work together on tough issues. The board and steering committee are able to see that the development of a briefing book builds ongoing capacity for leadership development and board training and orientations. Congregations that have chosen to use only parts of the process have usually chosen to create a briefing book. They have all found that it is helpful to get the community to get a consensus on the facts before they try to build a consensus on the implications of the data.

Multiple Paths

The briefing books vary a great deal. Some communities have helpful data from their federations. Others have outdated data or no data at all. Some teams have executive directors with accessible and user-friendly internal data; others have little useful data. Some teams have talented volunteers with consulting, publishing, and project management skills. They create very polished books. Others cut and paste the best they can. Recently I have worked to provide more of a template to help the congregations with fewer resources. I still believe developing some kind of briefing book is their hands-on responsibility.

Hopeful Steps

The briefing book process creates an opportunity for new gifts to come forward. Some leaders help craft well-written histories; others find someone skilled in creating graphs; some clergy write outstanding profiles of congregational programs; some financially oriented members create thorough financial executive summaries. All of the congregations I worked with created SVP briefing books that contain a values statement, strategic goals, and various action plans.

11. Creating a values statement demonstrates that collaboration is valued.

Most groups keep the values workshop in their process. The values workshop is perceived by most as meaningful, relevant, and fun! It is a great place to start. It honors what they can bring—not what they lack. We start by asking what is working well. The values workshop is not the same experience I had by going through three years of Melton or getting a master's degree at Spertus. I have had the opportunity to reflect over the last eight years about Jewish values. The values workshop at least puts the "V" word on the radar screen for most stakeholders.

When Jewish values are encountered in the planning process, stakeholders are in a more receptive position to absorb the new information. Those collaborative values are present in the workshop exercises and role modeled by steering committee members. Synagogue leaders have been preaching about values—often with disappointing results. I have found that stakeholders acquire new practices when they have a chance to try new things in a supportive collaborative atmosphere. The best results come when the stakeholders develop some key themes from the workshop and then the rabbi and some wordsmiths take the lead to weave them into a coherent statement that reflects their context and the Jewish tradition (see Resource 6 in the Appendix: Oceanside Jewish Center Values Statement). Combining their aspirations and traditional values of Jewish living, the SVP values statement can provide a framework for future adult education classes, family education programs, or leadership training sessions. If you have a values statement, you can weave it into the twelve-month board planner.

12. Public agreements about goals help people stay positive.

SVP is committed to creating public agreements about goals, objectives, and actions. In the teshuvah change process public confession is important: if you are changing your course, you need to say so in the presence of the community. The depth of the community consensus varies.

When stakeholders think about the future, they try to suspend old conflicts. Since they are dreaming, it doesn't pay to fight over future details. Good mediation focuses on the issues at hand. It tries to avoid chronicling all of the past conflicts. SVP seeks to mediate between new members and long-standing members, between the preschool parents and the empty nesters, between the observant and the less religious, etc. SVP encourages people to move forward. If members are to construct a new story, a positive vision of the future is critical. The new story helps build energy and reduces conflict over change.

> קיימה We had just come through a challenging rebuilding effort. SVP created an opportunity to engage seventy people in a positive, forward-looking project. New leaders and ideas emerged. As we face new decisions, we do so with some confidence.
>
> —Phil Perlmutter, Temple Avodah

Not all of the board participates in SVP. In the early congregations I worked with the planners simply referred the documents to the board for feedback. Just because they have been copied on the process does not mean they have really absorbed what is going on. Originally I overestimated the effectiveness of written updates. I found I needed to ritualize the practice of attaining steering committee and board agreements.

I came to consulting with the zeal of an entrepreneur. That passion served me in launching a variety of experiments. In my early years I was sometimes blindsided by the many and varied forces of resistance to change in synagogues. Sometimes my enthusiasm, or the enthusiasm of my planning leaders, had the effect of increasing elements of resistance.

Multiple Paths

As the SVP process has evolved, I have focused more attention on connecting the steering committee and the board in a dialogue about these emerging agreements. I encourage steering committee members and the board to meet to review the goals and to participate in a dialogue about the assignments to task forces and committees. In earlier groups the board was often only tangentially connected to SVP. I have found that it is extremely helpful to convene this conversation more formally.

Hopeful Steps

Developing a large coalition creates a memory of the commitments that are made. In this way it somewhat holds the feet of the leadership to the fire. The guiding coalition limits the power of some super-empowered individuals to stop initiatives. The large coalition allows the group to have the legitimacy to manage tough conflict issues.

13. More staff support helps build organizational discipline.

Developing organizational disciplines is a multi-year process. It is essential work. The investment will pay off over time. In the short term it can seem intimidating. To use Jim Collins's language, congregations need to get more staff resources "on their bus" (Collins 2005). I have found that many congregations with more than 450 members do not have a real executive director role. Rather than being staff-driven they are understaffed. Some just have an office secretary. Others have an administrator, but the person is often not empowered to do important community-building tasks. I have found that executive directors are able to help with the logistics of SVP. Some play an active role in recruitment. Others are very proactive in driving certain committees.

Executive directors can ease day-to-day burdens on lay leaders. They can also make a major impact on membership and volunteer development efforts. Lay leaders sometimes have to overfunction and micromanage many details because there is no one there to help. When the new staff person steps forward, it takes careful planning to ensure that he or she is empowered to perform the job. Lay leaders must learn when to step back. SVP congregations make a big investment in helping volunteers step forward. Increasing administrative support for volunteers helps their volunteer efforts to be more satisfying and productive. "SVP helped get us unstuck. It mobilized fundraising, facility, and welcoming committees. As they emerged, I could better resolve them" (Mike Schatz, Executive Director, Beth El).

14. SVP must work to be integrated with other planning processes.

SVP takes a great deal of energy. While SVP is in progress, sometimes staff are working to create new programs that would have a big impact on the plan. Some long-range planning groups or executive committees continue to move key decisions forward. Some personnel committees choose to give key staff serious feedback about their performance and contracts. Most of these are legitimate and appropriate tasks, but many of these groups would do better to sit back and take in the learning from SVP first. SVP gives them several alternative lenses relative to the decision they are making.

I have seen important goals developed outside of SVP. In other cases there are important issues that leaders decide to push forward without the consensus of the larger stakeholders group. In these cases, such side actions often demotivate the planning community.

Hopeful Steps

SVP works to ensure that the steering committee and board meetings on assignments and final recommendations. These meetings help bring to the surface emerging decisions that might otherwise happen outside of the stakeholder community. This is good learning for executive committee leaders who sometimes fail to keep the general board informed. Synagogue board development was created to help keep leaders on the same page.

15. Multiple strategies are needed for underdeveloped volunteer cultures.

SVP can increase the number of people willing to participate in parlor meetings, share in planning workshops, and volunteer for various projects. Some congregations with a low level of volunteerism must be careful not to create more evidence of volunteer weakness. Success breeds success, and frustration can breed frustration. SVP is ambitious. If the congregation's volunteer culture is very undeveloped, leaders can become discouraged just trying to recruit for parlor meetings. Planners must be realistic. Some stakeholders will come primarily to complain. They may fade after the first workshop. They may exit when Workshop 3 asks them to roll up their sleeves to develop more detailed plans.

Leaders can become frustrated even if forty-five people come to a workshop if they are planning for seventy. In early workshops I fell prey to this lack of perspective. I had a group that was only twenty-three people. I was very disappointed! In that congregation's culture that number represented an extraordinary number of people willing to work.

Multiple Paths

If a congregation is not able to do SVP in full, it is better to customize it (fewer parlor meetings, fewer stakeholders, etc.) than to try to push the team through a process they cannot succeed in. Planners have to ask if the team can really do the work. I am considering offering a design with the values workshop after Havdallah and the goals workshop on the following Sunday. One leaders said, "You are starting in the wrong place. We don't have leadership to do SVP. You need to start with our board." Out of this conversation Synagogue Board Development began to be sketched out.

16. SVP has the potential to provide critical assumptions for the future.

SVP was initially designed to be a leadership development process. Its secondary goal was to create consensus on facts, values, goals, and actions. Most early clients only hired me to work with them through two to three large stakeholder training workshops.

As SVP has evolved, I have tried to provide more guidance in implementation. If the steering committee stays focused, they can bring the board a set of assumptions about the internal and external environment and the community's shared aspirations. The assumptions about membership, programming, and staffing priorities need to be given to the finance committee after the task forces are formed, and they should be revisited every six months until the heart of the plan is completed. From these assumptions the finance committee will be able to create a financial model for the future that will shelter the community.

I do not guarantee the SVP will increase membership. Many congregations are facing well-established demographic declines in their areas. I do believe that SVP can clarify a congregation's position and make membership strategies more focused.

I do not guarantee that SVP will lead to greater fundraising, but several of the congregations I have worked with have gone on to raise significant new funds. I do believe that SVP can help leaders make the case for key projects and test them on a good sample of the congregation.

I also believe that having these discussions makes it easier to put some numbers into those five-year, best estimate budgets. In early SVP processes I simply assumed that the leadership would roll up the learning from the task forces and the workshops. I now build this step into my planning contract.

Hopeful Steps

The planning leadership needs to come back to the board six months later and ensure that the planning assumptions get put into a financial plan. Anchoring the plan in business terms helps make SVP initiatives more real and sustainable.

17. Leadership development keeps leaders stepping forward!

One of the most common outcomes of SVP is that it lays the ground-work for Synagogue Board Development (SBD). Leadership development programs are one way leaders institutionalize their learning. In order to create a program, you must figure out some basics. What do you want participants to know about themselves and others? How do you want them to feel? What do you want them to know about the congregation's organization and operations? What do you want them to know about its purpose and values? Many boards try to start up SBD programs without this groundwork. SVP provides a dress rehearsal for future leadership programs. Recruiting new leadership prospects requires just the kind of hope and optimism that comes from planning (and rehearsing).

Hopeful Steps

Leadership development is not a separate set of skills. It is intimately linked with the congregational leadership culture. SVP provides a taste of leadership development success as leaders gain confidence about their abilities. We have created a workbook called *Byachad: Synagogue Board Development* (Alban Institute, 2007). It provides a model for three three-hour training sessions with the board.

18. Leaders learn to hold themselves accountable for modeling the changes they seek.

Judaism is not just a technical strategic planning problem to be solved. It is a transformative process. In this book I chose to focus on certain leadership and management processes that are transformational. The underlying value that drives all of this is a journey of personal and com-munal spiritual maturity. Yes, I ask leaders to fill out some templates, but the reason is that I want them to learn to mediate between consumer and member, new member and long-standing member, lay leader and staff, and core and periphery. The word "Israel" means "to wrestle." I believe that leadership and management concerns are not problems to solve but tension to wrestle with. When leaders show that they can live within these tensions, they inspire others. Conflict is as old as Genesis. The wisdom to manage conflict with dignity runs through our tradition.

At Alban, we are taught that one of the tools consultants use is them-selves. I have shared some of my personal hopes and struggles in this book to model that there is nothing wrong about admitting you are wrong. Some of my experiments have worked. Others were less successful. I have successfully wrestled. Like Jacob, I carry my limp with pride.

Judaism starts by developing the holiness of the home. From here we reach out to be part of the community. As the community grows in wisdom and strength, it looks out to the needs of Klal Yisrael and the general community. When individuals and teams develop their capacity, they become more capable of stepping forward to support the repair of the world (tikun olam).

Hopeful Steps

Values Modeled	New Ritual	Impact on Culture
Inclusivity, welcoming	All are welcomed to parlor meetings and town meeting.	Leaders demonstrate more openness and trust.
Holiness, piety	Leaders are asked to struggle cognitively (with what they know) and affectively (what they feel toward others). They work through the briefing book and numerous group meetings.	SVP does not focus on worship services, but little of its work can be accomplished if people don't feel called to do leadership work that is different—separate from the norm, holy leadership.
Ruach, energy	Steering committee members make a major commitment for twelve months. They put themselves on the line. They personally solicit.	Others raise the bar about what they might consider doing.
Transparency, openness	Leaders communicate their shared facts, values, goals, and decision-making process to the whole community.	Transparency allows members to respond to emerging plans. It reduces resistance to change.

Values Modeled	New Ritual	Impact on Culture
Hope, optimism, looking forward	Leaders invite people to the process with clear expectations of strengthening the congregation.	Participants are more hopeful.
Accountability, responsibility, tenacity	Steering committee members hold themselves accountable for recruiting for parlor meetings and workshops, gathering data, and communicating about their work.	Stakeholders begin to hold themselves accountable for coming to meetings, participating, and stepping forward on action teams. The board observes the energy of a more accountable process and begins to explore how to be accountable to implement key values, goals, and actions (see SBD, p.230–31).
Communication, feedback	Stakeholders learn to share their views with less criticism and blaming.	Board members come to see opportunities to develop new ways of giving and receiving feedback (see chapter 16 discussion of covenantal caring conversations).
Tikun olam, external focus, compassion for the world	Leaders share their plans with the whole congregation. They encourage new mission and partnerships.	An external focus does not weaken internal programs. It creates more ruah, new leaders, and new missions.

Embracing Accountability:
God, Fellow Leaders, and the Congregation

SVP gives people the tools and the freedom to work. It expects them to set goals and be accountable for some actions. It asks them to expand the circle of leadership and put the question to other members. Will they help make a difference? What can we count on you to do? Before Workshop 1 planners create the stakeholder recruitment tracking form. It lists the steering committee table captains and the people they have solicited. SVP starts encouraging accountability early.

When I interview SVP prospects, I find that few congregations have any overall goals for the year. If there are goals, the board as a group has very little clarity about them. It is thus not surprising that there are very few rituals to encourage accountability.

The whole SVP process should help leaders reenvision their covenant with God, fellow leaders, and the congregation. What have they committed to do? Why have they stepped forward? SVP is about the power of a holistic approach to planning. I have described it as a way of developing hope and heart.

Some leadership groups start to really talk about accountability. Some leaders really step forward in each congregation. They feel called—deeply responsible—to work on this project. Some feel moved because of what stage they are in their lives. Others are engaged because of the quality of SVP leadership. Some of these individuals make a real difference. They join the executive committee. Some choose to become presidents. Some drive key committees. SVP is designed to create a critical mass for change, but in every congregation a few dedicated individuals who step forward can make a huge difference. Watching these special individuals emerge has been a transformational experience for me. One rabbi told me that he was honored to have been given the chance to be a witness to sacred moments in people's lives. I have been so honored.

SVP is not for everyone. Not every tool in this chest is right for every context. If the congregation has the readiness and the courage to jump into the waters, a lot of exciting, positive things can happen. I do not expect congregations to be great at all things. I do not ask that congregations be the best in their region. I do hope that they can articulate their congregations' strengths, the opportunities of their context, and a mission that is worthy of the Jewish tradition.

Final Thoughts

Ben Zoma would say, "Who is wise? One who learns from all people" (*Avot* 4:1). I have tried to learn from everyone. Those who made suggestions to me about the process may be pleasantly surprised to see these adjustments were made in the final work. I have tried to model the courage ('omets lev) to take feedback and grow from it—just as I ask the stakeholders to do so. I feel that synagogue leaders can learn from this book. They may not embrace the whole process. They may argue with some of my observations. They may challenge my understanding of the tradition. I have stepped forward faithfully to bring this to you. I am confident that there are tools in this book that provide leadership opportunities.

I have not tried to ask whether I was the best congregational consultant available. I will not ask if my program is as well designed as other management change models. I have a strong critical voice inside me that cries out, "It's not good enough. It's never good enough. This book will never be done," etc. I am challenging leaders to step forward and try new things. Not all of them will work. Leaders will have some awkward moments. As a relatively new consultant writing his first book, I can have compassion for a synagogue leader trying to take on a new task. The spies were overwhelmed with what the land was lacking—they did not move forward. If I focused on all of the critiques—the negatives—like the spies, I would have never stepped forward!

My rabbi, Irving Bloom, used to tell an old story about Zusia, who told his colleagues that he did not dread God's judgment because he had not measured up to Moses. He dreaded God's judgment because God would ask him if had been the best Zusia he could have been. That is the accountability (ḥeshbon nefesh) that I have been prepared to undertake in my six years working with congregations.

I began chapter 1 by discussing the challenge of motivating and managing the various gifts of the community. I would only ask of leaders what I have asked of myself. I have written this book to encourage them to be the best congregations they can be. I have not asked them to commit to my vision of their congregation, but I have asked them to be true to the values that have supported them when they were at their best as they address their will, the congregation's will, and God's will. I have asked them to read their documents, share their Torah, and reflect on shared meaning. I have challenged the board and steering committee to make efforts to anchor the changes in their culture and to work to make these sustainable.

SVP encourages leaders to develop new covenantal rituals to mark their path. Joshua asked the men to be recircumcised once they crossed the Jordan. I do not call for that (a tough sell!), but I do look for leaders to ritualize some new practices. The parlor meetings, congregational profile, twelve-month board calendar, key initiative tracking worksheet, self-assessment, and covenantal

קידוש I have not asked leaders to commit to my vision of their congregation, but I have asked them to be true to the values that have supported them when they were at their best.

caring conversation process are only tools. When they become disciplined practices, they reflect what leadership really values.

God warned Joshua that the road ahead would not be easy. There would be forks in the road, and the people would have to choose the path of blessing or of curses. Neither the leaders nor I have much control over the congregation's external environment. Joshua did not get to pick his adversaries when he entered the land, but he did get to say something about his practices and his partners. SVP partners (staff, steering committees, stakeholders, board, congregation, and God) are in most cases able to frame a new community conversation about their partnerships and their practices. These SVP leaders build their capacity to gather the community and help them choose faithfully. My prayer for those who embark on the journey of leadership development and planning is that they will be able to move forward with hope and heart from strength to strength.

Traveler's Prayer (Tefilat HaDerekh)

May it be Your will, Lord my God, to lead me on the way of peace and guide and direct my steps in peace, so that You will bring me happily to my destination, safe and sound.

Appendix

RESOURCE 1

Putting It All Together:

The Board Briefing Book

Introduction to Synagogue Visioning and Planning
- Letter to stakeholders from steering committee
- Steering committee members

Agreements
- Mission statement
- Values statement from Workshop 1
- Strategic goals from Workshop 2

Background
- Congregational history (could be from Web site, 1–2 pages)

Governance
- Organization chart
- Committees
- Job descriptions
    - Executive committee
    - Board
    - Expectations for individual member

External Data
- Jewish populations study data
- General community data
- Community trends
- Community Interviews: how others see us

Internal Data
- Membership
- School enrollment
- Demographics
- Sources and uses of funds—pie chart and detail
- Dues
- Fundraising
- Key programs

Report from Parlor Meetings
- Dominant themes report
- Parlor meeting summaries (optional)

Future Sections
Charges to committees and task forces
Committee and task force recommendations

Data Availability Worksheet–
Internal and External Data
Please rank all items so we can see what is readily available.

1= Data readily available
2= Data could be gathered with some effort
3= Data not available

Rank Availability	Internal Congregational Data (Examples; each team will customize their list)
	Membership
	History—10 years
	Why have they joined? What is the profile of the members who have joined over the last three years (ages, geography, practice, kids, etc.)
	Exit interviews, resignations by type (moved, joined other congregation, reasons for leaving, etc.)
	Religious school enrollment history—10 years
	Preschool enrollment—10 years
	Beney mitsvahs—5 years
	Weddings—5 years
	Funerals—5 years
	Demographics (numbers and percentages; if your system uses different groups, that's fine)
	Adults 65+
	Adults 50–64
	Adults 35–49
	Adults –34
	Children 14–18
	Children 7–13
	Children 1–6

Rank Availability	External Congregational Data (Examples; each team will customize their list)

Profile of General Area
- Population growth
- Value of homes
- Median income
- Jewish population and demographics

General Description
- Describe general community environment
- Overall economy
- Describe the neighborhood

Community Interviews: How do others see us?
1. Federation
2. City manager
3. Jewish family service
4. JCC director
5. Denominational regional director
6. Leaders from other congregations

Charts and Graphs
Provide two pie charts for all financial information.

Pie Chart 1: Expenses
- Preschool
- Religious school
- Debt service
- Professional staff
- Office staff
- Maintenance
- Mortgage
- Utilities
- Other

Pie Chart 2: Revenue
- Dues
- Fees
- Preschool tuition
- Religious school tuition
- Contributions
- Fundraising
- Other

Provide a table to show the percentage of change in key categories.

Table 2: Ten-Year History
- Membership
- Religious school enrollment
- Preschool enrollment
- Fundraising

RESOURCE 2

Congregational Membership Profile

Personal Information

Name: _____ M/F Date of Birth: _____

Address: _____

_____

Phone: (____) _____

E-mail: _____

Marital Status: Single   Married   Separated   Divorced   Widow(er)

Ages of Children: _____

Employer: _____

Occupation: _____

Work Phone: (____) _____

E-mail: _____

College Major: _____

Graduate School Field: _____

Growing up, with which branch of Judaism was your family affiliated?

Orthodox   Conservative   Reform   Reconstructionist

Nonaffiliated   Other: _____

Skills/Interests

For each of the following areas, please check the box that reflects your interest level. Please specify, if you like (for example, writing in "soccer" in the appropriate box after "Sports").

1= Very interested
2= Somewhat interested
3= Not interested

Skill/Interest	1	2	3
Art			
Clerical			
Computer			
Crafts			
Creative Writing			
Finance			
Grant/Proposal Writing			
Health Services			
Hospitality			
Humor			
Library			
Music			
Photography			
Sports			
Education/Teaching			
Torah Reading			
Drama			
Israel			
Holocaust			
History			
Hebrew			
Yiddish			
Bible			
Rabbinics			
Tefilah/Davening			
Other			

Committee Interests

For each of the following committees, please check the box that reflects your interest level. Also, indicate if you are a former/current chairperson or member of the committee.

1= Very interested
2= Somewhat interested
3= Not interested

Committee Interests	1	2	3
Adult Education			
Men's Club			
Building			
Cemetery			
Hesed (Caring)			
College Outreach			
Endowment			
Finance			
Seniors			
Honorials/Memorials			
Long-Range Planning			
Marketing/Public Relations			
Membership			
Parent Association/ Religious School			
Preschool			
Programming			
Worship			
School Committee			
Sisterhood			
Young Professionals			
Youth Commission			
Other			

RESOURCE 3

Steering Committee Debriefings

List SWOT results. Consolidate responses from four questionnaire questions (below). Ignore general comments such as "it's a good place."

1. Strengths	2. Weaknesses

3. Opportunities	4. Threats

Making the Connection

How might we use a strength to take advantage of an opportunity?

Strengths	Opportunities

Satisfaction Survey

The host will put the results from all of the satisfaction surveys into a summary using the satisfaction form.

Recording Suggestions

The host should also review all questionnaires and highlight *specific ideas or initiatives* that could be pursued. We do not want to focus on general concepts like "get people more involved." We do want to focus on specifics like "create a youth program with other Jewish organizations" or "create a young men's study group."

The questionnaire asks the participants to identify their top priority and what they would like to do to address it. It also asks them what the greatest unmet programmatic need is and what role they might like to play in developing the program. We need to record these responses so that we can capture the suggestions for change and identify the volunteers, by name, who are willing to support these initiatives.

Name	Priority from Satisfaction Survey	What leaders should do	The role I might play

Name	Greatest unmet programmatic need	The role I might play

Personal Debrief

One of the critical purposes of SVP is to *train leaders* to be more reflective. I encourage you to reflect on your experience and make meaning of it.

1. What was your experience in the parlor meeting?

2. What was a high point?

3. What was a low point?

4. When participants look into the future they have anxiety about:

5. When participants look into the future they have optimism about:

RESOURCE 4

Temple Beth El

Worship Task Force Report

The Worship Task Force of the Beth El Temple Strategic Planning Process was charged with the responsibility of exploring all aspects of the Beth El worship experience, with the goal of developing strategies for preserving cherished aspects of our practice, while invigorating it in new and exciting ways.

In a series of meetings and numerous e-mail exchanges from December 2005 through April 2006, the Task Force, comprised of eleven lay members with the professional staff assistance of Rabbi Cytryn and Mike Schatz, engaged in an enthusiastic, wide-ranging discussion of these topics. The results of that process—divided into Guiding Principles, Strategic Goals, and Strategies—appear in the outline below. The Task Force hopes that the Ritual Committee, whether it retains its current structure or, as we recommend, is reconstituted as a Spirituality Committee, will consider carefully each of the recommendations set forth in this report and will, with the approval of the Board, implement as many of them as possible in a timely fashion.

The consensus of the Task Force was that Conservative Judaism, as it is practiced at Beth El Temple, remains vital and relevant in the twenty-first century. At the same time, we recognize that if it is to remain so it must be open to creativity and change. Our recommendations are offered in the hope that they will start an ongoing conversation within our congregation that will lead to new ways of enriching both our collective and individual experiences of being Jewish.

I. Guiding Principles
1. Promote egalitarianism.
2. Encourage growth and change within the framework of Conservative Judaism.
3. Make maximum use of the Rabbi's creativity and leadership.
4. Recognize the diverse reasons why people attend services—religion, education, fellowship—and the reasons why people don't attend services.
5. Understand that there is no "magic bullet" or "one size fits all."

II. Strategic Goals

1. Increase participation and inclusion in Shabbat and holiday worship experiences.
2. Increase attendance.
3. Experiment with creative worship/learning experiences.
4. Increase participation in daily minyan.
5. Connect with younger (thirty- to forty-year-olds with children) cohort.

III. Strategies

A. Short-Term Strategies (things that can be done with existing resources)

1. Help English readers participate—prayer for country, congregation, Israel, responsive readings on Shabbat/Festivals and in daily minyanim.
2. Continue special programming—Third Friday, Sisterhood and Brotherhood Shabbats, Congregational dinners, family Shabbats.
3. Announce pages at minyan.
4. Place lay leaders on bimah—participatory role modeling (published schedule).
5. Balance sermons—focus on both textual study and current events.
6. Develop hevruta study—different study formats before, during, and after service (one-to-one outreach to encourage attendance at future sessions).
7. Recruit women for worship leadership.
8. Station greeters in the lobby.
9. Initiate "Fellowship" moments *during* services—greeting each other with a Jewish twist.
10. Draw upon congregants' expertise to illuminate Torah study— for example, lawyers, social workers, doctors.
11. Install better signs in the synagogue and new signage on Front Street/Second Street to give passers-by a better sense of what Beth El offers.

B. Mid-Term Strategies (things that are doable but may require some planning/development or a shift in allocation of resources)

1. Recruit more Torah/haftarah readers and daveners—training to increase competence and maintain standards.
2. Experiment with alternative English (evening) minyan— probably Sunday.

3. Create Kaddish outreach.
4. Provide name tags for congregants to facilitate interaction.
5. Identify formal and informal adult education programs to increase literacy in Hebrew and liturgical themes.
6. Identify resources—for example, USCJ COMPACT, home study, list of Web sites.
7. Integrate music—explore fullest use of music, both instrumental and with new melodies.
8. Invite congregants to services to recognize anniversaries, birthdays, bar and bat mitsvah anniversaries.
9. Offer more transliterated materials; purchase multiple copies of Or Hadash for congregational use.
10. Cultivate a culture of congregant-sponsored Kiddushes.
11. Promote social interaction (for example, coffee and Danish on Saturday morning) before services.
12. Reconstitute the Ritual Committee as a Spirituality Committee with the charge to pay attention to these broader considerations of participation, inclusion, and creative development of spiritual expression as well as its current work of examining ritual issues.

C. Long-Term Strategies (things that require significant planning/development)

1. Consider "Alternative" services—meditation, yoga.
2. Create a "Spirituality Checkup" campaign.
3. Make flexible use of space—don't foreclose worship opportunities; lessen the distance and increase the connection between leaders/congregation; eliminate the "performance" mentality; eliminate barriers to access—physical and audiovisual.

Respectfully submitted,

Worship Task Force   Rhea Gross
Harvey Freedenberg, Co-Chair   Dale Kaplan
Shalom Staub, Co-Chair   Andrea Lieber
Arthur Berger   Hope Pracht
Arthur Berman
Maury Brenner   *Professional Staff*
Sue Dym   Rabbi Eric Cytryn
Selwyn Friedlander   Michael Schatz, Executive Director

RESOURCE 5

Examples of Goal Topics
and Strategic Goal Statements

The following are examples of strategic goal statements that might be developed out of Workshop 2. The steering committee might have identified "family education" as a strategic goal topic. After the workshop, it might refine this to "help families practice together and have fun." We also ask that groups develop one SMART objective that will provide concrete details about how this broad strategic direction might be accomplished.

Goal Topic: Adult Education
Strategic Goal Statement: Provide Jewish Education without Walls

We will reach out beyond our facility through lunch-and-learns at hospitals, law offices, and community centers. We will break down barriers and pull in new ideas, new partners, and new approaches.

Goal Topic: Family Education
Strategic Goal Statement: Help Families Practice Together and Have Fun

We will connect the religious school curriculum to family home practices. We will create major events that celebrate the developing home practice of our members.

Goal Topic: Leadership Development
Strategic Goal Statement: Encourage Leaders to Commit to Learning

Leaders will commit to ongoing leadership development and Jewish learning. They will strive to grow in spiritual maturity, to contribute their unique gifts, and to work together. They will inspire new leaders and invite them to participate.

Goal Topic: Worship
Strategic Goal Statement: Create Worship That Is Wonderful

We are committed to respecting our worship traditions and having respect for our differences. We will plan different worship experiences throughout the years to help our members find a way to engage with worship and each other.

Goal Topic: Facility
Strategic Statement: Working to Sustain Our Sacred Space

All of our conversations are special when they happen within these walls. We will work to ensure that we have a facility that can hold and support our missions and aspirations.

Goal: Social Programs
Strategic Statement: There Is a Place at the Table for Everyone

Our synagogue is a place where you are welcome—there is always a seat at the table for you. We provide programs for young and old. We invite members to step forward to create a program or event, or join one. We strive to create a calendar that builds community.

RESOURCE 6

Oceanside Jewish Center

Values Statement

At the most recent meeting of the Oceanside Jewish Center's Synagogue Vision Project we explored a number of areas of congregational life, looking at our present situation and imagining what the future could hold for our congregation. We were struck by the diversity of points of view, the passion our members feel about their congregation, and the desire on the part of our members to help create a stronger and more vibrant community. Smaller groups of the gathering discussed various aspects of congregational life in terms of what is now happening and what we would like to see in the future. The following is an attempt to distill the results of that discussion into a series of values that should influence the continued growth of our congregation. We have also taken the liberty of adding other values that are essential to who we are as a congregation.

Tefilah, Ruaḥ: Joyous Celebration of Jewish Life

The members of our congregation are diverse and have different ways of connecting with the spiritual ideals of Judaism. For some the traditional practices are sufficient; for others there is a search for new ways to connect to our tradition, to God, and to the community. We need to find a way to address both groups by offering new opportunities while maintaining our traditional practices. What both groups are looking for is a spiritual practice that will inspire, encourage participation of both young and old, and infuse services with meaning.

Keruv/Hakhnasat Orḥim

As a congregation we must have a larger vision that extends beyond the synagogue to the larger community. How do we share Judaism with others? What can we do to create programs that will make OJC the kind of congregation people will want to join to celebrate Jewish life? We need to also create the kind of monetary base so that money is not an obstacle for participation in Jewish life. We must strive for more keruv—bringing people closer to God by doing hakhnasat orḥim, welcoming everyone into our midst. Whatever plan we create we must do so with a vision toward Klal Yisrael, the larger community of Jewish people.

Mitsvah, Commitment, and Involvement

There is a strong feeling in the group that we are not doing enough to keep our post–bar mitsvah teenagers and young adults involved. USY is not attracting enough teens, and few of our teens continue on in the Hebrew high school. Teenagers need to feel that they have a social community in the congregation. It must involve ruaḥ, Talmud Torah, and a commitment to tikun olam.

Kehilah, Community

The core of our congregation should be the board, but there is a lack of involvement and participation on the part of many of the board members. We need to find ways to nurture a sense of commitment to the community and active participation by board members. We must promote darkhey shalom—cooperation and mutual support—as well as a deep sense of community.

Talmud Torah and Beyond

Younger families in our congregation are deeply concerned about whether their children will remained involved in Jewish life beyond bar mitsvah. We need to give people a reason to hold on to their membership and a reason to be Jewish. While many families may be more concerned about bar mitsvah, others are looking for an entrance into more involved participation in Jewish life. We need to reach out door to door to recruit new families.

Tikun Olam

While this value was not specifically discussed at this meeting, we think it is essential to our congregational vision. There are people who may not be motivated intellectually or spiritually by the synagogue but who want to build a stronger community, promote the interests of Israel, and work for the good of humankind. Tsedakah, social justice, Klal Yisrael, and 'erets Israel need to be in the synagogue vision in a more meaningful way.

Mitsvah, Part 2: Jewish Observance and Living

We want to encourage members to explore their commitment to Jewish life through Shabbat, kashrut, holidays, and family life. We view Jewish living as a ladder we must climb—it is our job as a congregation to encourage this growth and ascent and to help people feel comfortable with each new level of observance. In the words of F. Rosensweig, it is our job to turn law into commandment by encouraging each person to make new commitments to Jewish living. A Conservative Jew is in a constant state of "not yet."

Talmud Torah

We have repeatedly defined ourselves as a community of learners. Yet we have not found effective ways to involve more adults in lifelong Jewish education. We need to explore new strategies for Jewish learning on all different levels.

Derekh 'Erets

We are here to help each member find the best within him/herself. Promoting positive midot—moral character and virtues—is essential to who we are as a congregation. Strengthening the family and encouraging a dialogue on moral values are part of why we are here.

For Further Reading

Aron, Isa. 2002. *The Self-Renewing Congregation: Organizational Strage-gies for Revitalizing Congregational Life*. Woodstock, Vt.: Jewish Lights Publishing.

Bolman, Lee G., and Terrence E. Deal. 2003. *Reframing Organizations: Artistry, Choice, and Leadership*. San Francisco: Jossey-Bass.

Buckingham, Marcus, and Curt Coffman. 1999. *First, Break All the Rules: What the World's Greatest Managers Do Differently*. New York: Simon & Schuster.

Butler, Lawrence. 2000. "Providing Meaningful Information for Governance." In *Building Effective Boards for Religious Organizations: A Handbook for Trustees, Presidents, and Church Leaders*, ed. Thomas P. Holland and David C. Hester, 204–10. San Francisco: Jossey-Bass.

Carver, John. 1997. *Boards That Make a Difference*, San Francisco: Jossey-Bass.

Collins, Jim. 2005. *Good to Great and the Social Sectors*. New York: HarperCollins.

Covey, Stephen R. 1989. *The Seven Habits of Highly Effective People*. New York: Simon & Schuster.

Denning, Stephen: *The Springboard: How Storytelling Ignites Action in the Knowledge-Era Organization*. Boston: Butterworth Heinemann, 2001.

Drucker, Peter F. 1990. *Managing the Nonprofit Organization: Principles and Practices*. New York: HarperCollins.

Eisen, Arnold M. 1997. *Taking Hold of Torah: Jewish Commitment and Community in America*. Bloomington: Indiana University Press.

Eisen, Arnold M., and Steven M. Cohen. 2000. *The Jew Within: Self, Family and Community in America*. Bloomington: Indiana University Press.

Gaede, Beth Ann, ed. 2001. *Size Transitions in Congregations*. Herndon, Va.: The Alban Institute.

Garfield, Jerry, and Ken Stanton. 2005. "Building Effective Teams in Real Time." *Harvard Management Review Update* 10 (November 2005): 1–3.

Goldstein, Raymond. 2006. "Greetings: A Message from the President." The United Synagogue of Conservative Judaism. http://www.uscj.org /Greetings6401.html.

Goleman, Daniel. 1995. *Emotional Intelligence: Why It Can Matter More than IQ.* New York: Bantam.

Hammer, Michael. 2001. *The Agenda.* New York: Crown Business.

Heifetz, Ronald. 1999. *Leadership Without Easy Answers.* Cambridge, Mass.: Belknap Press of Harvard University Press.

Holland, Thomas P. 2000. "Developing a More Effective Board." In *Building Effective Boards for Religious Organizations: A Handbook for Trustees, Presidents, and Church Leaders*, ed. Thomas P. Holland and David C. Hester, 83–108. San Francisco: Jossey-Bass.

Holland, Thomas P., and David C. Hester, eds. 2000. *Building Effective Boards for Religious Organizations: A Handbook for Trustees, Presidents, and Church Leaders.* San Francisco: Jossey-Bass.

Horowitz, Bethamie. 2000. *Connections and Journeys: Assessing Critical Opportunities for Enhancing Jewish Identity.* New York: UJA-Federation of New York.

Hudson, Jill M. 1992. *Evaluating Ministry: Principles and Processes for Clergy and Congregations.* Herndon, Va.: The Alban Institute.

———. 2004. *When Better Isn't Enough: Evaluation Tools for the Twenty-first Century Church.* Herndon, Va.: The Alban Institute.

Kiersey, David. 1998. *Please Understand Me II: Temperament, Character, Intelligence.* Del Mar, Calif.: Prometheus Nemesis.

Knowles, Malcolm S. 1973. *The Adult Learner: A Neglected Species.* Houston: Gulf Publishing.

Kotter, John P. 1999. *John P. Kotter on What Leaders Really Do.* Cambridge, Mass.: Harvard Business School Press.

Kouzes, James, and Barry Posner. 2002. *The Leadership Challenge.* San Francisco: Jossey-Bass.

Leventhal, Robert. 2003. "Teamwork in the Synagogue." *United Synagogue Review* (Spring 2003).

———. 2004. "Reimagning the Rabbi Lay Leadership Partnership." *Alban Weekly* (August 2004).

———. 2005. "The Synagogue Leadership Agenda." *Congregations* (Spring 2005).

———. 2005. "The Fair Report: What Do We Say When Bad Things Happen in Good Congregations?" *Alban Weekly* (November 2005).

———. 2006. "The Role of the Executive Committee." *Congregations* (Summer 2006).

———. 2007. *Byachad: Synagogue Board Development.* Herndon, Va.: The Alban Institute.

Lew, Alan. 2003. *This Is Real and You Are Completely Unprepared: The Days of Awe as a Journey of Transformation.* Boston: Little, Brown.

Light, Mark. 2001. *The Strategic Board: The Step-by-Step Guide to High-Impact Governance.* New York: Wiley.

Mann, Alice. 1999. *Can Our Church Live? Redeveloping Congregations in Decline.* Herndon, Va.: The Alban Institute.

Olsen, Charles M. 1995. *Transforming Church Boards into Communities of Spiritual Leaders.* Herndon, Va: The Alban Institute.

Palmer, Parker J. 1998. *The Courage to Teach: Exploring the Inner Landscape of a Teacher's Life.* San Francisco: Jossey-Bass.

Parsons, George D., and Speed B. Leas. 1993. *Understanding Your Congregation as a System: The Manual.* Herndon, Va.: The Alban Institute.

Rackham, Neil. 1988. *SPIN Selling.* New York: McGraw-Hill.

Rendle, Gilbert R. 1998. *Leading Change in the Congregation: Spiritual and Organizational Tools for Leaders.* Herndon, Va.: The Alban Institute.

———. 1999. *Behavioral Covenants in Congregations: A Handbook for Honoring Differences.* Herndon, Va.: The Alban Institute.

Rendle, Gil, and Susan Beaumont. 2007. *When Moses Meets Aaron: Staffing and Supervision in Large Congregations.* Herndon, Va.: The Alban Institute.

Rendle, Gil, and Alice Mann. 2003. *Holy Conversations: Strategic Planning as a Spiritual Practice for Congregations.* Herndon, Va.: The Alban Institute.

Rogers, Paul, and Marcia Blenko. 2006. "Who Has the D? How Clear Decision Roles Enhance Organizational Performance." *Harvard Business Review* 84, no. 1 (January 2006): 52–61, 131.

Rosenberg, Marshall B. 1999. *Nonviolent Communication: A Language of Compassion.* Del Mar, Calif.: PuddleDancer Press.

Sacks, Jonathan. 2000. *A Letter in the Scroll: Understanding Our Jewish Identity and Exploring the Legacy of the World's Oldest Religion.* New York: The Free Press.

Sales, Amy L. 2004. *The Congregations of Westchester.* Report on a study sponsored by the Commission on Jewish Identity and Renewal of the United Jewish Appeal Federation of New York.

———. 2006. *Synergy: Mining the Research, Framing the Questions.* Cohen Center for Modern Jewish Studies, Brandeis University, Waltham, Mass.

Schein, Edgar. 1988. *Process Consulting: Its Role in Organizational Development.* 2nd ed. Reading, Mass.: Prentice Hall.

Sellon, Mary K., and Daniel P. Smith. 2005. *Practicing Right Relationship: Skills for Deepening Purpose, Finding Fulfillment, and Increasing Effectiveness in Your Congregation.* Herndon, Va.: The Alban Institute.

Senge, Peter. 1990. *The Fifth Discipline: The Art and Practice of the Learning Organization.* New York: Doubleday/Currency.

Shevitz, Susan. 1995. "An Organizational Perspective on Changing Congregational Education: What the Literature Reveals." In *A Congregation of Learners*, ed. Isa Aron, Sarah Lee, and Seymour Rossel. New York: UAHC Press.

Snow, Luther. 2004. *The Power of Asset Mapping.* Herndon, Va.: The Alban Institute.

Telushkin, Joseph. 2000. *The Book of Jewish Values: A Day-by-Day Guide to Ethical Living.* New York: Bell Tower.

Teutsch, David A. 2003. *A Guide to Jewish Practice.* 2nd ed. Wyncote, Pa.: Reconstructionist Rabbinic College Press.

United Jewish Communities. 2003. *National Jewish Population Study 2001.* New York: United Jewish Communities.

Urban Institute. 2004. *Volunteer Management Capacity in America's Charities and Congregations: A Briefing Report.* Washington, D.C.: Urban Institute.

Wertheimer, Jack. 2000. *Jews in the Center: Conservative Synagogues and Their Members.* New Brunswick, N.J.: Rutgers University Press.

Windmueller, Steven. 2006. "The Second American Jewish Revolution." *Sh'ma* (June 2006): http://www.shma.com/june_06/second_american.htm.

Yoffie, Eric. 2005. Sermon. Union of Reformed Judaism 68th General Assembly. Houston, Texas. November 19, 2005.

Zevit, Sean Israel. 2005. *Offerings of the Heart: Money and Values in Faith Communities.* Herndon, Va.: The Alban Institute.